Regional Economic Integration in South Asia

South Asia today is among the most unstable regions in the world, riddled by both intra- and inter-state conflict. This book presents a comprehensive technical analysis of the trade–conflict relationship within the region, and explores how South Asia demonstrates underperformance of its potential for economic integration.

Using the gravity model framework, the book highlights quantitative estimates of the cost of conflict in terms of loss of trade for South Asia. Other variables representative of political and economic regimes are also included to make the model comprehensive, and the book goes on to discuss how the analysis reveals the overriding significance of the India–Pakistan relationship in the regional landscape. It looks at how the results of the econometric exercise reveal the extent to which a common border, when disputed, becomes a barrier rather than a facilitator to trade and, additionally, the extent to which long standing and persistent conflict can debilitate trade relationships.

The book is a useful contribution for students and scholars of South Asian studies and international political economy, and assists in formulating policy to correct the anti-home bias that is evident in trade patterns of the South Asian region.

Amita Batra is Associate Professor of Economics, South Asian Studies at Jawaharlal Nehru University, India. She has worked extensively in the area of economic and financial integration, with a special focus on Asia.

Routledge Contemporary South Asia Series

1. **Pakistan**
   Social and cultural transformations in a Muslim nation
   Mohammad A. Qadeer

2. **Labor, Democratization and Development in India and Pakistan**
   Christopher Candland

3. **China–India Relations**
   Contemporary dynamics
   Amardeep Athwal

4. **Madrasas in South Asia**
   Teaching terror?
   Jamal Malik

5. **Labor, Globalization and the State**
   Workers, women and migrants confront neoliberalism
   Edited by Debdas Banerjee and Michael Goldfield

6. **Indian Literature and Popular Cinema**
   Recasting classics
   Edited by Heidi R.M. Pauwels

7. **Islamist Militancy in Bangladesh**
   A complex web
   Ali Riaz

8. **Regionalism in South Asia**
   Negotiating cooperation, institutional structures
   Kishore C. Dash

9. **Federalism, Nationalism and Development**
   India and the Punjab economy
   Pritam Singh

10. **Human Development and Social Power**
    Perspectives from South Asia
    Ananya Mukherjee Reed

11. **The South Asian Diaspora**
    Transnational networks and changing identities
    Edited by Rajesh Rai and Peter Reeves

12. **Pakistan–Japan Relations**
    Continuity and change in economic relations and security interests
    Ahmad Rashid Malik

13. **Himalayan Frontiers of India**
    Historical, geo-political and strategic perspectives
    K. Warikoo

14. **India's Open-Economy Policy**
    Globalism, rivalry, continuity
    Jalal Alamgir

15 **The Separatist Conflict in Sri Lanka**
Terrorism, ethnicity, political economy
Asoka Bandarage

16 **India's Energy Security**
Edited by Ligia Noronha and Anant Sudarshan

17 **Globalization and the Middle Classes in India**
The social and cultural impact of neoliberal reforms
Ruchira Ganguly-Scrase and Timothy J. Scrase

18 **Water Policy Processes in India**
Discourses of power and resistance
Vandana Asthana

19 **Minority Governments in India**
The puzzle of elusive majorities
Csaba Nikolenyi

20 **The Maoist Insurgency in Nepal**
Revolution in the twenty-first century
Edited by Mahendra Lawoti and Anup K. Pahari

21 **Global Capital and Peripheral Labour**
The history and political economy of plantation workers in India
K. Ravi Raman

22 **Maoism in India**
Reincarnation of ultra-left wing extremism in the twenty-first century
Bidyut Chakrabarty and Rajat Kujur

23 **Economic and Human Development in Contemporary India**
Cronyism and fragility
Debdas Banerjee

24 **Culture and the Environment in the Himalaya**
Arjun Guneratne

25 **The Rise of Ethnic Politics in Nepal**
Democracy in the margins
Susan I. Hangen

26 **The Multiplex in India**
A cultural economy of urban leisure
Adrian Athique and Douglas Hill

27 **Tsunami Recovery in Sri Lanka**
Ethnic and regional dimensions
Dennis B. McGilvray and Michele R. Gamburd

28 **Development, Democracy and the State**
Critiquing the Kerala model of development
K. Ravi Raman

29 **Mohajir Militancy in Pakistan**
Violence and transformation in the Karachi conflict
Nichola Khan

30 **Nationbuilding, Gender and War Crimes in South Asia**
Bina D'Costa

31 **The State in India after Liberalization**
Interdisciplinary perspectives
Edited by Akhil Gupta and K. Sivaramakrishnan

32 **National Identities in Pakistan**
The 1971 war in contemporary Pakistani fiction
Cara Cilano

33 **Political Islam and Governance in Bangladesh**
Edited by Ali Riaz and C. Christine Fair

34 **Bengali Cinema**
'An other nation'
Sharmistha Gooptu

35 **NGOs in India**
The challenges of women's empowerment and accountability
Patrick Kilby

36 **The Labour Movement in the Global South**
Trade unions in Sri Lanka
S. Janaka Biyanwila

37 **Building Bangalore**
Architecture and urban transformation in India's Silicon Valley
John C. Stallmeyer

38 **Conflict and Peacebuilding in Sri Lanka**
Caught in the peace trap?
Edited by Jonathan Goodhand, Jonathan Spencer and Benedict Korf

39 **Microcredit and Women's Empowerment**
A case study of Bangladesh
Amunui Faraizi, Jim McAllister and Taskinur Rahman

40 **South Asia in the New World Order**
The role of regional cooperation
Shahid Javed Burki

41 **Explaining Pakistan's Foreign Policy**
Escaping India
Aparna Pande

42 **Development-induced Displacement, Rehabilitation and Resettlement in India**
Current issues and challenges
Edited by Sakarama Somayaji and Smrithi Talwar

43 **The Politics of Belonging in India**
Becoming Adivasi
Edited by Daniel J. Rycroft and Sangeeta Dasgupta

44 **Re-Orientalism and South Asian Identity Politics**
The oriental Other within
Edited by Lisa Lau and Ana Cristina Mendes

45 **Islamic Revival in Nepal**
Religion and a new nation
Megan Adamson Sijapati

46 **Education and Inequality in India**
A classroom view
Manabi Majumdar and Jos Mooij

47 **The Culturalization of Caste in India**
Identity and inequality in a multicultural age
Balmurli Natrajan

48 **Corporate Social Responsibility in India**
Bidyut Chakrabarty

49 **Pakistan's Stability Paradox**
Domestic, regional and international dimensions
Edited by Ashutosh Misra and Michael E. Clarke

50 **Transforming Urban Water Supplies in India**
The role of reform and partnerships in globalization
Govind Gopakumar

51 **South Asian Security**
Twenty-first century discourse
Sagarika Dutt and Alok Bansal

52 **Non-discrimination and Equality in India**
Contesting boundaries of social justice
Vidhu Verma

53 **Being Middle-class in India**
A way of life
Henrike Donner

54 **Kashmir's Right to Secede**
A critical examination of contemporary theories of secession
Matthew J. Webb

55 **Bollywood Travels**
Culture, diaspora and border crossings in popular Hindi cinema
Rajinder Dudrah

56 **Nation, Territory, and Globalization in Pakistan**
Traversing the margins
Chad Haines

57 **The Politics of Ethnicity in Pakistan**
The Baloch, Sindhi and Mohajir ethnic movements
Farhan Hanif Siddiqi

58 **Nationalism and Ethnic Conflict**
Identities and mobilization after 1990
Edited by Mahendra Lawoti and Susan Hangen

59 **Islam and Higher Education**
Concepts, challenges and opportunities
Marodsilton Muborakshoeva

60 **Religious Freedom in India**
Sovereignty and (anti) conversion
Goldie Osuri

61 **Everyday Ethnicity in Sri Lanka**
Up-country Tamil identity politics
Daniel Bass

62 **Ritual and Recovery in Post-Conflict Sri Lanka**
Eloquent bodies
Jane Derges

63 **Bollywood and Globalisation**
The global power of popular Hindi cinema
Edited by David J. Schaefer and Kavita Karan

64 **Regional Economic Integration in South Asia**
Trapped in conflict?
Amita Batra

Regional Economic Integration in South Asia
Trapped in conflict?

Amita Batra

Routledge
Taylor & Francis Group
LONDON AND NEW YORK

First published 2013
by Routledge
2 Park Square, Milton Park, Abingdon, Oxon OX14 4RN

Simultaneously published in the USA and Canada
by Routledge
711 Third Avenue, New York, NY 10017

Routledge is an imprint of the Taylor & Francis Group, an informa business

© 2013 Amita Batra

The right of Amita Batra to be identified as author of this work has been asserted by her in accordance with sections 77 and 78 of the Copyright, Designs and Patents Act 1988.

All rights reserved. No part of this book may be reprinted or reproduced or utilised in any form or by any electronic, mechanical, or other means, now known or hereafter invented, including photocopying and recording, or in any information storage or retrieval system, without permission in writing from the publishers.

Trademark notice: Product or corporate names may be trademarks or registered trademarks, and are used only for identification and explanation without intent to infringe.

British Library Cataloguing in Publication Data
A catalogue record for this book is available from the British Library

Library of Congress Cataloging in Publication Data
Batra, Amita.
 Regional economic integration in South Asia : trapped in conflict? / Amita Batra.
  p. cm. — (Routledge contemporary South Asia series ; 64)
  Includes bibliographical references and index.
 1. South Asia—Economic integration. 2. South Asia—Foreign economic relations. 3. South Asia—Commerce. I. Title.
 HF1586.5.B38 2012
 337.1'54—dc23   2012023868

ISBN: 978-0-415-60209-9 (hbk)
ISBN: 978-0-203-07715-3 (ebk)

Typeset in Times New Roman
by Swales & Willis Ltd, Exeter, Devon

This book is dedicated to my Father

Contents

List of figures — xiii
List of tables — xv

1 Introduction — 1
Regional cooperation in South Asia: SAARC, SAPTA and SAFTA 2
Nature of conflict in South Asia: implications for regional economic integration 5
Global context 9
Organization of the book 15

2 South Asia: the region — 17
Economic profile 18
Social development in South Asia 24
Contrasts 25
India's centrality 26

3 Trade and FDI patterns of South Asian countries — 28
Post-independence economic regimes in South Asia 28
New economic policy regime 29
Patterns and trends in trade and capital flows 34
India's centrality in regional trade 41
Role and quantum of informal trade 43
Non-tariff barriers (NTBs) to trade in South Asia 44
Capital Inflows in South Asia 51
South-south FDI and South Asia 56
Scope for production networks in South Asia 57

4	**Preferential trading agreements in South Asia**	61
	Trends in FTA formation: regional comparisons 61	
	Motivating factors for entering into PTAs/FTAs 62	
	South Asian context 63	
	Regional trade agreements in South Asia 65	
	Bilateral trade agreements 68	
	Inter-sub-regional agreements 71	
	Scope for reconciliation of overlap between FTAs and RTAs in South Asia 73	
5	**Conflict in South Asia**	75
	Nature of conflict in South Asia 75	
	Chronological sequence of conflict events and CBMs in South Asia 82	
	Impact of conflict on bilateral trade: visual impressions 91	
6	**Theoretical foundations of the economic integration and conflict relationship in South Asia**	99
	Theoretical foundations 100	
	Empirical analysis and bi-directional causality 111	
7	**Impact of conflict on intra-regional trade in South Asia: A gravity model analysis**	115
	The gravity model 115	
	Conflict augmented gravity model: estimation results 127	
8	**Summary findings and an assessment of the way forward**	135
	Summary findings 135	
	Way forward 143	

Appendix	152
Notes	156
Bibliography	165
Index	172

Figures

5.1	Bilateral trade	92
5.2	Impact of regional and civil conflict on bilateral trade: India–Pakistan	94
5.3	Impact of regional and civil conflict on bilateral trade: India–Bangladesh	95
5.4	Impact of regional and civil conflict on bilateral trade: India–Nepal	96
5.5	Impact of regional and civil conflict on bilateral trade: India–Sri Lanka	97

Tables

2.1	Economic indicators: relative regional performance	19
2.2a	Key economic indicators for South Asia	21
2.2b	South Asia: growth and macro-economic indicators	22
2.3	South Asia: sector-wise shares (per cent) in GDP	23
2.4	Social indicators in South Asian economies	25
3.1	Trade openness: regional and country comparisons	35
3.2	South Asia: FDI, net inflows (US$ million)	52
7.1	Conflicted augmented gravity model: estimation results	133
A.1	SAFTA sensitive list: revisions underway	152
A.2	Phase-out period for the SAFTA sensitive list	152
A.3	Textile and clothing sector: exercise details on production networks	153

1 Introduction

South Asia, comprising[1] Afghanistan, Bangladesh, Bhutan, India, Maldives, Nepal, Pakistan and Sri Lanka, has over the last decade been the subject of many discussions and debates, primarily for two reasons. One, owing to the region having been described by many as one of the most unstable in the world, and two, on account of the unexpected and unprecedented economic dynamism of its largest economy, India. The first revolves around the phenomenon of conflict that has been long-standing and varyingly intense through the history of the region and attracted renewed attention in the wake of global repercussions of terrorist attacks in the US in September of 2001. The second is an outcome of systemic economic reforms undertaken in India since 1991 that have altered its growth trajectory such that there is a shift in the centre of gravity of the global economy to Asia. A third more interesting but not as much analyzed characterization of South Asia is through the inter-linkages between conflict and economic exchange. As a unique exception to a well-proven 'natural trading partner' hypothesis,[2] the South Asian region demonstrates how historically and geographically proximate countries, when caught in persistent conflict, lead to underperformance of a region in terms of its potential for economic exchange. This intriguing inter-linkage between conflict and economic exchange in South Asia is the subject of this book. Specifically, this book is an attempt to quantify the extent to which conflict has prevented the region from exploiting its trade potential.

The subject assumes meaning and temporal significance as India that has been at the centre of exceptional global focus in the last decade owing to its economic dynamism is also central to the South Asian economy and trade. With over 80 per cent contribution to the region's GDP, over 60 per cent share in regional trade and 75 per cent of the regional population, India's economic centrality in South Asia is undeniable and is further reinforced by the geography and history of the region. India is the only country in South Asia that has a common border, land or maritime with all other countries of the region. Pakistan and Bangladesh have been a part of the erstwhile Indian subcontinent. While Pakistan is an outcome of British India's partition consequent upon its independence from colonial rule in 1947, Bangladesh was created out of Pakistan as a consequence of the 1971 war of independence. Given India's centrality and economic dynamism, the reasonably good growth of other countries of the region over the last decade and their geographical and historical proximity, intra-regional trade that has been stagnant at only about 5 per cent of the South Asian countries' total trade appears as a contradiction, and even more so when it is noted that the rate of global trade integration of the South Asian region has been the fastest among all the regions in the world in 2005 and 2007.[3] This development assumes further significance when it is noted that South Asia accomplished establishment of the institutional process for regional cooperation over a quarter of a century ago in 1985 with the setting up of the South Asian Association for Regional Cooperation (SAARC). These apparent contradictions in South Asia make it imperative to explore and identify the costs and barriers that inhibit trade and economic exchange within the region. The analysis in this book is therefore focussed upon the cost that, among other barriers, conflict may have inflicted on the region in terms of loss of trade. The paragraphs that follow establish the context for this analysis.

Regional cooperation in South Asia: SAARC, SAPTA and SAFTA

The process of regional cooperation in South Asia began with the establishment of the institutional mechanism, the South Asian Association of Regional Cooperation (SAARC), in 1985. The SAARC secretariat, headed by a Secretary General and comprising one Director from each member country, was set up in 1986 in Kathmandu, Nepal. The institutional mechanism of the SAARC operates through the annual summit meetings of the heads of government and states, the highest decision-making body, assisted by a council of ministers. Economic cooperation and integration became a part of the SAARC work agenda seven years later when the council of ministers of the member countries signed an agreement to form the South Asian Preferential Trade Agreement (SAPTA) in April 1993. The agreement was prompted by a desire of the South Asian economies to dismantle trade barriers following the move towards unilateral liberalization and global trade integration initiated first, in a systemic manner, in India in 1991[4] and later undertaken by the other economies of the region. The process of regional economic integration was simultaneously necessitated by the impending risk of isolation for South Asia as the rest of the world was increasingly formulating and entering into regional preferential trading arrangements.

The SAPTA that was aimed at trade liberalization and dismantling of trade barriers with no explicit objective of achieving a free trade area in the region became operational in December 1995. Four rounds of negotiations towards preferential tariff reductions were initiated, of which three were implemented and one was suspended. The three rounds, undertaken in 1995, 1996 and 1998, involved laborious and time-consuming negotiations having been restricted to product by product[5] and sectoral approaches. The negotiations resulted in more than 4,700 tariff lines being placed under preferential access. However, this had no impact on intra-regional trade that continued to remain stagnant at 5 per cent of South Asia's global trade. The inefficient and ineffective outcome of SAPTA's implementation was seen to be a consequence of the tariff preferences being largely irrelevant to trading interest of the partner economies in the region, inadequate tariff cuts, restrictive rules of origin and the erection of many hidden and obvious non-tariff barriers. Long-standing animosities and consequent distrust, lack of confidence vis-à-vis each other and the fear of major benefits accruing to the largest economy prevented member countries from giving real concessions that would have been meaningful in enhancing intra-regional trade. Work on the fourth round was initiated in 1999 but was put on hold after the military takeover in Pakistan in October of the same year and the nuclear tests by India and Pakistan. Both these events led to heightened political tensions between India and Pakistan. This was followed by a slowdown in the process of economic integration in South Asia for the next few years.

As the India–Pakistan situation normalized in 2003 the heads of the SAARC member nations agreed to launch the South Asia Free Trade Area (SAFTA) at the 2004 annual Summit that was held in Islamabad. The Agreement on SAFTA entered into force on January 1, 2006. As initially designed, SAFTA was restricted to trade in goods only and aimed at creating a free trade area in South Asia in a period of ten years through gradual tariff liberalization, removal of non-tariff barriers (NTBs) and introduction, strengthening and modernizing of trade-facilitating national infrastructure. The SAFTA Agreement provided for negative list specification and its periodic revision alongside a mechanism for dispute settlement. While aiming at the creation of a free trade area the Agreement suffered from many design-specific flaws, as well as problems of implementation. Exclusion of the more dynamic services sector from the liberalization schedule, large negative lists with no target specification for their elimination as well as the long periods required for dispute settlement among others stood out as major obstacles in the way of SAFTA becoming a beneficial instrument furthering the objective of trade integration in the region.[6] A bigger factor, though, that has contributed to undermining the SAFTA as an instrument of trade liberalization in the region was the defiance by Pakistan as it continued to specify a positive list for trade concessions vis-à-vis India, even though it is a signatory to the Agreement incorporating the provision of specification of a negative list by all members vis-à-vis their regional trade partners. Pakistan's stance is a reflection of its political hostility towards India and the strength of pressure groups that would not want trade enhancement with India, even if it is, economically, a more efficient choice. Conflict between India and Pakistan has stalled successful implementation of the regional agreement SAFTA.[7] Intra-regional trade has been observed to increase only marginally since the implementation of SAFTA in 2006, even though the period has been coincidental with economic growth in the region, unilateral trade liberalization and increased trade orientation of the South Asian economies.

While the initial slow progress of the South Asian regional economic integration agenda could be accounted for by the autarkic policies followed by all the regional member countries, it is difficult to stretch the argument for the period of the 1990s and after. In fact during the period of implementation of SAFTA the economic scenario in the region registered a dramatic improvement. India's 7 per cent plus average annual rate of growth over the decade 1998–2008 was the highest, while during the same period the average annual growth of GDP for all the other South

Asian economies was over 5 per cent.[8] Simultaneously the region displayed rapid integration with the global economy with South Asia experiencing one of the fastest growth rates of trade in the world, averaging 10.8 per cent in 2007 following a growth of almost 12 per cent experienced during 2005–06, which was the highest among all regions.[9] Notwithstanding these very positive trends, regional economic integration in South Asia has been anaemic. Intra-regional trade in South Asia is about 5 per cent of its total trade and about 5 per cent of regional GDP. India's trade with its regional neighbours is less than 3 per cent of its total trade and in contradiction with the global experience.[10] As India–Pakistan hostilities appear to have repeatedly got in the way of economic rationality, gains of economic integration seem to have been foregone by South Asia.[11]

The SAFTA has also been undermined by the successful implementation of bilateral preferential trade agreements in the region. India has bilateral trade agreements with three countries – Sri Lanka, Nepal and Bhutan – in the region and is negotiating a fourth with Bangladesh. Pakistan has a free trade agreement with Sri Lanka. The India–Sri Lanka trade relationship and bilateral FTA (BFTA) is an example of how economic rationality can assist the peace process and vice versa between two nations. The India–Sri Lanka BFTA that was implemented in 2001 helped ameliorate the tensions between the two nations that had arisen due to the perceived intervention by India in what was a domestic civil conflict in the smaller island nation. Having benefitted economically and politically, both India and Sri Lanka are keen to upgrade the bilateral trade agreement to its next stage of a comprehensive economic partnership agreement. The other long-standing bilateral trade treaties between India–Nepal and India–Bhutan, although not in the spirit of WTO defined FTA agreements, greatly facilitate trade between India and the less-developed countries of the region.[12] Trade between India and Nepal is conducted on the basis of the structure as provided by the 1991 Trade Treaty. The treaty has been modified several times and most recently in October 2009. The India–Bhutan Trade and Commerce Agreement that expired in 2005 has since been renewed for a period of ten years. The provisions of these agreements are such that a de facto free trade regime exists between India and Bhutan. Negotiations are also underway for a bilateral agreement between India and Bangladesh. The India–Sri Lanka bilateral FTA was followed by a bilateral FTA between Sri Lanka and Pakistan in 2005. The major economies of South Asia have therefore either already entered into or are negotiating bilateral FTAs among themselves. The bilateral FTAs underway in the region are working effectively in contrast with the regional FTA that is constantly encumbered by bilateral hostilities and conflicts. Given these developments it may not be easy to visualize the successful implementation of the regional FTA. Given that bilateral conflicts have consistently prevented onward movement of regional economic integration in South Asia despite the physical, historical and cultural proximity and economic prosperity of its member nations, a brief review of the nature and role of conflict in South Asia and its regional economic integration agenda helps to better understand the issues under discussion.

Nature of conflict in South Asia: implications for regional economic integration

Conflict in South Asia has been longstanding and multidimensional. Border, boundary and territorial disputes between India and Pakistan, India and Bangladesh, India and Nepal, and Pakistan and Afghanistan have dominated and persisted over the years. There have also been resource disputes and many water and river sharing arrangements have been at the centre of conflict between India, Pakistan, Bangladesh and Nepal. The region has also been characterized by ethnic domestic strife with adverse external spillover effects on inter-state relations, as evident in the cases of Sri Lanka and India, India and Pakistan, India and Bangladesh, and Pakistan and Afghanistan. Terrorist threats and nuclear and missile rivalry have only added to the regional tensions. India appears to be a part of almost all facets of this phenomenon owing to its common border with all countries of the region and the natural resources that cut across India, Pakistan and Bangladesh, irrespective of the boundaries drawn at the time of partition of the sub-continent in 1947 and subsequent independence of Bangladesh in 1971. India's large geographical and economic size coupled with its diversified production base has in addition meant that it enjoys a surplus in its trade with the other smaller economies in South Asia, much to their resentment. The inherent asymmetry has given rise to a fear psychosis among the smaller states of the region such that they have been less than forthcoming in their efforts to strengthen SAARC, anticipating and fearing larger gains for India. The asymmetry and attached fears have also simultaneously prevented India from assuming the role of a lead economy in the region. Overall a sense of commitment to common economic goals has eluded South Asia. This is in contrast with the experience of other regional organizations that have been largely driven by a common commitment to the idea of peace through economic interdependence (EU) or development through cooperation (ASEAN).

In South Asia, even though conflict is common to all the nations, it does not define the region in the sense of giving it a common purpose internally or externally. In fact, it underlies the difficulty in visualizing the region as one with a common interest – or, for that matter, a common perception – of external threat-conditions that invariably define other regional blocs and are at the core of regional leaders' desire and efforts towards regional cooperation and the general populace's acceptance of the loss of sovereignty that is inevitable in collaborative action. Differences are in fact more apparent and dominant in the South Asian countries' external relations than commonalities. Internal conflicts have led South Asian countries to follow and reflect different international alliances, preferences and voting patterns at international forums.[13] These regional differences have been further compounded by frequent changes in political regimes in member nations. In South Asia democracy has not been the norm. Only India and Sri Lanka have experienced democracy on a sustained basis. Pakistan and to some extent Bangladesh have had autarkic and military regimes with brief interludes of democracy, while Nepal and Bhutan have long histories of monarchy, with some episodes of attempted democracy in Nepal and a recent, nascent transition to democracy in Bhutan. As has been generally observed the world over that mixed political regimes such as autocracies and military regimes, unlike democracy, do not necessarily augur well for enhanced trade or peace,[14] so has been true of South Asia.

The South Asian experience is unique in terms of its inability to realize or effectuate the necessary placement of cooperation above conflict, even if it has been to the detriment of the region in terms of loss of peace, stability and economic benefits. Similar and probably more difficult regional situations in other parts of the world have been resolved and settled peacefully by giving primacy to economic gains over political interests. While the EU integration process may be considered *sui generis* and not easily replicable, there are other regions that have been able to overcome violent historical pasts. ASEAN, for example, is considered to have facilitated a transformation of the South East Asian region into a stable and peaceful zone through consultation and cooperation. The organization at its inception had the dominant countries in a state of dispute and suspicion, but a common need to come together following the communist threat in the region helped them overcome their differences.[15] Economic prosperity through cooperation was considered essential as a means of national and regional resilience to the spread of communism. Disputes were shelved, differences relegated to the background and agreements were arrived at for avoiding use of force to resolve bilateral discords.[16] Economic initiatives, like the ASEAN free trade agreement (AFTA) that was introduced in 1992, complemented by the ASEAN framework agreement on services liberalization (AFAS) signed in 1995 and the agreement for creation of an ASEAN investment area (AIA) in 1998, indicate ASEAN's commitment towards deeper economic integration. Record growth rates were experienced by these countries in the subsequent years as regional cooperation created a conducive and relatively secure environment. Diplomatic cohesion has since characterized the regional organization and was most evident when the member countries adopted a common stand on the Cambodian conflict. When the organization has been subjected to trials like the 1997–98 financial crisis, the effort has been to combat adversity by evolving regional mechanisms jointly by all member economies. The Chiang Mai Initiative (CMI) was established in 2000 as a bilateral swap arrangement in response to the currency and liquidity crisis experienced by the South East Asian economies in 1997–98. The CMI regional financial arrangement was made more substantive through its evolution into CMI multi-lateralization in March 2010 in the wake of the 2008–09 global financial crisis. The ASEAN charter released in 2007 for the establishment of the ASEAN Economic Community is the most recent evidence of the organization's evolving regional aspirations. The attempt by the regional economies to push forward the agenda of maintaining peace and economic prosperity as primary objectives of regional cooperation has helped facilitate region-wide production networks based on progressive evolution of comparative advantage of ASEAN economies, which has in turn led to increased intra-regional trade. During the two decades from 1986–87 to 2006–07, the share of intra-regional trade in total non-oil East Asia trade increased from 34.4 per cent to 54.1 per cent.[17]

The South East Asian example helps spotlight the contribution of regional peace and cooperation to successful economic integration. While the export-oriented economic growth models of ASEAN economies have been facilitating in establishing the production networks, it cannot be denied that economic cooperation has been allowed to happen despite ideological differences. Additionally, conflict prevention has been built into the ASEAN way of working, as decision making is based upon principles of consensus building and voluntarism. In contrast, the SAARC has deliberately and consciously kept bilateral issues out of the purview of discussion at the forum, revealing therein a prior lack of confidence in the cooperative mechanism. Conflict has in fact been allowed to obstruct the process of regional cooperation. Many SAARC summit meetings have been called off or postponed on account of bilateral conflicts. In 25 years of its existence, SAARC has had only 16 summit meetings. The SAARC summits in 1992 and 2005 were disrupted due to poor relations between India and Bangladesh, and the 1989 Colombo summit was cancelled because of Colombo's objections to the presence of Indian troops in Sri Lanka.[18]

Successful regional organizations, if not driven by a common agenda, have invariably been led by powerful motivation of either one or a pair of lead economies such that the joint determination and voluntary action filters down or seeps through the psyche of the region. For this to happen, though, the determined lead economy/economic duo has to be able to identify a common and beneficial-to-all economic programme. While EU had the Franco-German duo's desire to move away from conflict and war, other trade blocs have seen economic integration as means for accelerating the pace of economic development. In the case of Mercosur there was a long-standing desire on the part of Argentina and Brazil to enter into integration arrangements, as they perceived it as a means to strengthen their external position in a globalized world. The trade bloc was aimed at creating a more competitive position for themselves and despite later problems there was a continuous pursuit of integration, with efforts towards convergence of internal development policies with the external globalized world and attaining a position of strength externally. The initial attempts by Argentina and Brazil towards integration were made through strategic sector agreements in the 1980s.

The initiative for economic integration, it is observed, comes from either the conflicting nations (France and Germany in the case of the EU) or from the central economies, Argentina and Brazil in Mercosur. In the case of the latter, the importance of greater accommodation and shared vision of Argentina and Brazil cannot be denied either, particularly given the centrality of Argentina-Brazil bilateral relations for the Mercosur integration process. In addition, the process was able to move forward through conscious attempts by Brazil to contain and counter the dissatisfaction of the smaller members (Uruguay and Paraguay) from the integration process and prevent the grouping from disintegrating by establishing structural funds to be financed by Brazil to reduce asymmetries in the block. Brazil has also introduced a policy to increase its imports from its neighbours in general to reduce its large export surplus in the region and increase development.

In South Asia, India has provided for a duty-free import regime to all smaller nations of the region and has also entered into non-reciprocal and less-than-symmetric trade initiatives and agreements with Bhutan, Nepal and Sri Lanka. With Bangladesh, India has recently made an attempt to prune its negative list such that preferential treatment is offered in sectors/products of its export interest, even when this has raised doubts among its own domestic textile/readymade garments producers. These have all been unilateral attempts by India. The trade arrangements have helped the smaller countries to expand their export basket and consequently reduce their trade deficit with India. In the case of Bhutan, Indian efforts at trade expansion have been integral components of its developmental plans. But despite all these very positive factors the efforts have remained confined to the bilateral level and there is as yet little reflection of India's attempts to blunt the edges of asymmetry at the regional level. This failure to reconcile the bilateral with the regional in South Asia can be attributed, of course, to the fact that they are all very recent, have come after the region has for over a quarter of a century seen almost negligible success of the SAARC, and are all announced unilaterally by India outside the framework of SAARC – in a way more as a reinforcement of India's large economic position than as an effort to draw the smaller economies within the regional fold. The persistence of conflict between India and Pakistan, the pair that overshadows other pairs in the region, is the other factor that has prevented the emergence of a regional anchor economy. South Asia will see a success of regional economic integration only when, like in other regional arrangements, the dominant conflicting duo of India and Pakistan takes the initiative or lead to evolve the cooperative agenda as per a joint vision for the region.[19]

As a consequence of the slow pace of South Asian economic integration many economic advantages that would have been a natural outcome of integrating with one of the world's most dynamic economy, that is India, have not come to the smaller economies of the region. Simultaneously, since India has not found acceptability as the possible lead economy of the region there is now a possibility and even evidence of India looking elsewhere. India is actively following its economic integration with South East Asia that is getting reflected both in terms of increased trade and bilateral preferential arrangements with the region (ASEAN and the plus-three economies) and its individual member economies. Having formalized its relationship with the extended region through its 'Look East' policy, initiated way back in 1991 with an objective of drawing on the region's experience of economic liberalization, India has in the last decade added to it a new dimension of regionalism. The Indian leadership has repeatedly emphasized the need to actualize the potential of establishing a Pan Asian regional framework and this is amply reflected in its active membership of the East Asia Summit established in 2005 that includes members of the ASEAN, China, Korea, Japan and the US and promotes the idea of economic integration among the member economies. India has also formally signed comprehensive economic partnership agreements with Japan and Korea in 2009 and established a bilateral strategic economic dialogue with China in 2011. As an equal partner having rapidly increased trade with the regional economies as well as formal agreements/arrangements with all member economies, India is set to play a decisive role in this larger Asian economic integration initiative.

While the development augurs well for India and may in due course provide even South Asia with a window of opportunity to integrate with South East/East Asia, it does call for a re-examination and probably course correction for South Asia. Is trade trapped in the overpowering effect of politics and conflictual relations in the region? Does the potential for trade remain unexploited because of the protracted and persistent hostilities and frictions? This book makes an attempt to deal with this important question and undertakes a technical analysis to assess the extent of loss of trade potential that the region is subjected to on account of the phenomenon of persistent conflict. The thus obtained quantitative estimates of the cost that conflict is imposing on the region in terms of foregone trade benefits may just provide a basis for economic rationality to overrule political and historical animosities in South Asia. This, as discussed below, is significant in the evolving global context, wherein overcoming historical and political constraints will be necessary to make South Asia globally competitive.

Global context

Three major developments of the last decade that are potentially likely to impinge on the process of regional economic integration in South Asia are discussed below. These include the shift of the centre of gravity of the global economy to Asia, the global financial crisis and the renewed interest in SAARC as an organization for regional cooperation. The first is largely an outcome of the dynamism of the Indian and Chinese economies, the second with origins in the developed world has shown multifaceted implications for developing countries and regional economic integration as a process, and in Asia in particular, and, finally, the third is an interesting development that needs to be viewed in the light of the new membership and observers of the SAARC. Each of these issues is briefly discussed with its implications for economic integration in South Asia.

Rise of India and China

India and China have over the last two decades become the two fastest-growing economies in the world. The dynamism in their growth process has been a consequence of the timing, pace and nature of economic reforms that have spelt a major breakthrough in their growth strategies from inward-looking closed economies with minimal emphasis on the external sector and extensive state controls to more liberalized economic systems. Ever since the initiation of economic reforms in 1978, China witnessed a doubling of its economic growth by 1990 at an annual rate of growth of 9.3 per cent and a further increase to a double-digit level of 10.5 per cent annual growth over 1991–2010. India also experienced an increased pace of growth since its economic reforms in 1991. In comparison with a pre-reform almost stagnant annual rate of growth of between 3 and 4 per cent, the period from 1991 to 2010 saw a growth rate of 6.6 per cent per year. In the last decade, while China has relentlessly moved forward with a double-digit rate of growth, India too has seen an almost uninterrupted 8 per cent plus rate of growth since 2003. For both India and China, recovery from the global financial crisis of 2008–09 has been easier and quicker than the rest of the world. In 2010, China, with a rate of economic growth of 10.3 per cent, made a return to its pre-crisis double-digit pace of growth. India similarly recorded an almost untouched-by-the-crisis growth of over 8 per cent in the same year.

The economic dynamism of India and China, however, has differential implications for the process of economic integration in South and South East Asia respectively. This is largely on account of the differential growth strategies that these economies have followed in the past. China has made greater investment in manufacturing over the course of its development and trade liberalization process. China's manufacturing sector accounts for more than 40 per cent of its GDP, with manufacturing goods constituting over 90 per cent of its exports. This is in contrast with India's trade in manufacturing not being remarkable to date, with the sector's share being just about 20 per cent of GDP. The manufacturing sector development was further facilitated by the large-scale FDI inflows in China and availability of a large pool of cheap labour in the country, resulting in an evolving structure of comparative advantage. As a consequence, China assumed the position of a regional hub of manufactured production, mainly in the labour-intensive, low-value production in the 1990s and later in the more advanced electronic goods manufactures. ASEAN economies after the post 1997–98 financial crisis sought China in this new role and aligned themselves in the production chain. This trend is apparent from the changing export composition of the ASEAN economies with the relative share of intermediate manufactured goods in sectors like electrical machinery, computer chips and automobile parts increasing from 12 per cent in 1990 to 52 per cent in 2008 in the total export value of ASEAN to China. This production network-based and -led pattern of trade became central to the growth process of the ASEAN economies as well as China and the regional economic integration process in South East Asia. India, with a relatively lower share of the manufacturing sector, does not have the same linkages within South Asia. As all the economies in the region followed similar strategies of inward-looking industrialization post-independence, the comparative advantage structures have been largely similar. The scope for intra-regional trade has been consequently limited. Post-economic liberalization India, with its economic dynamism and growing middle-class population, has been able to develop a more diversified manufacturing base, which has not been true for the other economies in the region. India continues as an isolated player in the South Asian region with limited scope for collaborative production processes.

Interestingly, though, while India and China are differentially placed in their own regions, they are both highly coveted in each other's regions. India is being increasingly sought by the ASEAN economies as the balancing economic power vis-à-vis China in South East Asia. The initial Chinese hesitation to include India in the East Asia Summit (EAS) process and the support from Singapore and Thailand are evidence towards these sentiments. India is now a co-participant with other South East Asian and East Asian economies in the EAS. Similarly, China's presence in South Asia is marked by its recent economic relationships at the bilateral level with different countries of the region, apart from its longstanding strategic relationship with Pakistan. For a long time the Indian perceptions of the Chinese economy were dominated by the shadow of history and the India–China conflict of 1959–62 that culminated in the 1962 war between the two countries. However, it needs to be realized that while the conflict did cast a shadow on the region, it has by no means restricted the two economies from entering into a flourishing economic relationship. This is evident from the increase in India–China bilateral trade to US$42 billion from US$17 billion over the period 2005–06 to 2009–10.[20] The economic relationship was given an institutional format with the establishment of the Bilateral Strategic Economic Dialogue. The inaugural dialogue was held in Beijing in September 2011 with a comprehensive agenda of bilateral cooperation in areas like water, energy, environment and infrastructure. The new orientation to the India–China economic relationship has been accompanied by developments in other areas – like China recognizing Sikkim as Indian territory, the opening of the Nathu-la pass, and some progress on the border issues – all that have been in favour of reducing conflict and enhancing bilateral trade levels. Active trade partnerships have been established with other South Asian nations also. China's current trade volume with all South Asian nations is close to $20 billion a year. China has a trade surplus with all the South Asian trade partners, including India. There are massive investments by China in Bangladesh, Sri Lanka, Nepal and Pakistan, specifically in sectors like infrastructure development, socio-economic needs and energy production. The largest South Asian beneficiaries of economic aid from China are Pakistan, Bangladesh, Sri Lanka and Nepal, in that order. Apart from trade, China's interest in South Asia extends from strategic alignment with Pakistan, gas reserves in Bangladesh and the access that it provides to some of the northeast regions of India, the strategic location of Nepal between India and China and access to Sri Lanka's ports. China has also sought to formalize its relationship with South Asia, having expressed its interest in acquiring membership of the SAARC. China was granted observer status in 2005.

Expansion of SAARC

At the Delhi SAARC summit in 2007, seven countries were invited to join as observers. These included China, the US, Mauritius, the European Union, Japan, South Korea and Iran. At the next summit in Colombo two more countries, Australia and Myanmar, joined as observers. Expansion of SAARC to include Afghanistan as a full member happened in 2007 and is expected to have positive implications for stability in Afghanistan and at the same time allow South Asia to establish linkages with Central Asia. The development is beneficial in terms of increasing scope for trade and energy cooperation. India's large-scale aid programme and involvement in reconstruction of the Afghan economy is likely to contribute to greater stability of the country.

Since becoming an observer of SAARC, China has continuously attempted to deepen cooperation with the organization in areas of economy, trade and culture.

China has undertaken several initiatives including a China-SAARC business forum for exhibition of commodities from South Asian countries, and training courses for officials of political parties from South Asian countries. China has also donated US$300,000 to the development fund of SAARC.

The expansion of SAARC may be viewed as a reflection of the other countries' interest in the region's dynamism, as well as South Asia's desire to get rid of its stance of isolation in a more globalized world. This may be truer of India than the smaller economies that have always seen entry of other members as providing them with a sense of security against India's capacity to dominate the regional organization. However, the question of entry and thereby of future aspirants needs to be perceived within the larger issue of expansionism, being meaningful when economic integration among the seven founding members of the SAARC has been very limited. While expansionism and/or open regionalism has characterized many regional organizations, it is a beneficial step if it strengthens the existing regional bloc. The probability of providing strength to the regional bloc is greater if the member nations and the region as a whole are stable. It is important to consider this question, as there have been some calls in the past from both China and South Asian countries other than India asking to include China as a member of SAARC. It would be reasonable to say that there would have been benefits of enlargement if South Asia were a stable region, as then an additional member would mean an extension of the stable region. Given the present scenario of instability and persistent hostilities within SAARC, expansion and new entry can only mean the contrary. In particular with reference to China, the South Asian alignment, particularly of India and Pakistan as well as the other smaller countries, differs, so that expansionism may only lead to greater polarities in the regional body. The future course on expansionism should therefore be a function of positive outcomes of existing as well as prospective membership, both in terms of economic and non-economic gains.

Global financial crisis

The most significant implication of the global financial crisis for regional economic integration in South Asia is the alternative that the post-global-financial-crisis scenario presents for an alignment between India and East Asia. It is well known that Chinese trade expansion and surplus accumulation are considered by many as major factors responsible for the global financial crisis of 2008–09. The manner in which China can and may choose to undertake to adjust its trade imbalances and the underlying currency revaluation has been a matter of debate, concern and huge implications for the many Asian economies that are interlinked with the global economy through China. The US, which has correspondingly the largest deficit with the Chinese economy, has been deeply desirous of a revaluation of the Chinese currency that may in turn set the unwinding of the global imbalance in a favourable direction. However, the corresponding adjustment that this rebalancing between the US and China would require of the East Asian economies may not be simple, quick or without pain. With rebalancing and currency revaluations China will have to start looking inwards for a growth impulse, and the pursuit of growth, with the existing predominantly export-led growth strategy, may not be feasible. Domestic demand development in fact will be a necessity for China as the sharp drop in demand from the US and Eurozone will continue to have a detrimental impact on global growth. So far Chinese households have been heavily oriented towards accumulating savings that have been kept as deposits in state-owned banks and in turn invested in state-financed projects creating excess capacity in the economy. Deviation of savings to private consumption expenditure would call for social-sector reforms, in particular in sectors like education and health, to be undertaken in the immediate and medium term. Simultaneously, fundamental reforms in the financial sector would also be required to allow the interest rates to be market-determined and thereby correct the saving-investment balance in the Chinese economy. Greater public spending on social infrastructure in health, housing, and education would not only improve social welfare but also serve to reduce relatively high precautionary household savings. Other necessary accompaniments to ensure sustained onward growth and survival out of the current crisis based on domestic demand development in China include managing the apparent and rising labour discontent, regional inequalities and the existing pressures for currency correction. Given the political strength and ingenuity that would be required to undertake these reforms and the accompanying domestic economic management, it is entirely possible that China may not be able to maintain its linear growth trajectory too long into the future. As a consequence, it may be very likely that the market-led integration process in East Asia will lose its balancing centre point. Domestic consumption in China may in any case not be able to generate proportional demand for inputs from the East Asian economies. Also the import content of the domestic demand in China is likely to be much smaller than that of the export demand from the advanced economies in the pre-crisis period. A slowdown in growth accompanied by a loosening of the market-led inter-linkages seems a likely outcome. Alternatives to sustain economic integration in the region would need innovative thinking and institutional design. India as a market presents one such alternative for the region.

India's growth in contrast with China's has been achieved through maintaining a balance between consumption and investment as well as export and domestic demand. India has been relatively less impacted by the crisis and has almost no spill over impact on the region. The impact of the crisis that made its way into the economy through the liquidity crunch for investment financing was largely indirect. The crisis did impact the manufacturing sector exports, but the services sector and particularly the IT and related services were not as badly affected. Overall India has been protected from the global decline in export demand because exports constitute a relatively small proportion of GDP. Future growth projections remain predicated on the country's ability for fiscal consolidation that is more a matter of domestic policy correction than dependence on external corrective forces to play themselves out. India's conditions for sustained growth are far more manageable, though it may also be appropriate to state that even with a more secure growth process, in order to enter the double-digit growth phase and sustain its position among the leading emerging economies India has to undertake some major economic reforms. However, these reforms require domestic political consensus rather than imply a change in India's underlying growth strategy and orientation.

The emerging global and regional situation can therefore add to the existing momentum of economic integration between ASEAN and India. The evolving scenario makes it imperative that smaller economies in South Asia seriously rethink their economic integration strategy vis-à-vis India. The benefits of increased economic integration are to be derived not just from India but additionally from the ASEAN economies that India would provide linkages with. It is an opportunity that South Asia should not let go of and therefore must pursue its own regional economic integration agenda more vigorously.

EU emulation and re-questioning: Post-global financial crisis

The EU is at a critical juncture today with widespread speculation about its possible break-up in the post-global-financial-crisis period. The disintegration may not happen at all, especially given the concrete steps taken by the stronger economies of Germany and France, as well as the Union itself, to save their weaker co-members. Among the essential outcomes of the exposure of weaknesses of the EU experiment, one would be to seriously consider the extent of transfer of national sovereignty to supra-national institutions that is entailed in such Unions. Notwithstanding the recent questioning of the EU integration process, it is natural for any region to also seek lessons from the EU's experience prior to the crisis of 2008–09. This holds true for South Asia as well, especially given that the EU economic integration is an example of the coming together of former political adversaries. The important element to stress in this case, however, is the voluntary nature of collective action and the great joint determination on the part of political leaders to prevent future conflict and attached economic losses. It is noteworthy that the EU integration had some very special and unique circumstances that made the success of the experiment possible. The thinking towards the EU integration was against the backdrop of a war that had its origins in protectionism and trade barriers induced largely by the 1930s depression. Establishing economic interdependence was seen as the most potent and maybe the only available instrument that would help ensure peace in the continent. Maintaining peace was a necessity that all – especially France and Germany – wanted to establish in the post-WWII period. Internationalism and institutional supra-nationality was a common desire. Supra-national institutions were created deliberately so as to engender collective action and interdependence and peaceful co-existence. To a large extent the success of the European experiment lies in the desire of the member nations (certainly the founding members) for supra-nationality. The EU was at the start more homogeneous in terms of its income levels and more intent and committed towards deeper economic integration. What is absolutely essential to recognize and what emerges from the EU experience is that in making any regional organization a success there has to be an underlying commonality of interest that is all-encompassing – political, economic, social, cultural and historical – and the collective must aim at a common goal driven by this commonality of interest. It is this objective that the South Asian region needs to recognize and consciously work towards. In the hope that a numerical value of loss may motivate the regional leaders with a common objective to ameliorate this loss by looking beyond conflict and according the necessary priority to economic prosperity, this book undertakes to analyze the trade-conflict relationship in the South Asian context. The book is organised as follows.

Organization of the book

The overarching objective of this book is to quantify the loss of trade on account of persistent conflict in South Asia. The quantitative estimation of conflict-induced trade costs are undertaken using the gravity model[21] framework, augmented by features specific to the contextual realities and characteristics of the South Asian region. The idea is to present technically robust estimates of the costs of acceding priority to perpetuate conflict than to its resolution that would in turn ensure peace and economic prosperity in South Asia. Towards this purpose the book is organized in eight chapters, including this introductory chapter.

The following chapter introduces the South Asian region in terms of its member economies. Differential levels of economic development of member countries of the region are analyzed along with a profile of India's rise globally as a dynamic emerging economy. The central position that India occupies in the region – both geographically and in economic terms – is highlighted in the analysis. Chapter 3 undertakes an overview of the process of economic liberalization in South Asia with a detailed analysis of trends and patterns of trade and FDI of the South Asian economies. The chapter highlights the limited role that intra-regional trade has played in South Asia as against trade with the rest of the world. The role of non-tariff and other behind-the-border barriers in facilitating regional trade is discussed, as well as, in the context, the need to evolve a regional transit arrangement in South Asia. The chapter also presents a simple indicative example of production networks in the textiles and clothing sector as a means to economic integration in the region. The primary focus of Chapter 4 is on the nature of preferential trade agreements in South Asia. The multi-layered approach followed by South Asia with trading agreements at the regional, bilateral and inter-regional levels is analyzed. Chapter 5 presents a neutral and objective account of conflict in South Asia. The varied nature and sequence of conflict events as observed among the South Asian countries is also presented. While the focus is on inter-state conflict, a brief overview of confidence-building measures established in the region has also been included. In addition as a preliminary exercise to the more formal econometric estimation undertaken in the subsequent chapter, some analytical observations based on visual impressions of the relevant data on conflict and trade are presented. Chapter 6 discusses the theoretical foundations of the trade-conflict relationship as relevant to the South Asian context and as background to the formulation of a formal expression to be estimated econometrically in the following chapter. Given the fact that the ongoing preferential trade agreements among the South Asian countries at all levels – regional, sub-regional, bilateral – do not as yet cover, or are only as yet negotiating to incorporate, investment liberalization, and as the literature examining the effects of FDI on international relations is in its infancy, the trade-conflict framework is the mainstay of the analysis in Chapters 6 and 7 of the book. Current developments and extensions taking place in the trade-conflict literature are nonetheless presented. The analysis in Chapter 6 also highlights the possibility of bi-directional causality in the trade-conflict relationship. The estimation of the impact of inter-state conflict on intra-regional trade in South Asia is undertaken econometrically using a conflict-augmented gravity model in Chapter 7. The model incorporates and estimates the impact of conflict in its several dimensions on bilateral trade in South Asia. The estimation is undertaken for the period 1965–2000 that is marked by high levels of hostilities and tensions and bounded, at both ends, by major war/war-like situations in the region. The roles of region-, regime-political-and-economic- and dyad-specific characteristics have also been appropriately incorporated in the model and estimation process. The concluding chapter presents the main findings of the analysis in the preceding chapters, based upon which the chapter also discusses and proposes some initiatives to take the idea of economic integration in South Asia closer to reality.

2 South Asia
The region

A region is defined as a group of countries located in the same geographically specified area. Besides geographical proximity, it has also been considered that countries comprising a region are to be identified by a common culture, history and language, and sometimes political and economic ties. In fact, sometimes a regional identity has been based upon linguistic similarities without reference to geographical proximity. Commonality in the stage of development has been another basis of defining a region. More formally in the context of regionalism, countries that accord preferential treatment to each other in various trade and/or investment and comprehensive cooperation treaties, that is, in preferential economic arrangements, are said to constitute a region. Geographical proximity need not be a priority in this case.

Interestingly South Asia, comprising Afghanistan, Bangladesh, Bhutan, India, Pakistan, Nepal, Sri Lanka and Maldives,[1] appears to be an almost perfect fit as a region fulfilling almost all the conditions of regionalism. South Asia is a geographically well-defined and coherent region. The northern boundary of the region is defined by the Himalayan mountains, Karakoram range and Hindukush mountains, the eastern boundary by mountains and thick forests along the Myanmar border and the southern boundary by the Bay of Bengal, Indian ocean and Arabian sea. Only the western boundary is slightly open with deserts and mountains. The geography of the region is also unique. All countries of the region share a border with India but not with each other. Four nations – Pakistan, Bangladesh, Nepal and Bhutan – have a common land border with India, and two other nations – Sri Lanka and Maldives – share maritime borders with India. None of these countries have a common border with each other. Bhutan and Nepal are landlocked by India. Afghanistan and Pakistan border India and have geographical access to other SAARC members only through India.[2] Sri Lanka is an island and Maldives is an archipelago of low-lying coral islands in the central Indian Ocean.

Member countries of South Asia share a common colonial past and historical emergence as independent nations. They are bound together by historical ties, religious and cultural traditions, linguistic affinities, common values and social norms. The common colonial past has also conditioned their economic framework such that they have all followed the inward-oriented import substitution-based growth model till the late eighties/early nineties. Their growth objectives have been driven largely by a desire for self-reliance with minimum emphasis on the external sector. The shift in economic policies towards outward orientation has also been at almost similar junctures in their growth process in the late 1980s and early1990s, with the exception of Sri Lanka, which initiated the process of economic liberalization in 1978.

All the seven nations of the region are founding members of the regional organization, the South Asian Association for Regional Cooperation (SAARC). Afghanistan joined SAARC in 2007. All seven members established a preferential trading arrangement, SAPTA, in 1993 that was replaced by the South Asia Free Trade Area Agreement in 2004. Afghanistan is also a signatory to the SAFTA.

Economic profile[3]

In the last two decades South Asia has experienced high growth averaging 6 per cent annually. The average annual rate of growth that was 6.5 per cent during 2000–07 peaked at around 8.9 per cent in 2006–07 making South Asia the second fastest growing developing region after South East Asia. To a large extent the growth dynamism of the region has been an outcome of the process of economic reforms undertaken in the decade of the 1990s. The reforms that were broadly similar across many countries of the region included enhancing macroeconomic stability based on fiscal consolidation through tax and expenditure reforms, trade liberalization through introducing exchange rate flexibility and dismantling restrictive trade practices, reduction in state control of economic activities combined with increased private sector participation, strengthening and revitalizing the financial sector by deregulating interest rates, enhancing competition, easing private bank entry and introduction of prudential norms.

In the post-global-financial-crisis period South Asia has been one of the first regions to recover and demonstrate growth rates that are almost equal to the period before the crisis. As evident form Table 2.1, South Asia experienced growth at 8 per cent in 2009, higher than its pre-crisis levels and well above the rate for 2008, the year of the crisis. The rate of growth for South Asia in 2009 was the highest among all regions in the world, as the other regions recorded negative or very low rates of growth. However, as regards the gross national income per capita (GNI PC), South Asia at US$1,216 has recorded the lowest level among all regions in the world, even below that of sub-Saharan Africa. The picture is slightly different when the GNI is measured in terms of purchasing power parity (PPP), in which case South Asia ranks above the sub-Saharan African region but is still well below the other regions. South Asia's large population has an obvious role to play in its economic dynamism not getting reflected in per capita income levels.

South Asia has a combined population of 1.5 billion people and ranks second in the world after the East Asia and Pacific region, which has a population of 2 billion. Three of the world's ten most populous countries, including India, Pakistan and Bangladesh, are in South Asia. With about a fourth of the world's population and covering 3.8 per cent of the total world land area, South Asia is the most densely

Table 2.1 Economic indicators: relative regional performance

Region	GNI PC (US$)	GNI$_{PPP}$ PC (curr. int)	ROG (Annual %)	Population (milln)
East Asia & Pacific	7,118	9,750	7,(2),–1	2,159
Europe & Central Asia	23,335	24,155	2,(1),–4	887
Latin America and Caribbean	7,891	11,134	6,(4),–2	578
Middle East & North Africa	–	–	4,(5),2	376
South Asia	1,216	3,230	8,(5),8	1,567
Sub-Saharan Africa	1,187	2,166	5,(5),2	840

Source: World Development Indicators (WDI) (2011); figures in parentheses are for year 2008, preceded by 2010 and followed by 2009 figures. ROG: rate of growth

populated geographical region in the world. It has a population density of 331 in comparison with 124 for East Asia and only 18 and 29 for Europe and Central Asia and Latin America and Caribbean regions respectively. About 74 per cent of the total population of South Asia resides in India. The maximum percentage of South Asian population is concentrated in the age group of 15–64 years. This is an encouraging profile as the large percentage of youth in this age group is expected to join the work force in the coming years.

Global integration

In terms of global integration, South Asia moved from inward-looking to outward-looking trade orientation only in the 1990s. The inward-looking trade policies were focused upon import substitution through protection granted by high tariffs and customs duties. Tariffs have gradually been brought down in the region even though protection levels continue to be high relative to other regions of the world. South Asia maintains large differences between its bound and applied rates both for manufacturing and agricultural products. The bound rate for primary products is more than double the bound rate for manufactured products. Given that the applied rate (simple mean) in both categories of products is equal, the difference between the bound and applied is that much larger in terms of primary products and is thus indicative of the scope for greater protection in this category. It is therefore unsurprising that South Asia continues to be one of the least-open regions in the world and contributes only about 2 per cent of world trade.

Drawing comparisons with its immediate neighbourhood, the trade-to-GDP ratio in South Asia is 45 per cent (2010) relative to 70 per cent for the East Asia and Pacific region. In South Asia exports contribute only a fifth of GDP in contrast with almost 40 per cent in the East Asia and Pacific region. Overall South Asia is observed to have a deficit in its trade with the world, while East Asia has a surplus. Further, even though South Asia has made fairly rapid strides in integrating with the world (its rate of integration being higher than any other region over the period 2005–08) its export profile has not changed much. South Asian exports continue to be largely unskilled and labour intensive with high technology-intensive exports comprising only about 7 per cent of the total manufactured exports in contrast with 29 per cent for East Asia. High technology exports comprise 7 per cent of total exports for India, 2 percent for Pakistan and 1 each for Nepal and Sri Lanka. This is probably a reflection of the greater emphasis that East Asia places on the manufacturing industry, as well as the outward orientation of the economies. In the East Asia and Pacific region merchandise trade constitutes about 55 per cent of GDP in contrast with South Asia where merchandise trade is only about 33 per cent of the region's GDP. As regards trade in services, South Asia, with a 13 per cent share in GDP, is ahead of East Asia, with a 10 per cent share.

In terms of financial integration, South Asia has witnessed net private capital inflows in large amounts after its economic opening-up in the 1990s. Prior to the global financial crisis South Asia received private capital inflows to the tune of almost 8 per cent of its GDP in 2007. With almost a two-thirds share, net equity flows comprise a larger proportion of the total private inflows to South Asia. Inflows of FDI constitute 1 per cent of GDP in South Asia in contrast with about 3 per cent of GDP in East Asia. In terms of outflows, in both cases the proportion is about 1percent of the GDP. Post-crisis FDI flows to South Asia strengthened markedly in 2011. The FDI inflows as well as their recovery is largely due to the inflows to India, which accounts for about 90 percent of FDI to the region.

Overall trade and capital inflows combined have enabled South Asia to maintain total foreign exchange reserves in terms of seven months of imports. This is in comparison with East Asia that maintains reserves in terms of 20 months worth of imports. The reserves in both the regions are to a large extent a contribution of the larger economies of India in South Asia and China in East Asia. In 2010 India's reserve cover for eight months of imports was the highest in South Asia. In comparison Bangladesh's international reserves were equivalent to just three months of import cover. In East Asia, China's international reserves provide a 21-month imports cover.

Country-wise economic profile

Within South Asia, three of the eight countries, that is, Afghanistan, Bangladesh and Nepal, fall in the low-income category; four countries, including Bhutan, India, Pakistan and Sri Lanka, are classified among the lower middle-income countries; while Maldives is categorized as an upper-middle income economy.[4] India contributes nearly 81 per cent of the region's GDP, followed by Pakistan and Bangladesh with a contribution of 10 and 6 per cent respectively. Afghanistan, Bhutan and Maldives together account for less than 1 per cent of the regional GDP. The remaining about 3 percent comes from Nepal and Sri Lanka. About 74 per cent of the South Asian population resides in India, followed by Pakistan with about 13 per cent population and Bangladesh with 10 per cent population. Nepal and Sri Lanka have a population share of 2 and 1 per cent respectively. In sum, the seven countries other than India contribute 25 per cent of total regional population and 20 per cent of regional GDP.

As regards the economic structure, India, Bangladesh and Pakistan are relatively more diversified in terms of development; Maldives and Bhutan are small, specialized economies and Nepal and Afghanistan are landlocked and undiversified economies.

The South Asian regional growth is attributable largely to the economic dynamism of India. The annual GDP growth in India in the five-year period from 2003–04 to 2007–08 averaged an unprecedented high of 8.8 per cent. In fact in the last three years of this period economic growth in India soared to over 9 per cent. The other South Asian countries that have also experienced high growth rates of 5 per cent and more in this period include Bangladesh, Pakistan and Sri Lanka. In India the period of unprecedented high growth post-2003 also reflects the best average outcomes for other macro indicators like fiscal deficit, at a manageable 5per cent of GDP in 2007/08; external balance, which was in surplus in 2007/08 besides being at a low of around 2 per cent during this time; and inflation at a manageable around 5 per cent. In Bangladesh growth has been financed by growing remittances and exports. Bhutan's growth has been led by the large hydropower projects and is subject to little vulnerability as the power projects are financed by long-term capital inflows from India. Growth in Maldives, Sri Lanka and Pakistan has been accompanied by increased dependence on external finance and has therefore become more vulnerable. Pakistan has been the least stable of all the economies in terms of other macro-economic indicators. The South Asia growth dynamism was briefly interrupted by the impact of the global financial crisis during 2008–09. In fact, Bangladesh and India have shown resilience in the face of global crisis and this is evident from their over 5 per cent growth rate in 2008 and 2009. Sri Lanka and Pakistan have, however, experienced a dip in their growth rates over these two years, probably on account of the former's greater economic openness and the latter's greater dependence on external finance. The fall in growth in the case of Pakistan has also been much larger relative to that experienced by Sri Lanka. The broad macroeconomic profile of the South Asian economies is presented in Tables 2.2a and 2.2b.

Table 2.2a Key economic indicators for South Asia

Indicator	Population (mill)	GDP (bill. curr. US$)	Annual GDP RoG (%)
Afghanistan	29.80	–	8,(3),11
Bangladesh	162.22	89.36	6,(6),6
Bhutan	0.70	1.26	7,(5),18
India	1,155.35	1,310.17	9,(5),10
Maldives	0.31	1.47	10,(12),10
Nepal	29.33	12.53	5,(6),3
Pakistan	169.71	161.99	4,(2),6
Sri Lanka	20.30	41.98	8,(6),7

Source: WDI (2011) World Bank. Figures in parentheses are for year 2008 (crisis), preceded by 2010 (current) and followed by 2007 (pre-crisis) figures.
Note: RoG: rate of growth.

22 South Asia: the region

Table 2.2b South Asia: growth and macro-economic indicators

	GDP growth rate (%)			Current Account Balance			Inflation		
	1991–2000	2005–06	2008–09	1991–2000	2005–06	2008–09	1991–2000	2005–06	2008–09
South Asia	5.3	7.8	7.8						
Bangladesh	4.8	6.6	5.7	−1.4	1.3	2.8	5.7	7.2	6.7
Bhutan	5.1	6.7	6.2	−5.2	−4.3	−4.5	8.5	4.8	4.6
India	5.6	9.5	6.7	−1.1	−1.2	−2.5	8.7	4.2	9.1
Nepal	5	3.4	4.7	−2.9	2.1	4.7	9.6	8	13.2
Pakistan	4	5.8	2	−4	−3.9	−5.6	9.2	7.9	20.8
Maldives	8.3	−4.6	6.3	−5.7	−36.4	−51.4	7.5	1.3	12
Sri Lanka	5.2	6.2	6	−4.7	−2.7	−9.3	9.7	11	22.6
Afghanistan		16.1	3.4					9.4	3.2

Source: South Asia Economic Update (2010) World Bank.

Sector-wise growth pattern

The sector-wise growth profile of the South Asian economies has been at variance with the experience of other developing economies and many developed nations as well.

Already in South Asia it is observed that the services sector makes more than half the contribution to GDP in terms of value addition. In 2010 the sector-wise GDP structure of South Asia is close to that observed for the advanced economies in terms of industry and manufacturing, contributing less than a fourth of the total value addition in GDP. In contrast in the East Asia and Pacific[5] region, even while services is contributing more than half of the total value addition, industry and manufacturing continue to make a substantive contribution, while agriculture contributes less than 10 per cent to GDP.

Almost 50 per cent or more of GDP comes from the services sector for all South Asian economies except Bhutan and Afghanistan, in which case it is 37 percent. The proportion of GDP attributable to the services sector was highest for Maldives at 82 per cent. For India and Sri Lanka it was between 55 and 60 per cent, for Bangladesh 53 per cent, and for Nepal slightly less at 48 per cent. The growing importance of the services sector has been accompanied by a relative decline in the contribution of the agricultural sector, which is less than or around 20 per cent for India, Bhutan, Bangladesh, Pakistan and Sri Lanka. For Afghanistan and Nepal the agriculture sector has relatively greater significance, with its contribution to GDP being around 30 per cent. For Maldives the contribution of the agriculture sector is much lower at about 3 per cent. The industrial sector has undergone a slow decline or stagnation in these economies. This is in contrast with the experience of many developed countries and some developing economies where the declining share of agriculture in GDP has been absorbed by the industrial sector. In defiance of the growth experience worldwide the industrial sector in the South Asian

Table 2.3 South Asia: sector-wise shares (per cent) in GDP

Shares	Agriculture	Industry	of which – Manufacturing	Services
Afghanistan	30	22	13	48
Bangladesh	19	28	18	53
Bhutan	18	45	6	37
India	19	26	14	55
Maldives	3	15	4	82
Nepal	36	15	7	48
Pakistan	21	25	17	53
Sri Lanka	13	29	18	58

Source: World Development Indicators (2011), World Databank, World Bank.

economies has shrunk to around 20–30 per cent of the GDP. Of this the manufacturing sector has an even smaller share of around only 14–18 per cent. The implications of slow growth in industry and its manufacturing component are observed in terms of a much slower rate of employment or labour force absorption in the growth process. The South Asian economies, in particular India, are debating and discussing the possible solutions to this dilemma where high growth is not simultaneously leading to employment creation at an equally rapid pace. The service sector growth in India has been broad-based with both traditional services like construction, tourism and finance as well as the new-age services like ICT registering dynamism. The services sector has, however, not been able to generate employment at a rate consonant with its growth. The situation is further aggravated by the fact that almost 60–70 per cent of population in all the South Asian countries is based in rural areas where the primary activity of agriculture in terms of income and employment has undergone a declining share in total GDP.

Doing business in South Asia

Notwithstanding the changes in terms of its outward orientation, South Asia is still among the most difficult regions to do business. In terms of the *Doing Business Index* as reported annually by the World Bank, most of the South Asian countries rank in the bottom half with only Maldives and Sri Lanka in the top half at the 79th and 89th position respectively. Pakistan is at 105, Nepal at 107, Bangladesh at 122, India at 132 and Bhutan at 142 in a survey of 183 countries. As for the region's investment climate the Global Competitiveness Report (2010–11) reveals that India has moved down two ranks relative to its 2009 position and with regard to comparator countries, it stands way behind China, which is at rank 27 and has moved up by two ranks relative to its 2009 position. India is followed by Sri Lanka at rank 62 and Bangladesh and Pakistan are at 107 and 123 respectively. The ranking is among a set of 139 countries. Further, the report classifies four South Asian economies, including Bangladesh, India, Nepal and Pakistan, in the first stage of development that is characterized by factor-driven production and growth such that these economies continue to compete globally on the basis of given factor endowments. The South Asian economies have not yet evolved to the second stage where productivity levels are enhanced and economies become efficiency driven. Sri Lanka is the only South Asian country that is currently in the stage of transition to the second stage. In comparison, China has already made this transition to an efficiency-driven economy and is classified in the second stage of development.

Social development in South Asia

Despite the progress in economic growth South Asia continues to be challenged on the developmental front. The region presents a rather incongruous picture as regards the various social indicators relative to the pace of economic growth experienced over the same period. With the exception of Sri Lanka, all the South Asian countries rank below 100 in a survey of around 190 countries undertaken to assess the level of human development.[6] Sri Lanka ranks 91 and Afghanistan is at rank 155, while Maldives, India, Pakistan, Bangladesh and Nepal lie in between these ranks. It is observed that in 2010 India was at rank 119 and in the group of countries characterized at a medium level of human development. The value of Human Development Index (HDI) is 0.519 and this is close to the South Asian average of 0.516, which is less than the global average of 0.624. For India a one rank betterment over 2005–10 is clearly not in consonance with its growth story and economic dynamism. Similar marginal improvements in the ranking order are observed for the other South Asian countries also. Sri Lanka is, however, stationary at rank 91 and Pakistan experiences a fall of two positions in its overall rank from 123 to 125 over the same period. The UN classification describes Bangladesh, Nepal and Afghanistan as economies with low human development, while India, Pakistan, Maldives and Sri Lanka are among the economies with medium levels of human development. In terms of constituent indicators it is noted that on the index for multidimensional poverty (MP)[7] South Asian countries are in the segment of countries with a headcount ratio of 50 to 70 per cent, experiencing deprivations in 50 to 55 per cent of the weighted indicators – except for Sri Lanka, which has a relatively low level of headcount MP and average intensity of deprivation. As per the MPI, South Asia's poverty levels are comparable with those of sub-Saharan Africa. A comparison of states within India provides evidence of the poverty in absolute terms. Eight states in India with poverty as acute as the 26 poorest African countries are home to 421 million multi-dimensionally poor people, greater than the combined population of the multi-dimensionally poor people of 410 million in the 26 poor African states. The seriousness of this scenario is further reinforced looking at the poverty headcount ratio,[8] which at $1 a day was 40.3 per cent and at $2 a day was 73.9 per cent in 2005[9] for South Asia as a whole.

With regard to other components of HDI, Sri Lanka shows the highest life expectancy at birth of 74.4 years and is followed by Pakistan and India among the South Asian economies with a medium level of development. Among countries

Table 2.4 Social indicators in South Asian economies

Country	HDI Rank	Life expectancy at birth: male/female (years)	Adult literacy rate (% of people aged 15 & above)
Afghanistan	155	44/44	.
Bangladesh	129	66/68	55
Bhutan	.	65/68	.
India	119	63/66	63
Maldives	107	70/74	98
Nepal	138	66/68	58
Pakistan	125	67/67	54
Sri Lanka	91	71/78	91

Source: http://hdr.undp.org.

with a low level of development, Nepal has a life expectancy equivalent to that of Pakistan. Afghanistan has the lowest level of life expectancy at 44.6 years. The composite adult literacy rate for Sri Lanka is 90.8 and for Pakistan, Maldives and India the rate is 54.2, 97.3 and 68.3 per cent respectively. Significant improvement in this indicator is evident for India as it has increased from a value of 40 per cent in 1980 and 48 per cent in 1990. The indicator crossed the 60 per cent level only in 2000 and since then there has been a consistent rise in its value, even though it remains lower than Sri Lanka's 90 per cent. Bangladesh and Nepal have a composite adult literacy rate of 56.5 and 60.3 per cent, higher than that of Pakistan. Afghanistan, at 28 per cent, has the lowest composite adult literacy rate in the region. Sri Lanka has shown an exceptional performance with regard to social indicators in South Asia. In contrast, India, the lead economy in terms of rate of growth, has a lot of catching up to do in social development.

Contrasts

Our analysis clearly reveals that South Asia is a region of contrasts. High economic growth and global integration is coexistent with large-scale absolute poverty. While the percentage of poor below the poverty line and relative to the pre-liberalization period has declined, the number of poor in absolute terms is so large that poverty alleviation remains a challenge for the region. A study undertaken by the World Bank[10] shows that growth in South Asia has been unevenly distributed regionally, such that some regions have grown at faster rates than others. It is observed that regions that were poorer to begin with have experienced relatively slower growth leading to a perpetuation of existing inequalities. In addition the study highlights the aspect of economically lagging regions belonging to border economies that are either landlocked or geographically isolated. These include regions like northern Bangladesh, Bhutan, North East India, North West Pakistan and parts of Nepal. Better ex ante connectivity and access to regional and world markets has allowed some regions to better avail the opportunities of global integration, while those with a prior disadvantage have lagged behind or have been relatively poor beneficiaries of the process of opening up – regionally or globally.

Taking the growth dynamism to all its people and regions requires several more creative solutions than just reliance on growth itself. One of the means that is proposed through analysis in this book is trade. There is a need for the seven smaller economies in the region to accept that aligning with India –that is, growing rapidly and along a stable, sustainable path – is to their advantage. Regional trade is a useful instrument to take the idea of regional economic cooperation forward. In chapter 6 and 7 econometric modelling and estimation has been undertaken to show the extent of trade benefit that can accrue to South Asian countries if they shed their conflictual positions and attitudes vis-à-vis eachother. In the light of our analysis possible solutions to these issues are taken up for discussion in the concluding chapter.

India's centrality

An outstanding feature of the South Asian region is India's centrality both in terms of geography and economics. Economic centrality is apparent from the predominant position of India in terms of almost all economic indicators. The Indian territory constitutes 64 percent of the South Asian land area and is home to 1.2 billion people – that is 74 per cent of the total population of the region. India contributes nearly 80 per cent of the region's GDP. In comparison the seven countries other than India contribute 25 per cent of the total regional population and 20 per cent of the regional GDP. Further, India's GDP (PPP) is the fourth largest in the world while none of the other South Asian countries rank anywhere among the top twenty. Pakistan at rank 26 has a GDP (PPP) that is almost a tenth of India's GDP (PPP) (IMF, WEO, 2012).

India's central importance in South Asia is also evident from its contribution to regional trade and capital inflows. India accounts for 65 per cent of the total intra-regional trade and almost 80 per cent of the total capital inflows received by South Asia. As the only country that shares its land border with all the other South Asian countries, while the reverse doesn't hold true, India has a critical role in regional trade. Transit through India is necessary for all the other countries to access each other's market. Enhancement of intra-regional trade is therefore a function of India providing transit rights to the other economies. Further, owing to its larger market size and diversified production base, India as the region's major exporter is among the top-ranking trading partners for almost all countries in the region. The same doesn't hold true for other South Asian countries' contribution to India's total imports. Bilateral trade is therefore naturally in favour of India. India has bilateral trade treaties with three SAARC economies – Bhutan, Nepal and Sri Lanka – and negotiations are on with Bangladesh for an FTA agreement. India is also a member of all regional/sub-regional/inter-sub-regional groupings extending membership to South Asia, like the Bangkok Agreement (APTA), BIMSTEC and the South Asia growth quadrangle (SAGQ).

Notwithstanding its geographic and economic centrality India is not perceived as a central pole in South Asia. The smaller economies are overtly conscious of their size and limited production capacities. Fears of India's dominance and ability to draw greater gains out of the regional economic integration process has made the smaller economies trade with external partners through circuitous routes, even when economically this is a more expensive exercise. Such is the psyche of the region that rational thought and economic outcomes have been forgone and overlooked and irrational and costly hostile positions maintained, to the detriment of economic exchange in the region. These aspects are analyzed in a detailed description of the trends of intra-regional trade, investment and preferential agreements of the South Asian economies in the following two chapters.

3 Trade and FDI patterns of South Asian countries

This chapter presents a detailed analysis of trends and patterns of trade and FDI of the South Asian economies against a background review of their economic policy framework. The analysis helps emphasize the significance of economic regimes as a contributory factor in determining and estimating potential trade possibilities in the region.[1] The trends and patterns of trade in South Asia underscore the twin contradiction of the increasing rate of global integration of the region that is progressing with continued maintenance of trade restrictiveness in these economies at levels higher than the average in comparator income group countries, and an almost stagnant pace of intra-regional trade. Non-tariff and behind-the-border barriers that make informal trade a profitable alternative means of undertaking exchange in the region are also discussed. The centrality of India in regional trade and FDI is spotlighted in the discussion. Further, drawing on the experience of production-network-led economic integration in South East Asia, an attempt is made to identify the scope for establishing production networks in the textiles and clothing sector in South Asia.

Post-independence economic regimes in South Asia

Caught in the anti-colonial sentiment, South Asian countries followed a growth strategy aimed at self-reliance through import substitution. Starting in the 1950s, an active planning process was adopted to guide the inward-looking import substitution-based industrialization strategy for growth. Five-year plans were formulated for the agricultural and manufacturing sectors. In this phase growth process in these economies was characterized by large-scale state-owned enterprises, a highly regulated market process and state intervention in financial and labour markets. There was minimal emphasis on the external sector, with rigid controls in trade policies including an overvalued exchange rate and import controls. The outcome of these policies was a lack of competition, low productivity, high cost production and loss-bearing public-sector state production units, all reflected in a low-growth economic equilibrium in the region. For over three decades after independence India consistently registered an annual average rate of growth of only 3–4 per cent. Some ad-hoc attempts at economic liberalization were made in the late 1970s and 1980s but these proved to be only marginal in their impact on the economic growth process.

India undertook systemic economic reforms in 1991 when faced with a balance of payment (BOP) crisis as a consequence of the repercussions of the Gulf war that resulted in a dramatic fall in remittances for India and hence its foreign currency holdings. The crisis followed the prior disintegration of the USSR that had until then been India's role model for its heavy industry-based growth strategy. A shift to a more open economic regime as part of a structural adjustment programme that accompanied the IMF loan to resolve the BOP crisis was a necessity for India. The process of reforms was nonetheless adjusted to India's needs and capacity and based on political consensus that ensured its sustainability beyond the crisis.With India initiating the change towards a more open economy, other countries in the region soon followed with their own programmes of economic reforms and liberalization.[2]

New economic policy regime

Liberalization of trade and investment regimes[3]

India

India adopted an inward-looking development strategy after independence that focused on stimulating home-grown industrialization, based essentially on the infant-industry argument,[4] which called for shielding production for the domestic market behind high tariff walls and effective protection. This strategy of import-substituting industrialization created self-fulfilling biases against the export-producing sectors. The need to correct the anti-export bias was gradually recognized as low rates of economic growth started to sustain in successive decades after independence. Several export promotion measures were put in place to generate higher exports in the 1970s and the highly regulated trade policy started to give way to a more open regime in the early 1980s. A three-year export-import policy was introduced in 1985 to focus on the trade sector. Over the next three years the government reduced import duties and initiated liberalization of imports of capital and intermediate goods. This policy enabled easy access to essential capital goods, raw materials, and components from abroad to spur technological advances that would reduce production costs and improve the quality of India's exports. Notwithstanding these measures, trade regime in the late 1980s continued to be characterized by a cumbersome licensing mechanism as well as high tariffs. Systemic reforms were initiated only in 1991–92 after the Indian economy suffered a balance of payment crisis.

Large-scale reforms in the external sector were undertaken within an overall strategy of increasing India's integration with the global economy. Liberalization of trade policy with reduction in tariffs and quantitative restrictions first on capital goods, then on consumer goods and finally even on agricultural goods has been the hallmark of the process of opening up the Indian economy. Trade regime in India was further liberalized with a move to a market-determined exchange rate in 1993.[5] All foreign exchange receipts could now be converted at market-determined exchange rates. The peak rate of import duty on non-agricultural imports, which was 150 per cent in 1991–92, was gradually reduced to 25 per cent in 2003–04, 15 per cent in April 2005 and 10 per cent in 2007, where it has remained ever since. Tariff rates in agriculture, incorporating the concerns for the livelihood of a large section of population dependent on agriculture, are, however, higher and more variable. These tariffs range from 0 per cent to 100 per cent but are clustered around 30 per cent. Also, for social and religious reasons, special rates apply to alcohol products.

Quantitative restrictions on a wide range of goods (mainly consumer goods) were justified in India for several decades, for balance-of-payment reasons, under Article XVIII-2(b) of the GATT. In mid-1991, about 80 per cent of the Harmonized System tariff lines at the six-digit level were subject to some form of import licensing restrictions. India began removing balance of payment-related quantitative restrictions unilaterally in 1996. It removed quantitative restrictions on 488 items in 1996, 391 items in 1997, and 894 items in 1998. To meet its commitments to the WTO, on March 31, 2000, India removed quantitative restrictions on 714 items of the 1,429 items for which quantitative restrictions were maintained on balance-of-payment grounds under the GATT provisions. A year later, quantitative restrictions on the remaining items were removed. Export promotion schemes were extended to a large number of non-traditional and non-manufactured exports. Policy emphasis gradually shifted from provision of direct export subsidy to indirect promotional measures. At the multilateral level India undertook several policy measures for tariffication of the non-tariff barriers.[6] In 2004 India announced its first ever five-year integrated Foreign Trade Policy. The policy aimed at double the percentage share of India's trade in global merchandise trade over 2004–09 and using trade expansion as a means to growth and employment creation. The present trade policy aims at increasing India's share to 5 per cent in global trade for goods and services by 2020.

Capital inflows were liberalized both through foreign direct investment (FDI) and foreign portfolio investment (FPI) routes. In the former case in particular the policy has become increasingly simple and welcoming of foreign capital. Entry of FDI is allowed largely through the automatic route, that is, in most cases no prior permission is required. The Reserve Bank of India needs to be informed within 30 days of inflows/issue of shares. In cases where prior permission is required, proposals are to be approved by the Foreign Investment Promotion Board (FIPB). The procedures for granting permission by the FIPB have been simplified and permissions are granted within a short period of four to six weeks. Starting in 1991 upto 51 per cent FDI was allowed under the automatic route in 35 priority sectors, and by 2000 100 per cent FDI under the automatic route was allowed in all sectors except a small negative list. Foreign equity is limited and/or entry restrictions exist in sectors like arms and ammunition, atomic energy, nuclear power, agriculture and plantations, real estate business, multi-brand retail trading, atomic energy, gambling and lottery business, railway, coal and mining, of some items.[7] Equity route is also allowed in infrastructure services such as highways and roads, ports, inland waterways and transport, urban infrastructure and courier services.

Over time India's FDI regime has evolved into one of the most transparent and liberal FDI regimes among the emerging and developing economies. Indian law does not differentiate between an Indian and foreign-owned company once it has been incorporated in India. All investments made in India by foreign investors are given national treatment that is similar treatment as to domestic investors. India also allows for full repatriation of capital invested, dividend and profit. Additionally, other incentives like tax holiday in some locations, tax-free imports of raw materials and so on are provided to attract FDI in the country.

Pakistan

Pakistan embarked on a comprehensive programme of macroeconomic reform and structural adjustment at the end of the 1980s. Liberalization of trade regime and export promotion was seen as an integral component of this reform programme. Almost all non-tariff barriers were replaced by tariffs.[8] The maximum level of tariff was reduced to 45 per cent in 1997–98 from a high of 225 per cent in 1986–87, para-tariffs were merged into statutory tariff regime and all items were importable except for those whose entry was conditional upon health, religious or security considerations.[9] All exchange controls were lifted in 1991 and Pakistan made the shift from a fixed exchange rate system to a managed float.[10] In addition, export processing zones with one-window operations were set up and were supported by the introduction of several export promotion schemes. Pakistan further liberalized its trade regime as part of the Comprehensive Economic Revival Program launched in 1999 and its tariff rates have fallen dramatically since. To increase export competitiveness Pakistan has established the Trade Development Authority of Pakistan and the Trade Competitiveness Institute of Pakistan. In 2005 Pakistan announced a rapid export growth strategy aimed at trade diplomacy to increase market access, diversification of export markets, strengthening of trade promotion infrastructure, skill development and provision of modern infrastructure.

Notwithstanding earlier attempts and the Foreign Private Investment (Promotion and Protection) Act of 1976 that provided for an adequate legal framework for foreign participation, Pakistan implemented a liberal FDI policy only towards the end of 1980s. The new industrial policy in 1989 introduced several measures to attract FDI. The environment for FDI was liberalized further in 1991 eliminating the requirement for government approval and 100 per cent FDI was allowed. Some more initiatives were announced in the 1997; new industrial policy and foreign investment (less than 100 per cent) was allowed even in agriculture and the services sector, including telecom, energy and insurance. A board of investment was set up to help generate opportunities for FDI. Only a few sensitive sectors such as arms and ammunitions, high explosives, radioactive substances, alcoholic beverages and liquor are listed as exceptions for these policies. The liberalization of the forex regime further facilitated the FDI inflows in Pakistan. Special Industrial Zones (SIZs) have been set up to attract foreign investment in export-oriented industries.[11] Pakistan also allows for full repatriation of capital, capital gains, dividends and profits as well as several tax and concessional import incentives to the foreign investors.

Bangladesh

A three-year structural adjustment facility (SAF) under the auspices of the IMF was started in 1986 with reforms being undertaken in agriculture, industry and trade policy in Bangladesh. These were accompanied by changes in the fiscal and financial sector reforms. The process gained momentum in the 1990s.

Since 1992 Bangladesh has made continuous efforts to simplify and rationalize its trade regime. Nominal applied MFN tariffs have fallen by more than half from an average of 58 per cent in 1992–93 to 19 per cent in 1999–2000. The number of trade-related quantitative restrictions (QRs) have also been reduced with only some retained on safety, health and environmental grounds. However, trade policy regime in Bangladesh still lacks transparency in areas like customs administration, tariff concessions, border charges, subsidies and other regulatory framework. This lends a certain amount of uncertainty to the trade regime and consequently to costs of trade and doing business in Bangladesh. The applied tariff rates vary widely and, despite reduction, the protection levels continue to remain high.

As regards foreign investment, Bangladesh maintains one of the most liberal regimes in South Asia. There are few limitations on foreign equity participation. Among others, the liberal policy regime includes tax holiday, income tax exemption for exports of foreign enterprises, protection from double taxation, exemption from duty on imports of machinery and spare parts for 100 per cent export-oriented units, full repatriation of profits and dividend by foreign companies. Bangladesh is a signatory of the Multilateral Investment Guarantee Agency insuring investors against political risk. As a member of World Intellectual Property Organisation (WIPO) and World Association of Investment Promotion Agencies (WAIPA) the country further safeguards the interest of foreign investment.

Nepal

Nepal started its new economic policy regime in the mid-1980s. The 1987 Industrial Policy and Industrial Enterprise Act was the first concerted effort to attract FDI in Nepal. Reforms have since been executed in several areas like FDI, trade, fiscal and foreign exchange. Political instability, though, has been a constant obstacle in the smooth progress of economic reforms in the country. With the restoration of multiparty, parliamentary democracy in Nepal in 1990, the period between 1990 and 1996 was marked by market oriented reforms to accelerate economic growth and participation in the globalization process. As part of this process all quantitative restrictions and import licenses were removed, tariff structure was rationalized and investment incentives were extended.

Relative to other SAARC members Nepal was relatively late in joining the WTO in 2004. Nepal is committed to binding other duties and charges at zero and phase them out within ten years. Nepal's WTO accession package also includes the agreement to bind average tariff at 42 per cent for agricultural products and 24 per cent for all other products and the agreement to allow up to 80 per cent foreign equity participation in 70 services sub-sectors, including distribution, retail and wholesale services and audio visual.

Nepal permits FDI in all sectors except business management, consulting, accounting, legal services, defence, alcohol, cigarettes, liquor and retail sales. Further, Nepal allows 100 per cent repatriation of capital invested, dividends as well as incentives like tax holidays and concessional tax treatments. A new Foreign Investment and Technology Act was promulgated in 1991 to provide national treatment to foreign investors. The Investment Promotion Board was established in 1992.

Sri Lanka

Among the South Asian economies Sri Lanka was the first to have embarked on the path of economic reforms and liberalization in 1977 even though it was only a fitful start to easing of business-related policy restrictions. Incremental reforms since then have ensured that the country follows an open, liberal economic policy with a ratio of exports and imports to GDP of around 65 per cent. Initial reforms included dismantling of trade barriers, unification of exchange rate and reduced restrictions on pricing and investment by the private sector. Two significant developments since the beginning of the reforms in 1977 include the role played by the Export Processing Zones and a programme for privatization that was adopted in 1987 in pursuit of efficiency and profitability. This helped establish an enabling environment in Sri Lanka and attract export-oriented firms to the country. It also contributed a significant share to the country's industrial export earnings.[12]

In the 1990s the primary policy focus of the external trade strategy has been on pursuit of preferential trade arrangement. Rationalization of the import tariff regime received limited attention. More recently since 2006, the government of Sri Lanka has adopted the strategy of strengthening export growth through diversification, emphasis on small and medium enterprises and encouraging backward integration through policy-based measures for high-value added exports.

Significant changes in policy toward FDI were undertaken with the adoption of further economic reforms in 1990 under the second phase of liberalization. A statutory body called the Greater Colombo Economic Commission that was established in 1978, charged with attracting and supporting export-oriented foreign investment through an attractive incentive package to foreign investors and establishing and managing export processing zones (EPZs), was changed to the Board of Investment (BOI) in 1992 as part of an effort to increase its effectiveness to attract FDI. BOI is effectively the FDI regulator and promoter of FDI in Sri Lanka and all investments in Sri Lanka enter through the BOI 'gateway'. As per the liberalized FDI policy foreign and local investors are treated equally, other than in a few exceptional areas. Foreign ownership is permitted in all sectors except a few regulated areas. Investors are permitted to repatriate 100 per cent of their profits and exempted from most of the exchange control regulations.[13]

Maldives

Maldives is a small country, composed of 200 inhabited islands, that is very dependent on imports. Currently the tariffs levels continue to be maintained at high levels as they account for two-thirds of the tax revenues in Maldives. The government of Maldives is committed to making the country more open and diversifying the economy beyond fishing and tourism. The Maldives provides 'Most Favoured Nation' treatment to all WTO members and is eligible for 'special and differential treatment' under WTO Agreements. The export and import law of 1979 was changed in 2000 when Maldives formally adopted the harmonized system of trade classification.

Afghanistan

In 2001 Afghanistan inherited a highly differentiated import tariff regime including 25 tariff bands with a maximum rate of 150 per cent and a simple average rate of 43 per cent. Since then there have been major changes with the introduction of market exchange rate in calculating import duties, reducing the number of tariffs to six with a maximum tariff rate of 16 per cent. The simple average tariff rate has fallen to 5.3 per cent. As a consequence Afghanistan has the least-differentiated and lowest tariff regime in the South Asian region. In 2004 it also initiated the process of accession to the WTO. Afghanistan maintains import bans on some products, mainly owing to religious reasons. The country imposes no seasonal restrictions, quotas or other non-tariff barriers.

Patterns and trends in trade and capital flows

Having thus initiated economic reforms and liberalization, South Asian economies have made the transition from inward-looking import substitution-based industrializing nations to more outward-oriented economies with an increased emphasis on the external sector and developing export competitiveness. In this section an assessment of the extent of trade integration of the South Asian economies with the global economy is undertaken using alternative indices of openness and restrictiveness with respect to the external sector transactions.

Trade integration

Degree of openness

As a region South Asia registered an increase in the index of openness[14] during the period 1991–2010. The value of the index increased from 21 to 51 per cent in 2008 and then fell to 45 per cent in 2010. The decline in the last year would be attributable to the global financial crisis. The increase in the extent of openness of the region since 1991[15] is reflected in all South Asian economies except Pakistan, which is also observed to be the least open among all South Asian economies. Maldives is the most open economy in South Asia. The extent of openness in Pakistan declined between1991 and 2000 from 36 to 28 per cent and then recovered in 2008 to 37 per cent, close to the 1991 level, but has fallen again in the wake of the global financial crisis to 32 per cent. Since 2000 Sri Lanka and Nepal have also registered a decline in their degree of openness, even though an initial increase was observed between 1991 and 2000. The decline in trade to GDP ratio is smaller for Nepal and the ratio continues to be higher, though constant for the last three years (2008–10) than that in 1991, indicating a higher level of openness for the country over the entire period. For Sri Lanka the decline in trade/GDP ratio is larger and the level of openness in 2010 is lower relative to that in 1991. For India and Bangladesh the change has been positive and more than 100 per cent. For India the trade/GDP ratio has increased from 17 per cent in 1991 to 53 per cent in 2008 and 46 in 2010. For Bangladesh the index of openness increased from 19 in 1991 to 43 in 2010, having increased to 49 in 2008.

Despite the increase in individual economies' openness South Asia is the least open among all the regions in the world, less than even sub-Saharan Africa. In 2010 the trade/GDP ratio was the same as for Latin America and the Caribbean region but continues to be lower than the value of the ratio for all other regions (Table 3.1).

Global Shares

South Asia's increasing openness and global integration has not led to an increase in the region's contribution to global trade. South Asia's share in global trade has been stagnant at around 1 per cent almost throughout the period of reference. In 2008 South Asia contributed 1.4 per cent of world exports relative to 1 per cent contribution in 2000 and 0.80 in 1990. Of this the largest percentage contribution

Table 3.1 Trade openness: regional and country comparisons

Country	Trade/GDP (per cent)		
	2010	2000	1991
Afghanistan			
Bangladesh	43	33	19
Bhutan	137*	82	74
India	46	27	17
Maldives	161	161	160
Nepal	47	56	35
Pakistan	32	28	36
Sri Lanka	53	89	68

Region	2010	2000	1991
East Asia and Pacific	63	49	40
Europe & Central Asia	78	72	54
European Union	79	71	54
Latin American & Caribbean	45	44	32
Middle East & North Africa	85*	64	72
South Asia	45	30	21
Sub Saharan Africa	62	63	49

Source: http://databank.worldbank.org; *2009 data

of 1.10 per cent is made by India. As regards world imports South Asia's share is again small and amounts to 2.3 per cent, of which India's share of 1.8 per cent is the largest.[16] India's share in world merchandise trade was 1.45 per cent as per WTO estimates.[17]

Overall trade openness: alternatively viewed

Given that the South Asian countries have undertaken several policy measures to liberalize their trade regimes but still contribute only a small proportion of world trade as a region and in their individual country capacity, it may be useful to take a mirror view of the openness index by using alternative indices[18] to measure the extent of restrictions or trade distortionary measures that these economies continue to impose relative to other countries and regions in comparator income groups.

MFN TARIFF TRADE RESTRICTIVENESS INDEX (TTRI)

The average MFN Tariff Trade Restrictiveness Index (TTRI)[19] for South Asia stands at 11.7 per cent, for lower-middle-income countries at 8.6 per cent, and low-income countries at 11.6 per cent. On average, therefore, the region continues to be more restrictive in its MFN tariffs than countries in comparator income groups.

The MFN TTRI for overall trade for India stands at 12 per cent, which is slightly greater than the regional average, though significantly higher than that of its comparator income group,the lower-middle-income countries, and, disappointingly, higher than the average for low-income countries too. This is largely due to the relatively high protection that the government of India provides the agricultural sector (TTRI of 28 per cent) relative to the non-agricultural goods (TTRI of 11 per cent). India ranks among the top 20 per cent of countries with the most restrictive tariff regimes. Relative to the same comparator country group of low-middle-income countries and regional average, Pakistan's trade regime is more restrictive, though only slightly more,with an average MFN TTRI of 12.2 per cent. Pakistan, which is dependent on food imports, has established much lower import barriers for agricultural than non-agricultural goods, which have TTRIs of 7.9 and 12.5 per cent, respectively. Pakistan ranks as the 103rd least restrictive regime of a sample of 125 countries. In comparison, at rank 76, Sri Lanka's MFN TTRI for overall trade is 6.8 per cent, and compares favourably to the South Asian region average and the average for lower-middle-income countries. The government of Sri Lanka has taken many steps to increase reliance on domestic food production, including maintaining a high barrier for agricultural imports as measured by a TTRI of 16.7 per cent, compared to an average of 14.6 per cent for South Asian countries, and compared to 5.5 per cent for non-agricultural goods.Among the low-income countries, Bangladesh's trade policy has shown strong signs of liberalization, as demonstrated by the 2007 MFN Tariff Trade Restrictiveness Index (TTRI) of 11.3 per cent, which is just over half its value in 2001 and is lower than the regional average TTRI and that of its comparator country group (TTRI for the low-income countries of 11.6 per cent). In contrast, Nepal's trade policy remains somewhat restrictive toward imports, as judged by the MFN TTRI for overall trade of 16.4 per cent, which is higher than the regional and comparator countries' index value. Agricultural goods have a significantly lower TTRI (11.3 per cent) than non-agricultural goods (17.5 per cent). Based on the MFN TTRI, Bangladesh ranks 97th and Nepal 121st out of 125 countries.

In terms of their trade restrictiveness as defined by the TTRI, South Asian countries, with the exception of Bangladesh, lag behind their income comparator country groups. India and Pakistan are more restrictive, and Sri Lanka, even with an overall lower TTRI, maintains a rather high tariff barrier for agricultural goods.

SIMPLE AVERAGE MFN APPLIED TARIFF RATE

The simple average of the MFN applied tariff rate for the South Asian region and lower-middle-income countries are 13.5 and 11.4, respectively. Other than Afghanistan, all the South Asian countries, despite having undertaken reduction in tariffs as part of their trade liberalization programmes, continue to have higher average tariff rates relative to comparator income groups, as well as maintaining very high peak tariff rates for specific commodity groups.

In India the simple average of the MFN applied tariff rate has decreased significantly to 14.1, less than half of its value in 2004. It still remains higher than the averages for both the regional and income group comparators. India's maximum tariff (including ad valorem equivalents of specific duties) on all goods (excluding alcohol and tobacco) now stands at 301 per cent for cotton fabrics. The simple average of the MFN applied tariff rate in Pakistan has decreased significantly in the past several years to 13.5 per cent, less than one-third of its value a decade ago, and is now very close to the average for both the South Asian region and lower-middle-income countries. Pakistan's maximum tariff on all goods (excluding alcohol and tobacco) was 90 per cent in 2008. The simple average of the MFN applied tariff rate in Maldives has been virtually unchanged since 2000, and now stands at 20.4 per cent. It remains significantly higher than the average for the South Asian region and lower-middle-income countries, at 13.5 and 11.4 per cent, respectively. Based on the MFN applied tariff, it ranks as the 173rd of 181 countries. There is little difference between the treatment of agricultural and non-agricultural goods, with the latter having a slightly higher average tariff. Taxes on imports of non-agricultural goods are a means of taxing tourism, as a large share of merchandise imports is directly related to the provision of tourism services. Since 2006 the Maldives has increased its maximum tariff on all goods (excluding alcohol and tobacco) from 112 to 142 per cent. Afghanistan has a simple average applied MFN tariff rate of 5.6 per cent, which is lower than both the regional South Asian (13.5 per cent) average as well as its comparator country (low-income) average of 12.7 per cent. Bhutan's[20] simple average of the MFN applied tariff rate has increased considerably in the past decade to 21.9 per cent in 2007. Based on the MFN applied tariff Bhutan ranks 177th out of 181 countries. In 2006 this maximum tariff was applied to plastic packaging materials. The simple average of the MFN applied tariff rate in Nepal has decreased slightly since 2005 to 12.5 per cent. Nepal has not changed its maximum tariff of 80 per cent on all goods (excluding alcohol and tobacco) in the past several years.

TRADE POLICY SPACE

Trade policy space as measured by the wedge between bound and applied tariffs, indicative thereby of the scope for protection that a country maintains, stands at 54.8 per cent on average for South Asia and is significantly higher than the 29.5 per cent for lower-middle-income countries, modestly higher in comparison with the 50.9 per cent for low-income countries. Individual countries, though, reveal differential levels of potentially protectionist policies.

Bangladesh maintains the highest levels of trade policy space at 153.3 per cent and Nepal consistently the lowest, now for the past several years, at 13.9 per cent. For Maldives it has decreased slightly since 2000 and now stands at a relatively low 16.8 per cent. In comparison India, with 35 per cent, and Pakistan, at 46.4 per cent, are relatively more protectionist. For Sri Lanka, although the trade policy space was 15.1 per cent, approximately 62 per cent of its non-agricultural tariffs are unbound under WTO rules and can be increased at any time.[21]

In sum, it may be an appropriate conclusion to say that while major attempts have been made by the South Asian countries to open their external sectors the extent of restrictiveness of these economies is still very high relative to the average performance of countries in comparator income groups. This, it may be recognized, appears to be true of the major economies in the region like India, Pakistan and Bangladesh. Even Sri Lanka, which was an early starter in this regard, has taken retrograde measures in recent times. It is not surprising, therefore, that the region's contribution to world trade and extent of global integration through progressing remains among the lowest in the world.

Direction of trade

South Asian economies are increasingly observed to be moving away from their traditional markets like the US and EU and towards trading with other developing countries. The share of exports from South Asia to other developing countries in Asia (particularly China), Africa, the Western Hemisphere and the Middle East has increased significantly. Imports are also the largest from developing Asia. For India the most notable trend in the last decade has been the rapid rate at which its trade with China has increased. China surpassed the bilateral trade between India and the US in 2008 and has since emerged as the largest single country trade partner for India. Of particular relevance is the fact that trade between India and China held up even during the global financial crisis, whereas trade between India and the US registered a decline indicating that south-south trade is not just gaining in importance but has also been more resilient in the wake of global uncertainties. Other South Asian countries also show evidence in support of this trend. Pakistan's top three source countries for imports are developing Asian countries. Among its top ten export destinations, developing Asian countries of UAE, Afghanistan and

China surpassed its exports to the US in 2009. For Bangladesh and Sri Lanka, India and China together comprise 30 per cent or more of their total imports in 2009. The developed countries, however, continue to remain important as markets for services exports from the South Asian countries. This trend is likely to continue as higher income, growth of knowledge-intensive industries and differential demographics in the developed countries underlie a generation of demand in the service sector.[22]

Composition of trade

South Asian countries reveal concentration of exports in sectors like textiles, garments, gems and jewellery, carpets, handicrafts, leather and leather products, and primary goods. Since 2000 manufactured goods in sectors like machinery and equipment, electrical equipment and machinery and parts thereof, and pharmaceuticals have found a place among the top-ranking exports from India. For other countries like Bangladesh, Pakistan and Sri Lanka primary commodities, marine products, resource-based articles and textiles, and cotton and apparel continue to dominate exports, with machinery and equipment and pharmaceuticals also featuring among the major export sectors. For Nepal primary commodities continue to be the major export commodities. As regards imports of the South Asian countries there has been little change in the composition over the last decade and the predominant sectors continue to be minerals and mineral fuels, chemicals, fertilizers, machinery and equipment, and electrical equipment.

On average in South Asia manufactured exports comprise 62 per cent total exports, and agriculture raw materials about 1–2 per cent of total export/import. Specifically in India manufactured export comprises about 67 per cent of total export and 57 per cent of imports. Agriculture contributes only about a 1–2 per cent share of export and imports in India. In Pakistan the share of manufactured exports is higher at 75 per cent of the total but about the same as India for imports that stand at 53 per cent of total imports. In Sri Lanka manufactured exports and imports are 67 and 62 per cent of the total in their respective categories. For Bangladesh the share of manufactured goods to total exports is almost 95 per cent.[23]

The sectoral Hirschman index indicating the extent of concentration of exports of a country and hence the underlying vulnerability is the highest for Bangladesh at 0.57 and lowest for India at 0.25 with Pakistan and Sri Lanka at intermediate values of 0.32 and 0.37 respectively. India's exports include traditional sector products like gems and jewellery, R&D-based goods like pharmaceuticals, as well as resource products like petroleum products and iron ore at the top spots. For Sri Lanka and Pakistan the manufactured exports predominantly belong to the cotton yarn, textile and clothing product groups. For Bangladesh export trade is largely centred around one item: readymade garments.

Intra-regional trade

Intra-regional trade among the South Asian countries, at $1.2 billion, is low and only about 5 per cent of the region's global trade.[24] In fact evidence shows SAARC as having had the distinction of overseeing a reduction in intra-South-Asian trade. Intra-regional trade as a proportion of total trade within the region dropped from 3.2 per cent in 1980 to 2.4 per cent in 1990.[25] A predominant share of 87 per cent in intra-South-Asia exports is cornered by India. In intra-South-Asia imports, though, India's share is only 13 per cent. As a share of India's total imports the intra-regional imports comprise less than 1 per cent and exports to the region comprise about 5 per cent of India's total exports. Overall, therefore, India's intra-regional trade, at about 2 per cent of its total trade, is rather small. The relatively low importance of the region in India's trade is thus apparent. Relative to this the region holds greater importance in the smaller countries' total trade. For Pakistan the share is around 7 per cent while for Nepal and Afghanistan the proportions are higher at 58 per cent and 30 per cent of total trade respectively. For Bangladesh, Sri Lanka and Maldives the share of the region is 11, 16 and 15 per cent respectively. Imports from the region have a much larger weight in Bangladesh and Sri Lanka's total imports relative to exports. Relative to the other countries, therefore, India is the least integrated in the South Asian region. It is not inappropriate to say that while India is central to South Asia, South Asia is not central to India. However, India's rate of growth in exports to SAARC in 2010 is the highest among all member countries of the SAARC region. Import growth is positive in 2010 and even though not the highest in the region it augurs well after successive declines since 2005 and negative growth rates for 2008 and 2009. The previous two years' trends are surprising as India has announced giving special and favourable treatment on a non-reciprocal basis to least-developed countries of SAARC – that is, Bhutan, Bangladesh, Maldives, Afghanistan and Nepal – and, further, the government removed import tariffs on over 4,800 products from the four neighbouring countries on January 1, 2008, and in April 2008 the government announced that it was offering preferential market access to all least-developed countries. In addition the global financial crisis should have made the region and India particularly important as a market as many western markets underwent a decline in growth. Additionally this period has seen the implementation of the SAFTA agreement. Having registered negative growth in 2008–09, India's trade in South Asia has seen maximum increase with Bangladesh and Sri Lanka followed by Pakistan and Nepal at almost equal rates in 2010. Bangladesh exports with Sri Lanka and imports from Pakistan have undergone similar high and positive increases in 2010. The trends in 2010 may, however, have been only in response to India's better economic performance relative to the traditional markets of the South Asian economies. The point of relevance here would therefore be of sustainability of these trends in the long run.

Bilateral trade

All the major economies of the South Asian region experienced a positive growth in their trade with regional partners in contrast with negative growth that was registered in 2009 and for some even in 2008. The maximum increase was observed for India's trade (exports and imports) with Bangladesh and Sri Lanka. In fact Sri Lanka records a high and positive growth of over 25 per cent with its other major trade partners in the region. Bangladesh has a high positive growth of imports from Pakistan but its exports register a fall. India's exports and imports show an almost equal increase with Nepal while with Pakistan exports show a larger increase than imports. Nepal shows a fall in its trade with Bangladesh while showing almost equal increase with Pakistan and Sri Lanka. However, the positive trends in bilateral trade, while encouraging, do not appear to be sufficient to enhance intra-regional trade in South Asia. This is apparent when bilateral trade shares are seen relative to the individual country's global trade.

Trade with regional partners is a relatively small proportion of South Asian countries' total trade. This is true for exports and imports. Imports from India, though, hold a relatively greater weight than from any other country in the region. India's exports and imports from the regional trade partners comprise a negligible proportion of its total trade, but the country shows a very high level of trade intensity with Nepal, apparently as a reflection of the smaller country's trade dependence on India. Close to 60 per cent of Nepal's trade is with India. India has the highest share from the South Asian trade partners in Pakistan's total imports, even though the exports share is relatively small. Pakistan shows the highest trade intensity in the region with Sri Lanka, followed by Bangladesh. Sri Lanka shows the highest trade intensity with Maldives, followed by India and Pakistan. Exports from Bangladesh to India are about 2 per cent of its total exports, and imports from India around 13 per cent of its total imports, even while the country shows a high trade intensity index with India, Pakistan, Nepal and a little over 1with Sri Lanka.

Trade balance

In general it is observed that in recent years India has maintained a positive trade balance with all South Asian nations except Bhutan, which has a surplus with all its trading partners in the region. India has the largest trade surplus with Bangladesh, followed by Sri Lanka. Sri Lanka has a positive trade balance with Bangladesh and Maldives, but a deficit with Nepal, Pakistan and India. Pakistan has a negative trade balance with India, Bhutan and Nepal, and trade surplus with Maldives and Sri Lanka. Afghanistan has a trade deficit with Pakistan.

India's centrality in regional trade

Trends in intra-regional trade in South Asia reveal a unique feature in terms of the centrality of the Indian economy. Analyzing the trade patterns for South Asia over the last five years it is observed that India is among the top ten trading partners in value terms for all the South Asian countries, but the reverse is not necessarily true. Contributing about 20 per cent of total imports for Sri Lanka, India is in the top position for imports into Sri Lanka. This holds true both in 2005 and 2010. No other South Asian country figures among Sri Lanka's top ten trading partners. The same is also true for Nepal, but in this case India accounts for over 50 per cent of its imports and 60 per cent or more of exports. In varying proportions, similar trends are evident for other countries in the region. Sri Lanka and Pakistan do appear among the ten trading partners for Maldives and Afghanistan respectively but the overall South Asian picture is in contrast. Other than India, South Asian countries do not in general rank among the top ten trading partners for each other either as a source of imports or as a destination for exports. Further, as discussed above, for all countries in South Asia India has a far greater significance as a source of imports than as a destination for exports. As a consequence India maintains a trade surplus with all the countries of the region except Bhutan, with which it has small deficit. A similar consistent pattern is, however, not observed for other bilateral pairs in the region.[26] Furthermore, despite India's relative importance in total trade of the SAARC economies the relative significance of these economies in India's total exports is very small. Together the SAARC economies account for less than or just about 5 per cent of India's total exports.

This is in contrast with evidence available from other trade blocs with large economies. For example, it may be relevant to note that many studies have shown that US trade has increased more quickly with its NAFTA partners than with non-NAFTA partners. Since the announcement of NAFTA in 1993, real US exports to Mexico have increased by 95 per cent and Canada by 35 per cent in contrast with the 20 per cent increase observed for non-NAFTA partners. Real US imports from Mexico have increased by 190 per cent in comparison with 69 per cent for Canada and 59 per cent for non-NAFTA partners.[27]

It is, however, not difficult to understand the contrasting picture with respect to the central economy's share in intra-regional trade in South Asia. Given its large size and middle-class population with increasing per capita income, a larger production base and economies of scale have made possible efficient expansion and diversification of production in India. The small size of the domestic market in the other economies does not allow for such diversification. Trade with a larger economy also often enables smaller partners to overcome their short-term production imbalances. For example, in May 2005, Pakistan, in an attempt to meet domestic demand and bring down prices, allowed private traders to import meat and vegetables directly from India without duty. There is therefore a natural economic dependence of the smaller South Asian economies on India while the reverse does not hold true. India's major imports are in the semi-manufacture category. The rest of the region has neither the capacity nor the comparative advantage in this product category. The meagre share of the smaller South Asian economies in India's imports is therefore only natural. However, the imbalance in this relationship has become a major reason to prevent consolidation of efforts towards economic cooperation in South Asia. There is a fear among the smaller South Asian nations that any cooperative trade pact would result in Indian goods further flooding their small domestic markets and the enlargement of the existing trade deficit. Thus the perceived greater benefits to India have in fact led many South Asian countries to look for imports from the rest of the world, even though many products could have been sourced at cheaper prices and lower transaction costs from India, implying lower overall trade deficit for these economies. It may be noteworthy in this context that Pakistan's international trade is suffering from a huge amount of deficit that stood at US$3.946 billion in 2010. Over the years items like tea, auto parts and spices have been imported from countries other than India, even though it is estimated[28] that imports from India in some cases could have led to a US$900 million saving for Pakistan. Given Pakistan's huge trade deficit this is a very substantial amount that has been foregone only due to political compulsions in the country. Political and historical frictions have consistently overruled the application of economic rationality in South Asia. Larger bilateral trade deficits with India are considered difficult to justify politically in the South Asian economies relative to the economically second-best outcome of a burgeoning trade deficit with the rest of the world. Larger trade deficits with other economies have been accepted by Pakistan. For example, trade deficit between Pakistan and China was to the tune of US$5.2 billion in 2010[29] and, interestingly, an FTA is in operation with China. As a means of resolving the issue of a large deficit the two countries actually discussed expansion possibilities with regard to the FTA. The differential approach adopted by Pakistan vis-à-vis its 'large' trade partner in South Asia versus outside the region is thus apparent.

Role and quantum of informal trade

There is high incidence of informal trade in the SAARC region and between India and her neighbours in particular. India and Pakistan are observed to carry out trade other than as officially recorded through third country routes (also called the circular trade) and illegal/informal channels through the borders of the two countries. Often illegal trade or smuggling takes place across the unfenced border between the two countries through the Amritsar–Wagah route and/or the Mumbai–Karachi route by boats and across the Rajasthan and Gujarat borders with Sindh in Pakistan. The circular trade happens when goods from one country are exported to the destination country through a third country, in which case the latter becomes the country of origin for these goods. The circular routes through which trade between India and Pakistan is undertaken include India–Dubai–Iran–Afghanistan–Pakistan, Mumbai–Afghanistan transit trade that lands in Pakistan and goes to Afghanistan to be exported back to Pakistan through the land route. The most frequently used third-country routes are India–Dubai–Karachi, India–Singapore–Karachi, and India–Hong Kong–Karachi.[30] Further, the illegal and circular trade is almost unidirectional – from India to Pakistan – and this is only to be expected given that India has granted Pakistan MFN status so that Pakistan exports to India through the formal channel and, moreover, that India's exports are highly valued manufactured commodities. Historically, the black market and circular trade between the two countries have outweighed levels of formal trade.[31] There has also been substantial informal unrecorded trade across the India–Bangladesh land borders. It is classified under two categories, one referred to as 'bootleg smuggling' that involves a large number of local people individually transporting small quantities, often just head loads or by bicycle rickshaw; and two, trade, called 'technical smuggling' in Bangladesh, which goes in larger quantities, mostly by truck, through the formal legal/customs channel but which involves explicit illegal practices such as under-invoicing, misclassification and bribery of customs officials. Illegal trade and smuggling is one of the oldest challenges to border management for India and Bangladesh. The main informal trading centres on the India–Bangladesh border are Assam (Fakiragram, Mankachar and Karimgunj), Meghalaya (Lichubari and Dawki), Mizoram (Tlangbunj), Tripura (Kailashahar, Agartala, Sonamora, Bilonia and Sabroom) and West Bengal (Petrapole, Bagdha, Mejdia, Lalgola, Mohedpur, Radhikapur, Kaliagang and Hilli). Availability of a large market and railways near the border make it easier and attractive for smugglers to indulge in informal trade.

Informal trade in the South Asian region is often a reflection of difficult practices and non-tariff barriers that individual countries follow and impose when trading with regional partners. These may be overt policy measures – like Pakistan not having granted India the MFN status – or hidden barriers – like port restrictions – or may be simply on account of technological backwardness of some of the South Asian countries – reflected in technical and sanitary and phyto-sanitary (SPS) specifications for goods to be traded across borders. In all cases the phenomenon is indicative of a high potential for trade to be directed towards formal channels, which is then going to imply greater benefits to both countries in terms of commodity prices and revenue earnings for the state. While complete information on all kinds of NTBs in operation in South Asia is not yet available, some that have been explicitly cited by traders are discussed below.

Non-tariff barriers (NTBs) to trade in South Asia

The types of non-tariff restrictions imposed by the South Asian countries are multi-fold but broadly include complex and protracted customs procedures, port restrictions, rules of origin (RoOs), preferential access, packaging and labelling requirements and restricted transit facilities across the region. It is indicated that of the total NTBs faced by the SAARC region, the majority (86.3 per cent) fall in the category of SPS, TBT and other related measures, followed by tariff quotas (9.8 per cent), anti-dumping measures (7.4 per cent) and licence requirements (5.3 per cent), and countervailing measures (1.2 per cent).[32] With tariff rates having declined as part of trade liberalization programmes undertaken by all the South Asian countries, it is the NTBs that have taken centre stage as the main challenge for trade negotiators in their attempt to reduce trade costs and enhance the level of trade in the region.

Country-specific NTBs in bilateral trade are cited as follows. Nepal lists problems of SPS requirements, complex quarantine rules on agricultural products and uneven implementation of trade treaty measures by state governments in India, in addition to disagreement on customs clearance procedures for cross-border rail operations and CVDs (countervailing duties) as major NTBs imposed by India on its goods. Bangladesh for all seven countries, and especially for India, specifies laboratory testing of food items, chemical testing, packaging requirements, SPS, pre-shipment inspection (PSI) certification, product standards and CVDs as NTBs. Bangladesh

Bank Letters of Credit rules and, more generally, the credibility of the Bangladesh banks have been reported to constrain Indian exports to Bangladesh, and as one of the factors responsible for illegal practices in the border trade, especially at the Petrapole–Benapole border crossing. An important general non-tariff constraint on Bangladesh's imports from India is the fact that only four out of the 42 customs posts on the land border with India are allowed to clear all imported goods – the others are limited to dealing with a very short list of products and must obtain case-by-case authorization from the National Board of Revenue for clearing anything not on the list. Additionally, apparently in a bid to restrict illegal imports, since 2002 July, Bangladesh has required that two of its principal imports from India – textile yarn and sugar – can only be imported through its seaports. Both Bangladesh and India have periodically constrained imports of certain products by specifying the ports at which they can be cleared by customs. In June 2005, India restricted the ports that can administer its various export incentive schemes. Many of the alternative ports are prohibitively costly for the North East and Eastern states in India, effectively implying a ban on exports from these states to nearby regions in Bangladesh and providing an incentive to send these goods illegally. Pakistan considers PSI as the main obstacle in exporting to Bangladesh and refusal of letters of credit when it exports to India. In addition, Pakistan exporters have also reported sampling, customs inspection, TBTs and SPS as other NTBs in the region.[33]

More generally, Bangladesh is known to impose non-automatic licensing and prohibitions as quality control measures on goods that are imported into the country. Prohibitions are imposed to ban products like drugs and related goods, live animals and animal products, and the like. Bangladesh also imposed technical measures such as standard and certification on processed food items, marking, labelling and packaging requirements, in addition to the requirement of a Letter of Credit Authorization (LCA) form for importing goods on the restricted list.

Bhutan imposes non-automatic licensing in a way of import permits for the importation of some agricultural products. Technical measures such as Sanitary and phyto-sanitary (SPS) certificates, marking and labelling requirements also act as non-tariff barriers.

India imposes anti-dumping measures as a price control measure to protect domestic production. India also insists on prior authorization for sensitive product categories specially focusing on the genetically modified (GM) food category. Citing damage to the environment or wildlife and human life, India has placed restrictions on certain animal products, and fresh fruits and vegetables coated with edible and non-edible wax. The goods that enter India are required to fulfil the marking and labelling requirements of the country. India is in the process of identifying the barriers and removing them as far as possible. Recently the government of India has taken a decision to waive the stipulation for testing and certification of products by Indian laboratories as a precondition for imports. Instead of testing and certification by the Indian entities, it would now be enough if the job was done by laboratories in the SAARC countries accredited by the Bureau of Indian Standards.

Maldives has imposed non-automatic licensing, quotas and prohibitions due to human health, safety, security, environmental concerns and religious reasons as a quality control measure. Sanitary certificates on live animals and phyto-sanitary certificates on live plants have also been made necessary. Labelling also became a significant requirement, especially when importing food items. Sri Lanka also engages in setting prohibition on some meat products. Agricultural products are subjected to licensing and prior authorization is necessary for some imports, for example GM foods.

Recent initiatives notwithstanding, liberalization and easing out of the technical barriers to trade (TBTs) and other NTBs for intra-regional trade enhancement may not be so simple in South Asia. In other regions, especially in the case of the EU, success achieved in this context has to be understood in terms of the role of the supra-national organizations. The acceptance of the EU court as a superior court made possible the liberalization of TBT measures[34]. The possibility of the court rejecting the national business/state argument for imposition of TBT made lobbying for TBTs a high-cost activity. Rents earned from imposition of stringent TBTs were often negated by the costs to fight for these in court when challenged by business. This logic made easy the implementation of acceptance of national standards by all EU members. It has to be realized that the supra-nationality (acceptance of the EU court rulings to supersede the national Parliament) was an outcome of the Treaty of Rome, which itself was an outcome of the extraordinary circumstances of the devastation of WWI and WWII. It is not possible to replicate the same in South Asia. South Asia will have to devise other ways for acceptance of national standards and enter into mutual recognition agreements to simplify trade procedures. As the existing information base on NTBs in the region is weak a very basic initial step for South Asia is to identify and create a database for NTBs in a diligent fashion. This may then be followed by the SAARC member nations drawing a consensus on existing cross-border NTBs so as to facilitate negotiation on their elimination on a bilateral or regional basis. The process of the creation of the database has been initiated, as, after a 2006 meeting of the committee of experts and the council of ministers, a sub-group was constituted by the SAARC to identify, review and recommend measures for removal of NTBs/PTBs regionally and bilaterally.

Role of transit agreements in facilitating intra-regional trade in South Asia

Currently transit restrictions act as barriers to the movement of goods across South Asia.[35] The transit barriers in particular impinge negatively on the ability of the landlocked countries to trade – regionally and globally. Landlocked countries are dependent on their contiguous neighbours for facilitating trade across borders. In South Asia, Afghanistan, Bhutan and Nepal, all least-developed countries, are landlocked. Both Bhutan and Nepal are unique in having only one transit neighbour, India.

India provides transit facilities to landlocked Nepal under the Treaty of Transit. The current Treaty, which was renewed in January 2006, would be in force for a period of seven years up to January 5, 2013. This Treaty provides for free movement of traffic-in-transit across each other's territories through mutually agreed routes for trade with third countries, subject to taking measures to ensure that this does not infringe the other's legitimate interests/security interests. Traffic in transit is exempted from customs/all transit duties. The Treaty provides for exit/entry points as may be mutually agreed upon. India has allowed 15 transit routes to Nepal, but so far has not availed of this facility from Nepal. Merchant ships of Nepal are accorded treatment no less favourable than that accorded ships of any other foreign country. Presently Kolkata/Haldia are the operational entry points for Nepal's trade with third countries.

India and Bhutan signed a new agreement on trade, commerce and transit in 2006 in place of the extant agreement on trade and commerce, which was signed in 1995. The new agreement provides for four more exit/entry points in place of the twelve exit/entry points in the protocol to the existing agreement. The new exit/entry points in India include two road routes via Phulbari and Dawki and two sea and air routes via Mumbai and Chennai. The procedures for export and import have also been simplified, including those for movement of goods from one part of Bhutan to another through the Indian territory.

The three landlocked LDCs have transit agreements with their trading neighbours but the implementation of these agreements is a function of bilateral political relations, neighbours' administrative frameworks and domestic stability, and its own bargaining power. The bilateral transit arrangements between the landlocked developing countries and their principal transit neighbours in South Asia are not observed to work equally well, as is evident in case of Bhutan and Nepal. Bhutan, owing to its special relationship with India, enjoys better transit procedures in comparison with Nepal. Bhutan is like an exception to the administrative burden of transit as all Bhutanese transit trade through India is handled by Bhutan's own customs agency. While part of the ease of transit is because of its good working relations with India, it is also on account of the small size of transit trade in case of Bhutan. Nepal has a generally positive relationship with India but when bilateral relations have been strained India has exercised its inherent advantage over Nepal. This advantage was most evident from the 1989 Indian blockade of Nepal. Even in normal times, Nepal does not enjoy the hassle-free transit enjoyed by Bhutan. In particular, Nepal has had to deal with the Indian regulations emanating both from the central government as well as state governments of West Bengal, Uttar Pradesh and Bihar.[36]

Pakistan and Afghanistan signed a trade and transit agreement (APTTA) in 2010, according to which Afghanistan exports can be carried in Afghan trucks to Pakistan seaports as well as to the Indian border. The long-desired treaty will, if implemented in its true spirit, help augment trade and development prospects for Afghanistan and may also be a stepping stone to more trade-facilitating agreements in the future. In particular it is considered that the treaty may create sufficient pressure in the future for transit facilities for Indian goods across Pakistan to Afghanistan. The Agreement does not presently provide for transit facilities for Indian goods across Pakistan to Afghanistan but states an intention towards considering the feasibility of such a proposal at an appropriate time in the future.

The absence of transit arrangements between bordering non-landlocked countries such as India and Bangladesh and India and Pakistan has impeded South Asian economies' efficient integration into the global economy, as well as diversification of their intra-regional trade. However, apart from the formally signed agreements, transit in South Asia is also regulated and conducted as part of overall bilateral trade agreements. In the case of India and Bangladesh, for example, a bilateral agreement called the Protocol on Inland water Transport and Trade, signed in 1999 and renewed in 2007, derives directly from the provisions of the bilateral trade agreement between the two countries. In 2010 India and Bangladesh signed agreements on regional connectivity whereby India has agreed to provide transit facilities from the Mongla and Chittagong ports in Bangladesh to destinations in Bhutan and Nepal. Simultaneously, Bangladesh has agreed to sell seaport services to Bhutan, India and Nepal and a new port of call and transshipment port on the inland waterways of Bangladesh for onward connectivity to Tripura in India has been designated. There are also specific agreements for movement of goods by rail through specific border routes between the two economies. Nepal and Bangladesh have a bilateral transit agreement that provides transit rights/facilities for accessing overseas markets, but the agreement does not deal with their bilateral overland trade. India provides transit for bilateral overland trade between Bangladesh and Bhutan. A trade agreement signed in 2003 between Bangladesh and Bhutan also specifies the transit route for undertaking bilateral trade.

A major concern for India is to provide access to its North Eastern states. Transportation through the narrow passage referred to as the 'chicken neck' that connects the rest of India with the North Eastern region is slow and implies high time-costs. Also, the North Eastern states of India do not have access to sea, except through Kolkata, and this adds to their transport costs for trade. Bangladesh, which provides an easier transit route for North Eastern states, does not allow Indian goods transit rights/facilities through its territory, and, similarly, India did not allow Nepal and Bhutan to access Bangladesh ports through transit facilities in its territory until recently.

Given that efficient transit continues to be lacking, even though many kinds of bilateral transit arrangements operate in the region, it is imperative that a regional transit agreement be evolved to better facilitate trade integration in South Asia. Regional trading agreements help create a level playing field and address the problem of the low bargaining power of the smaller and vulnerable nations, particularly landlocked ones. Through a regional agreement, the landlocked countries stand to secure better transit rights, as they are then less dependent on their political relationship with any particular country, as any restriction and the resultant dispute will be a regional issue as opposed to a bilateral issue. Regional transit agreements in South Asia are also necessitated by the large-scale informal and illegal trade in the region. Better inspection and regulation of goods in transit has to be undertaken so as to prevent entry of third-country goods in the course of transit across a nation. This is relevant for India–Nepal transit and Afghanistan-Pakistan transit, among other possible means and routes for smuggling in South Asia.

South Asia does not have a regional transit arrangement to date. The SAFTA under Article 8 provides for adoption of trade facilitation measures; transit facilities for efficient intra-regional trade, especially for the landlocked member states; and development of communication systems and transport infrastructure. However, little progress is evident in these areas, apparently on account of Article 8 being more a reflection of member states' positive intent rather than a concrete specification of implementation strategy or design. The need for formulating a regional transit agreement has also been recognized by the SAARC, and the country transport ministers in the region have agreed to evolve a regional transport and transit agreement.[37]

Pakistan, India and the MFN issue

Pakistan's denial to grant India the MFN status has acted as another barrier that restricts normal trade between the two countries. Pakistan has so far denied India the MFN status even though the same was accorded to Pakistan by India in compliance with the WTO norms in 1996.[38] The MFN clause is a mechanism that is used to liberalize trade on a non-discriminatory basis. Granting MFN status to trade partners assures them that any preferences in the form of tariff reductions granted to any one nation will be extended automatically to all trade partners with MFN status. It therefore extends equality to all trading partners, and Pakistan not doing so in its trade policy towards India reflects an act of discrimination and conscious direction of trade away from India.

Pakistan cites import surge from India and further enlargement of Pakistan's existing trade deficit with India as a possible adverse consequence of extending MFN status to India. The economic rationale is, however, flawed and is apparently proposed with a narrow political perspective. Even if according MFN status to India is likely to lead to an increase in Pakistan's trade deficit with India, the reduction in costs by importing from India the commodities that are otherwise imported from distant countries at higher costs may ultimately imply a much lower overall trade deficit for the country. This would contribute to improving Pakistan's external position, which is currently extremely vulnerable and the reason for the economy's increased external dependence.[39] The fear of being flooded by cheaper and better-quality goods is also only short term as cheaper imports from India are likely to initiate more competition in the otherwise protected market. In the short term this may lead to elimination of some domestic industry in Pakistan, but over the longer term it can only lead to increased productivity and efficiency levels.

It is also noteworthy that the denial of MFN status to India and imposition of restrictions on imports from India is sometimes redundant as many of the restricted items are imported through third channels like Dubai, Singapore, Afghanistan and other countries, or else even smuggled illegally to Pakistan through the long, porous and unfenced land border between the two countries. Granting MFN status to India would reduce transaction costs, bring the illegal trade into official channels and thereby generate revenue for Pakistan. In fact it is considered that more than economic logic, it is only parochial national sentiments that are being perpetuated through this policy.[40,41]

Behind-the-border barriers and ease of trade facilitation

In addition to the above barriers that have been brought to the fore by traders there is another set of barriers behind or at the border[42] that add to costs of trade. These include difficult and protracted customs regulation, port fees and charges, lack of transport infrastructure and logistics services. The Word Bank, in its Logistics Performance Index (LPI), makes an evaluation of the extent of trade facilitation with regard to such barriers. The composite measure rates country performance with regard to behind-the-border constraints on a scale from 1 to 5, with 5 being the highest performance.

The average LPI for the South Asian region is 2.3, which is lower than the index value of 2.47 for the lower-middle-income group of countries and only marginally higher than the 2.29 index value for the low-income group. The LPI for India at 3.07 compares well with the average for the South Asian region and comparator countries in the lower-middle-income group. As per these scores India is ranked 39th in the world and leading in the South Asian region. India performed best in the LPI components of timeliness of shipments in reaching their destination, but needs most improvement in increasing the efficiency and effectiveness of customs procedures. Afghanistan's LPI score is 1.21 and is ranked 150th in the world and last in the South Asian region. The area in which it performed the best was domestic logistics costs and its weakest performance was in the ability to track and trace shipments. Bangladesh, with a LPI score of 2.47, ranked 87th in the world and 3rd in the South Asian region. The area in which it performed the best was the timeliness of shipments and its weakest performance was in the area of customs procedures. Bhutan is at 2.16 and ranks 128th in the world and 5th in the South Asian region. The area in which it performed the best was domestic logistics costs, and its weakest performance was in the area of customs procedures and the quality of transport and IT infrastructure. The LPI rates Nepal at 2.14 with a ranking of 130th in the world and 6th in the South Asian region, with its best performance in the area of domestic logistics costs and weakest performance in the quality of transport and IT infrastructure for logistics. Nepal faces transportation challenges for manufactured goods because of the fact that it is landlocked and most of its goods must travel through India. Pakistan is at 2.62 on a scale and ranked 68th in the world and 2nd in the South Asian region. The area in which it performed the best was the timeliness of shipments in reaching their destination, and it needs most improvement in the quality of transport and IT infrastructure. Sri Lanka at 2.4 is ranked 92nd in the world and 4th in the South Asian region. It performed the best in domestic logistics costs and lagged in the quality of transport and IT infrastructure.

Individual performance for South Asian economies thus reveals the areas of customs procedures and transport and IT infrastructure as those most in need of improvement to further ease the behind-the-border constraints for trade enhancement in the region. This requires individual country efforts to improve these areas so as to reduce trade costs. These are also areas where a coordinated approach among the South Asian countries is possible and coherent and similar regional performance across a range of business and trade facilitation areas could significantly increase trade competitiveness. Gains from improvements in business regulatory coherence in Asia could generate an additional 3 per cent average increase in bilateral exports in the region.[43]

Capital inflows in South Asia

Trends in capital inflows: foreign direct investment

The liberalization of the policy for capital inflows and facilitating investment environment has over the last decade-and-a-half led to the South Asian economies emerging as some of the most attractive destinations for foreign investment in the world. India, with its high growth and accompanying stability, has emerged as the most attractive destination for capital inflows in South Asia. In fact India is among the highest recipients of net capital flows among the emerging market economies of Asia. Also, South Asia's share in total FDI flows to developing countries is rising even though it remains small in absolute magnitude. Of the total FDI to developing countries the share of South Asian countries has more than doubled from around 3 per cent to around 8 per cent over 2004–08.[44] Since 2005, South Asia has experienced accelerated inflows with an annual average rate of 68 per cent. Around 90 per cent of the total FDI to South Asia is directed to the Indian economy. It would therefore not be incorrect to attribute the increased flows to South Asia and the increasing share of South Asia in the total developing country inflows to an increasingly attractive Indian economy as a destination for FDI. The period from 2004 to 2008 also coincides with an unprecedented growth and macroeconomic stability in India.[45] Also, as per the aggregate assessment provided by the international investor confidence survey rankings undertaken by A. T. Kearney, India has moved from 6th position in 2003 to 2nd position in 2005, then to 3rd in 2010 when the US took over in 2nd position. UNCTAD's World Investment Prospects Survey (2010–12) ranks India second after China in the top priority host economies for FDI in the world. The *Doing Business* report (2010) published by the World Bank ranks India higher relative to other South Asian economies with regard to the financial aspects of undertaking business. Getting credit is relatively easier in India than in other South Asian economies and at the same time regulatory institutions are well established so as to ensure investor protection in the country, even though overall India is classified among the more difficult countries (at rank 132 in a survey of 182 countries, 2011 and 2012 *Doing Business* report) in terms of doing business.

Other economies in South Asia are also catching up with this trend, though the magnitude of inflows to these economies is very small in comparison with India. For example, while Pakistan has received substantial investment capital in 2009 these inflows (net FDI inflows) were less than a tenth of the net inflows to India. Bangladesh and Sri Lanka receive much smaller inflows. Overall in 2009, India received 90 per cent and Pakistan in 2nd position received 6 per cent of the total FDI inflows (net) to South Asia. In absolute terms, the inflows to Pakistan have increased from US$0.5 billion in 2003 to US$5.6 billion in 2007 and US$5.4 billion in 2008. According to the *Doing Business* report (2010) Pakistan has the most conducive environment in South Asia with reference in particular to investment climate features like getting credit, protecting investors, closing a business and dealing with construction permits. The positive investment is, however, marred by political instability in Pakistan that may in fact be responsible for the small magnitude of flows to the country. Bangladesh has also experienced an increase in FDI inflows over 2003–05, after which there was a decline in inflows upto 2007. In 2008, a recovery was registered and the inflows reached a level of US$1,086 billion. Owing to early initiation of reforms, Sri Lanka experienced an initial spurt in FDI inflows but this was interrupted by the onset of the civil war in 1983.The flows recovered to some extent in the 1990s and during the mid-1990s, with the implementation of a divestiture program of state-owned enterprises, higher inflows were recorded. Nevertheless, total FDI inflows stagnated for the first five years of the last decade. FDI inflows increased only in 2006, and in 2008 amounted to US$752 million. Sri Lanka does well on aspects like starting and exiting business and Bangladesh performs well in terms of dealing with permits, payment of taxes and exiting business[46] as per the assessment of investment environment. Afghanistan has also in recent years emerged as an important destination for FDI inflows, and in 2008 it received around US$300 million of FDI inflows. Bhutan and Nepal receive very small amounts of FDI, while Maldives is an insignificant host country for FDI. While net FDI inflows in 2009 are relatively lower for all the major South Asian countries, reflecting the adverse impact of the global financial

Table 3.2 South Asia: FDI, net inflows (US$ million)

	2001	2008	2009
World	820,430	1,770,873	1,114,189
Developing Economies	215,421	630,013	478,349
Developing Economies: Asia	113,936	372,739	301,367
Afghanistan	1	300	185
Bangladesh	355	1,086	674.25
Bhutan		30	36.37
India	5,472	40,418	34,577
Maldives	12	12	9.60
Nepal	21	1	38.18
Pakistan	383	5,438	2,387
Sri Lanka	172	752	404
South Asia (share in Developing Asia)%	5.6	12.9	12.7
South Asia (share in Developing Countries)%	3	7.6	8

Source: World Development Indicators, (WDI), World Bank.

crisis on global movement of capital, the share of South Asia in net FDI inflows to developing economies as a whole, as well as to developing Asia, undergoes little change relative to the previous year's flows.

Source of FDI to South Asian nations

Most of the firms investing in India are from the USA and Western Europe. MNCs from Germany and the UK are the leading European investors.[47] In Sri Lanka, Singapore is the largest investor, followed by the UK and then by the Asia-Pacific countries of Japan, Republic of Korea, Hong Kong and Australia. India has also become an important investor in Sri Lanka as a result of the India–Sri Lanka FTA (ISLFTA) that has facilitated exports to the Indian market. In 2002 India was the largest investor, and investment was oriented towards industries responding to demand originating from the Indian market. Other foreign investments in Sri Lanka have been similarly motivated towards exporting to the Indian market. For Pakistan the major sources of FDI include the US and UK, followed by Germany, Japan and UAE. Of the 50 countries that have their commercial presence in Nepal (up to 2005–06), 33 are developing countries, accounting for 66 per cent of FDI in the country. Very few FDI projects have been commissioned in Bhutan.

Sector-wise distribution

The sectors that have attracted the largest amount of FDI vary across the region, from infrastructure being the predominant sector for India, and power for Pakistan. Bangladesh and Sri Lanka both have textiles as the most attractive sector for FDI.

MNC investment picked up in India only after 1994. Most of the early entrants into India were in the intermediate goods, machinery and equipment and IT sectors. The data reveals a shift in the FDI patterns in the periods 1991–99 and 2000–05. In the first period the transportation industry, electrical equipment and telecommunications, along with the services sector, were the dominant sectors. Primary sectors like paper and paper pulp, including paper products, also appeared in the top ten sectors attracting FDI in the first period. Post-2000, however, this sector does not appear as a priority sector for foreign investors. In the manufacturing sector, the previous priority areas, notably chemical industry, have experienced steeply decreasing shares in overall FDI stocks. Yet FDI stocks in nominal terms have multiplied even in these industries. Priority areas have changed within the manufacturing sector and electrical equipment has replaced the transport industry as the top ranking with its share in 2000–05 being double that of the latter in the period 1991–99. The sectors that received the highest cumulative inflows of FDI over the period 2000–08 are the services sector (22.4 per cent), computer software and hardware (14.0 per cent), telecommunications (7.2 per cent), and construction activities (5.5 per cent). Country-wise, much of the European investment in India is concentrated in the intermediate and machinery and equipment sectors. The majority of the North American firms, almost all of which are from the USA, have invested in the IT and financial services sectors. Much of the investment of Japanese and East Asian firms has been concentrated in the 'old economy' machines and equipment sector and in the 'new economy' IT sector. Only a small fraction of the MNCs investing in India are large. Most of the larger affiliates are concentrated in the infrastructure and machinery and equipment sectors. A significant proportion of the MNC affiliates in India (23 per cent) contribute to a significant proportion of the worldwide turnover, that is, greater than the 5 per cent of the parent MNCs. Most of the firms contributing significantly to the parents' global output are in the IT and machinery and equipment sectors.

Among the sectors attracting foreign investment in Pakistan are power, chemicals and pharmaceuticals, telecommunications, and mining and quarrying. This can be attributed to the increasing needs and demand for energy in Pakistan and natural resource advantages in case of mining.

The bulk of foreign investment in Bangladesh is concentrated in the gas sector owing to availability of considerable reserves. In other sectors FDI has been limited owing to slow pace of privatization, inadequate basic infrastructure, an inefficient financial sector and generally uncertain political climate. Significant inflows were observed in the period 2005–08. More recently in 2009–10, the new investment projects were in the services, engineering, clothing and agriculture sectors. The services sector has attracted the maximum investment, followed by IT and engineering and manufactured goods. Agro-based industries have also attracted investment, as Bangladesh is a predominantly agrarian economy, and the second most important industry in the country is textiles.

As regards sector-wise distribution of FDI in Sri Lanka, initially it was focused in the manufacturing sector – mainly in the textile and garment sector – but in the 2000s this was outpaced by FDI in the services sector, driven apparently by the opportunities available in the telecom sector. The most popular sectors to attract FDI over 1997–2007 have been services, textiles, chemicals, food and beverages, and manufacturing products.

In Nepal, tertiary sectors like hotels and restaurants and transport have attracted maximum investment.

Bilateral investment promotion and protection agreement (BIPA)

Bilateral investment protection and promotion agreements have been initiated by South Asian countriessince the liberalization of foreign investment regime with a view to providing confidence to foreign investors. The elements of protection offered by India in BIPAs include, inter alia, national treatment for foreign investment and MFN treatment for foreign investors and investment, free repatriation/transfer of returns on investment, recourse to domestic dispute resolution and international arbitration for investor-state and state-state disputes and nationalization/expropriation against compensation only in public interest on a non-discriminatory basis.

As of 2010, India has signed bilateral tax treaties with 57 countries and has agreements of double taxation avoidance with 63 countries, Pakistan has signed bilateral tax treaties with 23 countries and agreements for double taxation avoidance with 52 countries. Nepal has signed double taxation avoidance agreements with

India, PRC, Austria, Korea, Mauritius, Sri Lanka, Pakistan, Norway and Thailand. Nepal has also signed investment protection agreements with France, Germany and the UK. A draft regional agreement on promotion and protection of investment within SAARC, under consideration of the members since 1997, when initiatives for the agreement were first launched, was finally signed at the 16th SAARC Summit meeting held in Thimpu, Bhutan in 2010.

Intra-regional FDI

Intra-regional FDI in South Asia is small but increasing. The dominant investor in the region is India. Indian MNCs are investing not only within South Asia but the rest of the world also. Indian investment in Nepal and Bhutan has been significant. Nepal's opening up in 1990 resulted in major FDI inflows from India using the bilateral trade agreement between the two countries that was signed in 1996. The treaty allowed free access to the Indian market for goods manufactured in Nepal. Due to this provision many Indian joint ventures were interested in investing in the manufacturing sector in Nepal, particularly where production/output was aimed at the Indian market. However, following the 2002 revision of the rules of origin in the treaty the FDI flows registered a decline.[48] Bhutan also has similar agreements with India. Bhutan introduced its FDI policy in 2002, replacing the previous case-by-case system of approving foreign investments. For Bhutan, FDI typically is investment from India. Bhutan's major industry – hydropower – has all Indian investment. After the India–Sri Lanka bilateral FTA Indian investment in Sri Lanka has increased. A major attraction for Indian investors has been the ability to re-export to India while benefitting from lower tariffs in Sri Lanka. India became the biggest investor in Sri Lanka in 2002, 2003 and in 2010 India was the largest source of FDI to Sri Lanka with US$110 million. A number of Sri Lankan companies are also investing in India, although in small magnitudes.[49]

None of the SAARC countries are among the major investors in Pakistan. In the case of Bangladesh, firms from India, Pakistan and Sri Lanka have invested in a wide range of sectors.[50]

FDI outflows from South Asia

India has emerged as a major source of FDI among the developing/emerging economies in the world. Within a span of seven years from 2001 to 2008 India's overseas stock of FDI has grown from US$1.3 billion to US$56 billion. Indian outward investment in 2008 was US$18 billion and even after the impact of the global financial crisis in 2009 it amounted to almost US$15 billion in 2009.[51] The emergence of the Indian multinational on the global stage has been a notable development reflecting the strength of Indian enterprise that is supported by large-scale economic policy reform. Capital outflows from India are largely in the manufacturing sector, followed by the non-financial services sector. Major multinational corporations are sourcing high-quality components from India. Prominent among these are Volvo, GM, GE, Chrysler, Ford, Toyota, Unilever,

Cliariant, Cummins and Delphi. Outflows from India are directed towards both the developed and developing countries. It is interesting and useful to note that for the first time in 2008, five MNCs from South Asia, all from India, were ranked among the top 100 non-financial trans-national corporations.[52] Apart from reinforcing the individualistic rise of India in South Asia, this trend is indicative of FDI becoming a driver of trade and integration in South Asia. As outflows from India gain strength it is natural that neighbouring countries are seen as potential markets, and FDI as means of economic integration. Indian companies have already been observed to invest within the South Asian region and outflows from India to Sri Lanka and Nepal provide evidence towards this phenomenon. Pakistan, Bangladesh and Sri Lanka are also observed to be sources of FDI outflows from the SAARC region, though with relatively miniscule shares.

South-south FDI and South Asia

The contrast with South East Asia and implications for regional economic integration

In the last two decades from 1990 to 2007 south-south FDI has increased from US$3.7 billion to over US$73.8 billion. It is observed that in a region-wise distribution of total world outward stocks South, South East and East Asia are the largest investor regions with a 10.4 per cent share of the total. However, within this it may be noted that South Asia contributes an insignificant 0.2 per cent. Even this miniscule share is observed only after 2000. Prior to this, South Asian contribution to total outward stock of capital was non-existent. In this negligibly small share of the total, India makes a contribution of about US$29.4 million. In the region of South, South East and East Asia, India is the only country from South Asia that figures among the top ten FDI recipients and source of outflows. The FDI outflows from India are close to those from Latin America in terms of magnitude, yet when compared to the top-ranking economies it is negligible. China, for example, has a total FDI outflow of US$75.8 million.[53] As regards intra-regional FDI share in total south-south FDI, South Asia has the lowest share at 2.1 per cent, and the largest shares are evident for Latin America, South East Asia thus representing the level of regional integration as promoted by or on account of the FDI flows in these two regions.

In South East Asia in particular it is well known that large-scale and growing intra-regional investment has helped in recycling comparative advantages, transferring technology and enhancing competitiveness. This phenomenon has been instrumental in the sequential upgrading of industries across countries at various stages of development, resulting in establishment of regional production networks that have been at the core of regional economic integration in South East Asia. Given the liberal policy environment and availability of liquidity with Indian and other South Asian multinationals that can facilitate regional production, we make an attempt to examine the scope for such sequentially integrated production processes in South Asia. The exercise is undertaken for the textile and clothing sector, which is one of the top ten exports for the major economies of the region – India, Pakistan, Sri Lanka and Bangladesh. For these four economies potential commodities for integrated production networks are identified at the six-digit level of harmonized system (HS) of product classification, as follows.

Scope for production networks in South Asia

It has long been considered that the South Asian economies have a similar industrial structure and hence the scope for complementarities among these economies is limited. But it must be recognized that with transformation of economic regime the South Asian countries and their subsequent high growth, in particular since 2000, it is entirely possible that the structure of comparative advantage of these countries could have evolved such that new complementarities may be identifiable, and hence scope for intra-regional trade and investment may now exist. We set out to identify these complementarities by undertaking a simple exercise for two sectors: textile (HS-50–60, 63) and clothing (HS-61 and 62) for the primary South Asian exporters and importers in these categories, which includes Bangladesh, India, Pakistan and Sri Lanka. The analysis is undertaken at the HS six-digit level of commodity classification and the years 2007–08,[54] as follows.

For all possible trade dyads all non-overlapping exports and imports to and from the world are identified and matched to draw a set of common commodities. This set would thereby comprise commodities that one country in the pair can export and the other is a potential importer but for which the importer-exporter relationship is not as yet established. This helps identify an opportunity for trade and production network creation in the South Asian region. The exercise provides us with the following insights.[55]

Overall possibilities of trade within these two predominant sectors exist such that network production among South Asian countries is a real possibility. Specific commodities and country pairs that can take this idea forward are as follows.

i) Bangladesh exports – Sri Lanka potential importer
    a) 560721: Binder or baler twine, of sisal or agave (textile fibre)
    b) 570490: Carpets of felt of textile materials, > 0.3 m^2

For both of the above commodities China is currently a major source of imports for Sri Lanka.[56]

ii) Pakistan exports – Sri Lanka potential importer
    a) 520623: Cotton yarn <85 per cent single combed 232–192 dtex, not retail
    b) 520624: Cotton yarn <85 per cent single combed 192–125 dtex, not retail
    c) 520833: Twill weave cotton >85 per cent <200g/m^2, dyed
    d) 521021: Plain weave cotton <85 per cent + man-made fibre, <200g, bleached
    e) 521131: Plain weave cotton <85 per cent +man-made fibre, >200g, dyed
    f) 540781: Woven fabric synthetic filament, <85 per cent +cotton, nes

g) 550190: Synthetic filament tow, nes
h) 551030: Yarn of artificial staple fibres and cotton, not retail
i) 551634: Woven fabric <85 per cent artificial staple + wool/hair, printed
j) 570249: Carpets of yarn nes, woven pile, made up, nes
k) 600521: Warp knit fabrics, incl. those made on galloon knitting machines (excl. of . . .)

For the above commodities the existing major source of imports for Sri Lanka are the East Asian economies of China, Hong Kong, Republic of Korea, Singapore and Thailand.

iii) Pakistan exports – Bangladesh is potential importer
　a) 520534: Cotton yarn >85 per cent multiple uncombed 192–125 dtex, not retail
　b) 551030: Yarn of artificial staple fibres and cotton, not retail
　c) 551221: Woven fabric >85 per cent acrylic staple fibres, unbl./bleached
　d) 551641: Woven fabric <85 per cent artif.staple + cotton, unbl./bleached
　e) 600524: Warp knit fabrics. incl. those made on galloon knitting machines (excl. of 60.01–60.04), of cotton, printed
　f) 600644: Knitted/crocheted fabrics, nes in Ch. 60, of artificial fibres, printed
iv) Bangladesh exports – Pakistan potential importer
　a) 520291: Garnetted stock of cotton
　b) 570490: Carpets of felt of textile materials > 0.3 m^2
　c) 610331: Men's, boys' jackets and blazers, wool or hair, knit
　d) 611530: Other women's full-length/knee-length hosiery, measuring per single yarn less than 67 decitex, knitted/crocheted
　e) 620191: Men's, boys' anoraks, etc., of wool or hair, not knit

Imports of these commodities are currently being sourced by Pakistan from China and in some cases from the US.

v) India exports – Sri Lanka potential importer
　a) 520533: Cotton yarn >85 per cent multiple uncombed 232–192 dtex, not retail
　b) 520535: Cotton yarn >85 per cent multiple uncombed <125 dtex, not retail
vi) Pakistan exports – India is potential importer
　a) 510111: Greasy shorn wool, not carded or combed
　b) 551634: Woven fabric <85 per cent artificial staple + wool/hair, printed

These commodities are currently being sourced by India from Australia, Turkey and Italy.

vii) Bangladesh exports – India potential importer
　a) 611231: Men's, boys' swimwear, synthetic fibres, knit (currently sourced from China)

vii) India exports – Bangladesh potential importer
   a) 520614: Cotton yarn <85 per cent single uncombed 192–125 dtex, not retail
   b) 521222: Woven cotton fabric > 200g/m², bleached, nes
   c) 551644: Woven fabric <85 per cent artificial staple + cotton, printed

All of the above three commodities are currently being sourced by Bangladesh from China.

China is the source of imports in almost all commodities for almost all South Asian economies.

The trade pattern apparent from the above analysis suggests, at the very least, production linkages in the textile sector whereby yarn and fabric flows from India and Pakistan in different categories to Bangladesh, and the latter can supply garments to both these countries. Both Bangladesh and Pakistan can supply textile material and fibre to Sri Lanka. This process of vertical integration in the textiles and clothing sector can be potentially oriented in the following manner:

1. Pakistan to Sri Lanka: cotton yarn, man-made fibre, woven fabric, synthetic filament
2. Pakistan to India: wool, woven fabric
3. Pakistan to Bangladesh: yarn, fabric
4. India to Pakistan: cotton, yarn
5. India to Bangladesh: yarn, fabric
6. Bangladesh to India: garments
7. Bangladesh to Pakistan: garments
8. Bangladesh to Sri Lanka: textile material, fibre

While the evident longstanding links with South East Asian and East Asian economies as suppliers/source of imports for South Asian economies have been discussed earlier by some analysts[57] what needs careful analysis and policy attention is that the South Asian importers are adjusting to the shifts within the South East Asian region as well. This is evident from Vietnam emerging as one of the exporting countries in the above commodity categories to South Asian destinations. In the context it may be hard to understand why the same adjustment is difficult for India or other South Asian countries. Performance and variety[58] have been identified in earlier analysis as South East Asian economies' outstanding attributes, but there again in our analysis commodities have been identified at the six-digit level such that existing specializations in the region permit trade in a vertical integrated manner. Conflictual frictions that may be reflected in tedious processes or other kinds of NTMs may be the only factors that prevent traders from forming these networks in the region. For example, although Bangladesh's long-standing ban on the import of textile fabrics was removed in 2005,[58] textile fabric protective duties remained very high and continued to provide a strong motive for fabric being smuggled from India rather than being legally traded. Additionally, the incentive for 'technical' smuggling through under-declaration of the quantities of duty-free shipments of inputs for exporters – especially yarns, fabrics, dyes and other inputs for use by readymade garments exporters – has not changed greatly and remains considerable. Identification of non-tariff measures (NTMs) that may currently be the reason for South Asian countries looking eastward for textile imports in these sectors would therefore be helpful and should be taken up as priority task at the policy level. Networked production linkages can be a stable means for enhancing intra-regional trade and a strong integrating force in the region, as they would be driven by the profit-oriented private sector and therefore are likely to be sustainable in the long run.

The detailed analysis of the trends and patterns of trade and FDI of the South Asian region make very apparent the anti-home bias of the South Asian region. It is critical to identify the underlying factors that continue to inhibit trade within the region, even when trade with countries outside the region is expanding, and south–south cooperation is emerging as the predominant global trend. Even though South Asian countries are moving away from their traditional markets they are not yet confident of expanding towards their own region. In the next chapter the analysis is carried forward to examine the role of preferential trade agreements in consolidating trade and economic integration South Asia.

4 Preferential trading agreements in South Asia

South Asia's attempts at bilateral and regional trade agreements date back to 1949–50 when India signed the Trade and Transit treaties with both Nepal and Bhutan, though as part of an overall developmental strategy of the smaller nations. The trade treaties have since been renewed and revised with additional and sometimes more stringent new-age components. As the spirit of regionalism gathers momentum in the rest of the world, the bilateral FTA between India and Sri Lanka implemented in 2000 has been the first to herald the trend of bilateral preferential trade agreements (PTAs) in South Asia. This was later followed by a bilateral FTA between Sri Lanka and Pakistan in 2005. At the regional level, preferential trade agreements were initiated with the South Asian Preferential Trade Agreement (SAPTA) in 1993 and then the South Asia Free Trade Area (SAFTA) in 2004. The former was suspended in 1999 on account of, among other reasons, domestic political changes in Pakistan and the ensuing worsening of India–Pakistan bilateral relations. As tensions between India and Pakistan started to ease out, the heads of the SAARC member nations agreed to launch the SAFTA at the Islamabad Summit in 2004. The agreement on SAFTA that was restricted to trade in goods only, entered into force on January 1, 2006. An agreement for liberalization of services in South Asia was signed in 2010 at the 16th SAARC summit held in Thimpu, Bhutan, and the agreement towards investment liberalization among the member countries is under negotiation.

South Asia has thus followed a dual approach of regional and bilateral trade agreements. The design and implications that have been varied across these agreements are discussed below against a brief background of trends and motivation for PTA formation in the region.[1]

Trends in FTA formation: regional comparisons

A regional classification of the Asian FTAs[2] shows that as of January, 2011, South Asia has a total of eight FTAs within the sub-region. Of these, five bilateral trade agreements have already been notified to the WTO. Of the other three FTAs, one is under negotiation and two more have been proposed. In comparison with the other sub-regions South Asia fairs well with regard to the number of 'within sub-region' FTAs. It is second to the Central and West Asian sub-region that has

17 bilateral FTAs, nine in effect and notified to the WTO and eight signed and yet to be notified to the WTO. East Asia, like South Asia, had no bilateral FTAs notified to the WTO in 2000, and in 2011, at almost the same pace as South Asia, has formulated seven bilateral FTAs, of which only two have been notified to the WTO. South East Asia and the Pacific sub-region have the lowest numbers with one and two bilateral FTAs within the sub-region. As regards the bilateral FTAs across sub-regions in Asia, South Asia has 19 FTAs across Central, South East and East Asia and the Pacific sub-region. The largest number of bilateral FTAs (30) has been formulated by the South East Asia sub-region across East, South, and the Pacific sub-regions of Asia. In terms of bilateral FTAs with non-Asian countries, South Asia lags behind South East Asia, East Asia and the Central Asian sub-regions. None of the South Asian economies has an FTA in effect with either the EU or the US.

In South Asia as well as Asia as a whole, India has been the most active in forming bilateral FTAs. Being the most dynamic economies in South Asia, 33 FTAs at various stages of formation[3] may not have been a very surprising trend but for the fact that India is followed by Pakistan (26), which has seen many economic and political vicissitudes during this period. India already has 11 FTAs in effect, while Pakistan has only six in effect with ten at the proposal stage and another five for which the framework agreement has been signed. Maldives in South Asia has formed the lowest number of FTAs, only two: one that is in effect and another under negotiation. The distance in terms of time between framework agreements, negotiations, signing and the agreement coming into effect varies across the region.

Motivating factors for entering into PTAs/FTAs

PTAs across the world have been driven by economic and non-economic considerations. Broad categories of motivational factors underlying formulation of preferential trading arrangements are briefly discussed below so as to provide a contextual background to the South Asian experience. The factors are not mutually exclusive and, as evident for South Asia, policymakers may have had multiple reasons for entering into a PTA with another state, and many of these may actually be other than the following three broadly specified categories in the theoretical literature.[4]

Economic welfare enhancement

It has been observed that trade creation and enhancement is one of the most desired objectives, theoretically, for establishing preferential trade agreements. PTAs are considered to be welfare-enhancing, as preferential trade liberalization through tariff reduction can potentially lead to an increase in trade among the member countries. And when member countries are in close physical proximity, a further reduction in transportation costs implies additional gains in trade. A priori, though, it may be difficult to estimate the potential welfare benefits of PTAs. Nevertheless, PTAs are entered into particularly in circumstances when the global trading system is unable to deliver, as is true of the conditions today, both on account of the increased protectionist tendencies evident from the developed world in the wake of the global financial crisis and the inability of the WTO members to reach a consensus agreement on the Doha Development Agenda (DDA).

It has also been observed that growth in PTAs around the world provides an incentive to countries to acquire membership owing to the competitive effect and fear of isolation as an increasingly larger proportion of world trade is conducted on a preferential basis.

Domestic political economy and geo-political considerations

The basic political economy argument comes into play when countries tend to sign preferential trade agreements with economies that may not, in the traditionally understood sense, be 'natural trading partners'.[5] This tendency can be attributed to domestic political conditions wherein some industrial sector lobbies may be more powerful than others in influencing the foreign economic policy formulation such that countries may sign deals with otherwise minor trading partners. Sometimes the industrial lobbies are driven by fear of being overtaken by foreign goods competition, and sometimes by loss of FDI collaborations if trade deals are not signed with host countries. In each case the industrial lobby's scope for influence may be a function of political institutions/regime of an economy, which, if democratic, may provide greater scope for such influence to be evident in policy.[6]

Geo-political considerations influence PTA alignments and are evident when support is extended to PTAs, even if they yield minimal or no economic benefits but are considered as beneficial for national security, or when PTAs, even if economically beneficial, are not signed with countries that are considered as political adversaries. India and Pakistan are suitable examples in this case.

An interesting observation has been made in the context of a large number of FTAs being signed by the former Soviet Union economies – apparently reflecting a desire to preserve the 'Union' through economic integration in the aftermath of the collapse of the political union.

South Asian context

The FTA exercise in South Asia appears to be within an overall framework that is defined less by economic and more by political parameters. In the case of South Asia, even while the 'naturalness' of trading partners is a given with geographical, historical, cultural and linguistic similarities inherited by all member nations, the level of intra-regional trade has been low and stagnant for several decades. The natural advantage of physical proximity of the member nations has been limited initially by highly protectionist economic regimes and more recently by overriding political and historical frictions. There has been little enthusiasm to take forward the agenda of enhancing intra-regional trade, at least with regards to the regional FTAs. The only economic factor that may and in fact should propel the region towards preferential trade arrangements is the slow-moving and close-to-suspension

64 Preferential trading agreements in South Asia

DDA of the WTO that has made apparent the lack of support that the developed countries are willing to offer for issues of interest and concern to developing countries. As regionalism gradually becomes the only course of action, south–south cooperation through preferential trade agreements with other developing countries will increase even further. South Asian countries need to, in this context, take forward the idea of economic integration of the region. As per existing trends, however, it appears that South Asian countries are more keen on participating in extra-regional FTAs rather than focus on the South Asian trade partners. This is evident from South Asia's growing links with South East Asia, with India as the lead economy in terms of both forming FTAs and rising trade levels. The trend of integrating South Asia with East Asia is growing and may be a forerunner towards Pan Asian integration. In the latter half of the last decade, as India's trade policy towards preferential trade agreements gathered momentum, the maximum number of PTAs were signed/initiated with the ASEAN and East Asian economies of Japan and South Korea.

Regarding political factors, other than the India–Pakistan hostilities, an additional factor that may be held responsible for the slow pace of economic integration in South Asia is the variety and volatility of political regimes and institutions across South Asia. Democracies and autocracies or military regimes cater to different interest groups in the society. The significance of signalling policy orientation towards economic welfare of the median voter does not prevail across all regimes. It is likely that, given the volatility of political regimes in South Asian countries like Pakistan and the prevalence of regimes other than democracy that are not necessarily favourably inclined towards India in Bangladesh, this may have been a reason for this trend. That democracy has a role to play in facilitating trade is evident from the ongoing pressure and demand from Pakistani businessmen for opening up trade with India and from the steps that have already been initiated in this direction, like the announcement for granting India the MFN status. However, given the past record of frequent and unpredictable changes in Pakistan polity, these announcements may not see fruition, as in the earlier instances of these declarations in 1975 and 2004. As it is, the present political scenario in Pakistan is considered to be very fluid owing to the divisions between the elected government, judiciary and military that have become very apparent in the first half of 2012. In the case of SAFTA, Pakistan's thus-far positive-list approach to India was not only in violation of the provisions of the agreement but also of economic rationality, only in deference to its domestic political constituencies. Domestic political economy influences are also apparent in South Asia's FTAs with countries outside the region. A case in point is the India-ASEAN FTA where the protracted negotiations were largely in deference to a section of the farming community that was a politically sensitive constituency for the ruling coalition government in India. The delay in signing the FTA implied economic costs in terms of trade benefits as well as late entry relative to other regional players.[7] The India–Thailand FTA, the framework agreement for which was among the first to be signed by India in 2003, is another example where domestic pressures from industrial lobbies have prevented an economic deal. The FTA has not progressed beyond the initial opening up of 83 commodities under the early harvest programme (EHP) of the framework agreement and the full deal is still under negotiation. This is largely attributable to the strong opposition from the Indian auto-industry lobby that feared competition from Japan via Thailand through this agreement.

Unlike the case of disintegrated USSR, South Asia seems to have no desire to economically unite the one-time political union of three member states of SAARC-India, Pakistan and Bangladesh. On the contrary, their subsequent partition at the time of their independence is the primary reason for persistent conflict and limited economic cooperation in the region. In fact the South Asian regional PTAs that have been announced in the spirit of WTO-defined FTAs have neither been designed nor implemented thus far in terms of coverage and concessions so as to increase intra-regional trade. As will be evident from the discussion below, the agreements at some stage or other appear to be constrained by domestic or bilateral political compulsions of member countries.

Regional trade agreements in South Asia

South Asian Preferential Trade Agreement (SAPTA)

The SAARC member nations signed an agreement to form the South Asian Preferential Trade Agreement (SAPTA) in April 1993. The Agreement, which became operational in December 1995, was aimed at trade liberalization and provided for exchange of tariff preferences among member nations with no explicit aim of achieving a free trade area in the region. SAPTA made a distinction between the least-developed countries (LDCs) and developing nations of the region and provided a special and differential treatment for the LDCs. The agreement also included a regional 'MFN' provision so that any preference extended within the SAPTA framework was to be automatically extended to all SAPTA members. The rules of origin (RoO) were finalized, after a prolonged debate, at 40 per cent local content requirement for non-LDC members and 30 per cent for LDC members, with a 'cumulative' origin requirement of 50 per cent, thereby implying that goods produced in more than one SAPTA member state have at least 50 per cent of FOB value as value added in SAPTA countries.

Three rounds of preferential tariff reductions were implemented under SAPTA. The first round that concluded in 1995 was modest in its coverage and tariff cuts. About 226 products at the six-digit level of the Harmonized System (HS) of tariff classification, which is only 6 per cent of traded goods, were covered under preferential treatment and the important issue of non-tariff barriers was deferred. The second round of SAPTA, negotiations for which were concluded in 1997, was more ambitious as it covered 1,800 six-digit HS items and also incorporated provisions about easing some non-tariff barriers. The third round, signed in 1998, was the most ambitious with product coverage extending to 2,700 items. In the first two rounds negotiations were undertaken on a product-by-product basis and in the third the negotiations were done chapter-wise. Work on the fourth round was initiated in 1999 but put on hold after the military takeover in Pakistan on

October 12, 1999, and the consequent worsening of bilateral relations between India and Pakistan.

Despite three rounds of preference negotiations the impact of SAPTA on intra-regional trade that remained at around 4 per cent of the region's global trade in the period 1995–2000[8] was negligible. Apart from the hugely time-consuming product-by-product approach of negotiations, two main factors may have been responsible for SAPTA's inability to raise intra-regional trade levels by substantial amounts. First, at the time of implementation of SAPTA, the region was characterized by a highly restrictive economic and trade regime, so that the few tariff cuts that were offered did not mean much given the initial high level of protection in the South Asian economies. Second, and more importantly, concessions offered extended to only a few sectors, like chemicals, textiles and clothing, and machinery and appliances, and some in the category of live animals and animal products. Taking advantage of the more liberal enabling clause[9] of the GATT, the number of goods for which trade preferences were offered under SAPTA did not constitute a significant proportion of the total number of goods traded among the member countries. It has been estimated[10] that the proportion of intra-regional imports covered by SAPTA preferences was highest for Pakistan (39.6 per cent), followed by Nepal (35.2 per cent), India (30 per cent), Bhutan (17 per cent) and Sri Lanka (12 per cent). The import value coverage for Bangladesh and Maldives was marginal.

South Asia Free Trade Area (SAFTA)

The agreement on SAFTA for trade in goods only entered into force on January 1, 2006. The governing principles of SAFTA included overall reciprocity and mutuality of interests of member countries. Provisions of the agreement have been laid down taking into account the contracting countries' differential level of economic and industrial development. The agreement is designed with the objective of strengthening intra-SAARC economic cooperation to maximize the region's potential for trade and development through elimination of barriers to trade. Towards achieving its objective SAFTA outlined a trade liberalization program that called for tariff reduction from the then-existing rates within two years. For non-least-developed countries this was to be reduced to 20 per cent and subsequently within five years to between 0 and 5 per cent. For least developed economies the tariffs were to be reduced to 30 per cent and subsequently within eight years to between 0 and 5 per cent. The agreement provided for sensitive lists specification that were to be subject to a maximum ceiling of 20 per cent of all tariff lines and were to be reviewed every four years or earlier. For LDCs the sensitive list specification was more flexible. The SAFTA agreement covers tariff reductions, rules of origin, safeguards, institutional structures, and dispute settlement. It also calls for the adoption of various trade facilitation measures such as harmonization of standards and mutual recognition of test results, harmonization of customs procedures, and cooperation in improving transport infrastructure. The implementation of the SAFTA schedule has to be undertaken in cognizance of the differential levels of development of member nations and hence with the provisions for special and differential treatment.

The SAFTA agreement at its initiation was only a shallow trade agreement that dealt with trade in goods only. Many issues that were crucial for trade enhancement and that are regularly incorporated in regional trade agreements (RTAs) elsewhere were either not included at all or, if included, were not dealt with in a sufficiently detailed and workable manner. Many SAFTA provisions indicated members' intent but negotiations for their implementation were left for later. These include rules of origin, institutional arrangement of the agreement, specification of safeguard measures, details regarding consultations and dispute settlement procedures and additional measures of trade facilitation. The provisions of the agreement with regard to these elements reflected intent but were left unaccompanied by the means to convert this intent into action. For example, SAFTA member countries agreed to the following two principles concerning trade facilitation in Article 3 of the agreement. One, SAFTA shall involve the free movement of goods, between countries through, inter alia, the elimination of tariffs, para-tariffs and non-tariff restrictions on the movement of goods, and any other equivalent measures; and two, SAFTA shall entail adoption of trade facilitation and other measures, and the progressive harmonization of legislations by the contracting states in the relevant areas. This statement of principles in the agreement, however, has no corresponding action programme or a timeline for realizing these intentions. So, while SAFTA was definitely a well-intentioned step forward in regional economic integration in South Asia its scope was very limited.

Over the years some flaws that were identified initially in the agreement have been corrected. For example, one of the missing elements of SAFTA, that is, the liberalization of services, was formally incorporated when member countries signed the SAARC Agreement on Trade in Services at the 16th SAARC Summit held in Thimpu, Bhutan, in 2010. The initial negative lists comprising over 50 per cent of exportable items were large. In a recent move to enhance the intra-regional trade potential of the Agreement it has been decided that all SAFTA signatories will reduce their negative list by 20 per cent of the tariff lines and the commodities thus excluded will be accorded preferential treatment from January 1, 2012, with a specified phase-out period. As per the revised list, India will have the least number of products on its negative list for LDCs (384) and for non-LDCs (NLDCs) the 695 items are next only to Maldives' specification of 545 products. Nepal has the longest list with 1,036 items, followed by Bangladesh (993), Pakistan (936) and Sri Lanka (834). The exception in this regard is Bhutan, which will consider requests, if any, from member states. The phase-out period for tariff reduction (0–5 per cent) is three years for NLDCs to NLDcs, six years for Sri Lanka, eight years for LDCs to all contracting states and three years for NLDCs to LDCs.[11] Pakistan has also notified a negative list of 1,209 items for India in March 2012, thus eliminating its positive list approach that had so far stalled SAFTA's progress. Other flaws relating to trade facilitation, dispute settlement, and so on, remain, even though some progress is observed in terms of identification and construction of the NTB database by SAARC.

It is to be noted that many initiatives towards regional economic cooperation in South Asia as now being undertaken by SAARC, such as in trade-related areas of connectivity, transit, creation of the NTBs database, trade facilitation, which follow a project-based approach and are not strictly within the SAFTA framework. It is possible that this may be a consequence of political resistance to the implementation of the regional FTA for fear of its outcomes benefitting the larger economy of India more than the smaller economies. Project initiatives, on the other hand, are cooperative and invariably technically and financially supported by regional multilateral lending agencies such as the ADB[12] and may therefore be seen as a preferred and more effective mode for regional cooperation.

Bilateral trade agreements

Since 2000 many bilateral trade agreements within the WTO framework have been proposed and signed by countries in South Asia. Not all the agreements that have been proposed or signed, however, are in effect or with other South Asian countries. Some of the existing bilateral treaties that India has with Nepal and Bhutan have been operational in the manner of a free-trade agreement, though not formally so designed. The main features of the bilateral preferential trade agreements that are in effect in South Asia are discussed below.

India–Nepal

Nepal signed its first Treaty of Trade and Commerce with India in 1950. The Treaty envisaged a customs union between the two nations. This was followed by trade treaties signed in 1960, which allowed Nepal to pursue an independent tariff policy by removal of the customs union clause of the 1950 treaty; 1971, which permitted favourable treatment to products from Nepal imported into India with a 90 per cent or more Nepalese/Indian content; and 1978, when trade was de-linked from transit and separate treaties were signed in respect of each. The treaty expired in 1988. A new agreement was signed only in 1991,[13] which was renewed in 1996, 2002 and most recently in 2009. The Treaty of 1996 was a turning point in the history of India–Nepal bilateral trade as it provided duty-free access to the Indian market for all Nepalese-manufactured goods on the basis of only a certificate of origin issued by the Nepalese authorities. The elimination of the rules of origin requirement resulted in a phenomenal growth in India's imports from Nepal, which increased by almost 94 per cent in the following year (1997) over its pre-treaty (1995) level. The increase in India's exports to Nepal was significantly lower, only about 7 per cent over the same period.[14] The 2002 revision of the agreement was undertaken with a clause for an automatic renewal every five years. In addition new rules of origin were introduced taking into account the issue of trade deflection and entry of some Nepalese goods overtaking the Indian market.[15] According to the new rules Nepalese-manufactured goods were required to fulfill the twin criteria of CTH (change in tariff heading) at the four-digit level of HS trade classification and 30 per cent VA (value addition) for duty-free access to the Indian market. Other revisions included the introduction of tariff quotas and safeguard provisions. Tariff quotas were imposed with regard to four commodities that included vegetable ghee, acrylic yarn, zinc oxide and copper products. MFN duty was to be applicable beyond the quota imports. Further major changes have been made in the treaty in the recent revision undertaken in 2009. The validity of the treaty has been increased from five to seven years with the additional provision for automatic extension for a further period of seven years. This is expected to provide stability to India–Nepal trade as well as promoting investments in Nepal based on preferential access provided by the Treaty to Nepalese products. The treaty has for the first time introduced trade via air and introduced/relaxed several trade facilitation measures, like granting recognition to sanitary and phyto-sanitary certificates provided by competent national authorities, establishment of land customs stations and annulling the export of vanaspati via contentious channelling agencies. With regards to the RoOs, it has also allowed the value of Nepalese goods to be considered on a FoB basis as opposed to the earlier 'ex-factory' basis. The Indian side also agreed to allow Nepal access to the Bangladesh port through Indian territory.[16] Quota restrictions for the four products were maintained, however, though with provisions for review and simplification. The quota for copper was raised.

Bilateral trade between India and Nepal greatly benefitted from the trade treaties and the provision for duty-free access to the Indian market for Nepalese goods. Except for a short period between 1998 and 2002, bilateral trade has been in favour of India. India's imports from Nepal have recorded a positive rate of growth since 1996, except in the years 2002 (the slowdown possibly on account of the introduction of RoOs and imposition of quota for four commodity groups), 2006 and 2009. Exports to Nepal have also registered a positive rate of growth since 1996, except in 1998, 2000 and 2009. The duty-free provision encouraged Indian joint ventures to operate in Nepal. Almost 200 Indo-Nepalese joint ventures operate in Nepal, and Indian investments account for 36 per cent of total FDI in the country. India is Nepal's principal trading partner, accounting for 50 per cent of Nepal's total trade, as well as Nepal's largest industrial collaborator and foreign investor.

India–Bhutan

Bhutan is the only South Asian country that is not a member of the WTO although it is an observer and in the process of joining. India–Bhutan trade relations are governed by the trade agreement of 1949 and four Indo-Bhutan trade agreements have been concluded in 1972,[17] 1983, 1990, and 1995.The India–Bhutan's Trade and Commerce Agreement signed in 1995 expired in 2005. It has since been renewed for a period of ten years.Under the various free-trade agreements in place since the 1970s imports from India are not subject to tariff. A de facto free-trade regime exists between India and Bhutan. The Agreement on Trade and Commerce also provides for duty-free transit of Bhutanese merchandise for trade with third countries. India is Bhutan's major trading partner and accounts for 80 per cent of its imports and 94 per cent of its total exports.[18]

Bhutan maintained a chronic trade deficit with India, and its ability to supply exports to India was limited for a long time. With India's help, Bhutan developed a hydroelectricity project and exported energy to India.[19] This has helped correct bilateral trade balance in favour of Bhutan. The trade deficit did resume after 2003 but that was on account of increased imports by Bhutan for development activities, like construction of hydro power plants.

India–Sri Lanka

The India–Sri Lanka FTA that was signed in 1998 and operationalized in 2000 has been a landmark development in India–Sri Lanka bilateral trade relations. The FTA was designed taking into account the economic asymmetry between India and Sri Lanka. Being a smaller economy, Sri Lanka was given a longer period of adjustment to undertake the process of tariff removal and phase out. In addition the negative list specified by Sri Lanka as per the Agreement had India agreeing to remove tariffs on 1,351 products and to phase out tariffs on the balance items over a span of three years. Sri Lanka, on the other hand, was to provide immediate duty-free access to India on 319 products and 50 per cent margin of preference was offered on 889 products. This was to be raised to 70, 90 and 100 per cent over a period of three years and the duty on the balance products was to be phased out over a period of eight years. The negative list from India comprised 429 items as against Sri Lanka's 1,180 (i.e., 13 per cent vs. 21 per cent of bilateral exports). With regard to some specific products that were of export interest to Sri Lanka but on India's negative list, such as tea and garments, market access was initially provided in a limited manner through tariff rate quotas and product-specific rules of origin. Later in 2007 these provisions were relaxed by increasing the port entry points for tea and by increased quota and duty-free entry with no sourcing requirements for garments. The RoOs were defined with relatively easier terms at 35 per cent of value addition.[20] Both countries are now eager to elevate the partnership to a deeper form of economic integration through a comprehensive economic cooperation agreement that would include services and investment liberalization.

The positive outcome of the ISLFTA is evident in the trends in bilateral trade. The balance of trade, which in 1999 favoured India 11 to 1, had by 2002 tilted somewhat towards Sri Lanka, when it favoured India by 5 to 1. Sri Lanka's exports to India, which were worth US$47 million in 1999 and 1 per cent of its total exports, increased to US$515 million in 2007, accounting for about 7 per cent of Sri Lanka's total export. Similarly its imports of US$511 million from India in 1999, about 6 per cent of its total imports, increased to US$2.8 billion in 2008 and US$1.7 billion in 2009, accounting for 23 and 18 per cent of its total imports respectively. Almost 90 per cent of Sri Lankan exports to India received preferential treatment in 2008–09 versus 22 per cent in 2001.

As a consequence of the FTA, Sri Lanka has become a popular destination for foreign direct investment (FDI) because many countries now see Sri Lanka as providing access to the huge Indian market. More than 50 per cent of India's investment to SAARC countries goes to Sri Lanka. In 2010, India was the largest source of FDI to Sri Lanka. Most of the FDI (71 per cent), it may be noted, is in services-related industries.[21]

India–Afghanistan

A bilateral FTA between India and Afghanistan was signed in March 2003 and became effective in May the same year. The Agreement is aimed at enhancing trade through preferential access to each other's market and working towards the development of national economies.

Pakistan–Sri Lanka

In 2002 Sri Lanka signed a FTA with Pakistan, with the objective of establishing a FTA by 2010 through the process of tariff liberalization. The Agreement came into force in 2005. Noting the asymmetries between the two economies the number of items on offer for tariff concessions were larger in case of Pakistan in comparison with Sri Lanka. The period for undertaking tariff liberalization was also longer for Sri Lanka. Pakistan offered 206 tariff lines for immediate zero duty, while Sri Lanka offered 102 lines. The remaining products outside the negative list were to be liberalized by Pakistan over the next three years and by Sri Lanka over the next five years. Pakistan's negative list of 540 items was smaller than the 697 items in Sri Lanka's negative list. Tariff Rate Quotas (TRQs) in some products were provided by both Pakistan and Sri Lanka to eachother and Pakistan also gave margin of preference in betel leaves, ceramics and cosmetics to Sri Lanka. Twin criteria (VA and CTH) RoOs were applied in the PSLFTA, also with the domestic VA, like in the ISLFTA, being 35 per cent with the CTH requirement specified at the six-digit level.

The economic impact of the Agreement has been limited, however. As a proportion of its total exports Sri Lanka has not experienced any increase in its exports to Pakistan even though in absolute value terms the exports have increased. Pakistan has experienced an increase in its exports to Sri Lanka such that as a proportion of its total exports they account for 1.6 per cent in 2007 versus 1 per cent in 2003. Pakistan accounts for 2 per cent of Sri Lanka's total imports.[22] Additionally the composition of the export basket has undergone little change for either of the economies over this period.[23]

Inter-sub-regional agreements

In addition to the regional and bilateral agreements, South Asian countries are also members of trade agreements that comprise countries from both the South and South East Asian regions. The trend towards this inter-regional economic integration began with the Bangkok Agreement.

The Bangkok Agreement

Now called the Asia Pacific Trade Agreement (APTA), the Bangkok Agreement was signed in 1975. Its members are Bangladesh, China, India, Republic of Korea, Laos and Sri Lanka. Further, the agreement is open to all developing member countries of the Economic and Social Commission for Asia and the Pacific. The agreement has been limited in scope for a long time, with coverage extending only to tariff concessions on goods. The Agreement was revitalized in 2001 with the entry of China. At the end of the third round of negotiations that came into effect in 2006 the participating states had exchanged concessions on 4,270 products plus 587 for LDCs, making a substantial improvement from the pre-third-round position of 1,721 products and 112 products for the LDCs respectively. The margin of preference[24] extended by China is 55.1 per cent versus 38.2 by Korea, 32.2 per cent by India and 14 per cent by Sri Lanka. The Agreement is now aiming at deepening trade cooperation and integration and is extending into areas beyond the traditional tariff concessions to trade facilitation, non-tariff measures, trade in services and investment. In 2009, the participating members entered into a framework agreement on promotion, protection and liberalization of investment and the framework agreement on trade facilitation. The institutional arrangement of the Agreement includes a ministerial council as the highest decision-making authority, which meets at least once every two years. APTA is administered by a standing committee and the Trade and Investment Division of the UNESCAP functions as its secretariat.[25]

The South Asia Growth Quadrangle (SAGQ)

The SAGQ was launched in 1997 and comprises Bangladesh, Eastern India, Bhutan and Nepal. The sub-regional initiative has been subjected to the bilateral frictions between India and Bangladesh. The SAGQ is aimed at accelerating sustainable development among the member countries through projects in targeted sectors that include multimodal transportation and communication, energy, trade and investment facilitation and promotion, tourism, optimal utilization of resource endowment and environment. Relevant projects are encouraged within the framework of SAARC. On invitation from the member countries the ADB extends help in the implementation of the SAGQ projects through the South Asia Sub-regional Economic Cooperation (SASEC) initiative.

BIMSTEC

The Bay of Bengal Initiative for Multi Sectoral Technical and Economic Cooperation (BIMSTEC), comprising Bangladesh, India, Myanmar, Sri Lanka, Thailand, Bhutan and Nepal, is an inter-sub-regional initiative for economic cooperation between South and South East Asia that was established in 1997. This initiative includes countries from both SAARC and ASEAN and was formulated with the objective of becoming a bridge between the two Asian sub-regions – that is, the more inward-oriented South Asia and the more outward-oriented South

East and East Asia. The underlying philosophy of BIMSTEC was derived from both the Look West Policy of Thailand and ASEAN with the Look East Policy of India. The first ever summit-level meeting for BIMSTEC was held in July 2004. The BIMSTEC draft FTA agreement provides for, inter alia, a two-track tariff reduction/elimination programme, liberalization of trade in services, investment and cooperation in identified sectors of technology transportation and communication, energy, tourism and fisheries.The timeline for negotiations for tariff reduction and investment and services has been pre-specified. However, progress of BIMSTEC has been slow owing to bilateral tensions among the various members of the organization as well as the loss of initial interest of Thailand, which has since been caught first in the financial crisis of 1997–98 and then in internal political turmoil. The negotiations on individual aspects of the Agreement have been prolonged and the proposed FTA, though signed in 2009 by member nations, is yet to be implemented.[26]

Scope for reconciliation of overlap between FTAs and RTAs in South Asia

The South Asian region has thus followed a multi-layered approach to regional economic integration. If the bilateral FTAs were to complement the regional FTAs this would be a useful strategy. Otherwise the bilateral FTAs, particularly those that have been successfully implemented, could make SAFTA irrelevant for the region. In fact this is a scenario that is very likely to emerge in South Asia, with bilateral agreements out-performing the regional agreement in terms of content and pace of implementation. Policymakers need to take cognizance of this likely development and take necessary steps to accelerate the pace of implementation of SAFTA. Alternatively the regional FTA needs to be operationalized in a manner such that it either subsumes the bilateral FTAs within itself or renders them irrelevant or relatively less beneficial. This can be made possible if the regional FTA undertakes deeper and wider tariff cuts over a comparatively shorter period of time. This, however, is not true of SAFTA. A successful bilateral FTA like that between India and Sri Lanka may not be easily replaceable by a relatively less ambitious regional FTA like SAFTA. It may help if the policy formulators evolve a conscious programme of gradual reconciliation of bilateral FTAs with the regional FTA. This again may not be easy in practice. It may instead be more practical if the regional FTA is by itself more beneficial to adhere to. Similar dilemmas prevail with regard to overlapping membership in regional and inter-sub-regional FTAs like the SAFTA and BIMSTEC. While differentially designed, both trade agreements have been equally plagued by political frictions among member countries, resulting in as yet unimpressive outcomes.[27] Multiple agreements, if differentially beneficial, should automatically lead to elimination of the inefficient and establishment of the most efficient or beneficial agreement. Over time the least beneficial will be least used and hence rendered ineffective. In South Asia regional or inter-sub-regional trade agreements are yet to become effective instruments of trade enhancement. One reason that is apparent and has been emphasized in the analysis thus far for the less-than-optimum performance of the region in trade or trade agreements is the overriding role of politics and conflict in South Asia. The next chapter, after a preview discussion of the nature and pattern of conflict in South Asia, presents some initial observations on the relationship between trade and conflict in South Asia.

5 Conflict in South Asia

Perceived as one of the most unstable regions in the world, South Asia is home to persistent inter- and intra-state conflicts among member countries. Some of these were inherited at the time of independence and can be attributed to the process of creation of South Asian nations. These include disputes on the demarcation of boundaries and territories as well as disputes that are a consequence of the accompanying distribution of natural resources across borders. Others are of more recent origins and include phenomenons like cross-border illegal migration and terrorism. The most persistent bilateral conflict in South Asia has been between India and Pakistan. Bilateral political relations among other country pairs in the region have also not been devoid of tensions. Political regimes that have alternated between democracy, monarchy and military rule at different time points in Nepal, Pakistan, Bangladesh and Sri Lanka have in their own way contributed to the hostilities and to its varying intensity over time. Given below is a brief and neutral account of the nature of inter-state conflicts observed in South Asia, followed by a chronological presentation of specific conflict events, which are also interspersed with confidence-building measures that these nations have attempted to establish among themselves from time to time. An attempt is also made to draw some initial impressions of the extent to which regional, bilateral and civil conflict impacts bilateral trade from a graphical analysis of these variables for the region. This exercise is undertaken as a prelude to the formal econometric estimation of trade costs of conflict undertaken in the next chapter.

Nature of conflict in South Asia

Border/boundary/territorial disputes

India–Pakistan

The longest-standing territorial dispute between India and Pakistan has been over Kashmir. The two countries have fought three wars in 1947, 1965 and 1999 over the disputed territory. The origins of this conflict are to be seen in the sequence of events starting with the initial indecision of the maharajah regarding the accession of Kashmir at the time of partition of India,[1] rebellion by Pakistani-backed forces and later accession to India by the maharajah in return for military support that resulted in the first full-fledged war over Kashmir in 1947. The 1965 war followed Pakistan's 'operation Gibraltar', which was designed to infiltrate forces into Jammu and Kashmir to precipitate an insurgency against rule by India. India and Pakistan were also involved in a militarized armed conflict that took place in the Kargil district of Kashmir and elsewhere along the Line of Control (LoC) between May and July 1999. The conflict was attributed to infiltration by Pakistani soldiers and Kashmiri militants into positions on the Indian side of the LoC that serves as the de facto border between India and Pakistan.

Other than Kashmir, Siachen, which is an icy northern border wasteland, has for years been the scene of border skirmishes between Indian and Pakistani troops. The Siachen conflict stems from the incompletely demarcated territory beyond the map coordinate known as NJ9842. The 1949 Karachi Agreement between India and Pakistan contained a generalized statement which said that the UN-supervised ceasefire line (CFL) 'moved thence north to the glaciers'. India has used this line to justify its claim that most of the Siachen glacier is unambiguously and lawfully part of its territory. Pakistan rejected this interpretation and insisted that the delimitation agreement of 1949 contained no reference to the CFL beyond NJ9842. The 1972 Simla Agreement restated the same position. India and Pakistan have fought intermittently since 1984 when India, during the 'operation meghdoot', successfully wrested control of the glacier from Pakistan, forcing it to retreat. A ceasefire went into effect in 2003. Both countries maintain permanent military presence in the region at the height of about 6,000 mts, making Siachen the highest battleground on earth. There is also the Sir Creek demarcation issue and the related dispute regarding the small coastal strip along the Rann of Kutch. Though the creek has little military value it has significant economic value, as much of the region is rich in oil and gas and can contribute to energy potential of the controlling country. Despite many rounds of negotiation, there has been no resolution so far.

India and Pakistan also fought a conventional war in 1971. As a result of the denial of victory to the Awami league in the 1970 elections, the first general election in Pakistan since independence and the military excesses in the eastern wing of Pakistan, an open rebellion followed. Millions of refugees fled East Pakistan across the border to India and the support by India led to the battle in December 1971 that resulted in a humiliating defeat for Pakistan and the carving out of Bangladesh from the country.

Pakistan–Afghanistan

For these two nations the porous international border of the approximately 1,500-mile-long Durand line has been contentious. The poorly marked border cuts through the Pashtun tribal areas dividing ethnic Pashtuns (Afghans) on both sides of the border. Kabul has never recognized the line as an international border, instead claiming the Pashtun territories in Pakistan that comprise the Federally Administered Tribal Areas (FATA) and parts of North West Frontier Province along the border. During the 1980s, Pakistan-supported militant groups were used by the US to destroy the Soviet-backed Afghan government. After the collapse of the Soviet backed Afghan government in 1992, Pakistan created a puppet state in Afghanistan run by the Taliban, which continued to resist the Durand line. After the removal of the Taliban government in 2001, the new government led by Hamid Karzai has also not accepted the Durand line.

India–Bangladesh

Hundreds of border enclaves left over from the 1947 boundary demarcation had not been streamlined and were reason for continuing bilateral trouble between India and Pakistan. The Bangladeshi officials maintained that the absence of ratification by India of the 1974 treaty on the modalities to deal with the outstanding border concerns, including enclaves and undemarcated boundaries, is the root cause of the disputes along the 4,096km-long border between India and Bangladesh. India did not ratify the agreement on the plea that the demarcation of the border had not yet been completed. In 2011, the two countries signed a historic agreement on the demarcation of land boundaries and resolved the status of enclaves and adversely possessed areas.

Muhurichar river island has been a disputed area since the birth of Bangladesh. The Indian Border Security Force (BSF) and the Border Guard of Bangladesh (BGB) have exchanged fire in 1976, 1979 and 1985. Although the two countries decided to treat the midstream as an international boundary, complications arise on account of the changing course of the Muhuri river, one of the trans-border rivers of India and Bangladesh, and the appearance of new stretches of land.

Bangladesh also has problems with India in the Bay of Bengal regarding the New Moore island that emerged as a result of a cyclone in the Bay of Bengal and disappeared at a later point. Sovereignty claims are made by both India and Bangladesh over the island for the speculated oil and natural gas existence in the region. The natural disappearance of the island seems to have resolved the issue.

India–Nepal

This boundary has long been a subject of disagreement between the two neighbouring states. The two countries disagree on the interpretation of the 1816 Sugauli Treaty that delimited the boundary along the Mahakaliriver. The dispute intensified in 1997 as the Nepali parliament considered a treaty on hydro-electric development of the river. Most of the boundary separating the two countries was agreed in December 2007 when strip maps were signed by experts from both sides. However, some 2 per cent of the boundary relating to the Susta and Kalapani areas (respectively in the Nawalparasi and Darchula district of Nepal) remained unresolved. The most common border disagreements concern river boundary sections where rivers have changed their course.

Natural-resource-based conflicts

Water in South Asia is used not just for drinking but also for food and industrial production. With the largest rural population, the agriculture-dependent subcontinent relies heavily on water resources for irrigation (The World Fact Book, CIA, 2012). In India 90 per cent of annual freshwater withdrawals is for agricultural use (The World Data Bank, World Bank). Seventy five per cent of the water used in India in 2007 came from international rivers, namely the Indus and the Ganges–Brahmaputra basin that India shares with Pakistan, Bangladesh and Nepal (ADB, Water Knowledge Centre: Country Profiles – India). Due to regional scarcity of water and because a number of rivers in South Asia flow across countries irrespective of man-made political boundaries, India and its neighbours have had long-standing disputes over the regulation and distribution of shared water resources, particularly rivers. So far, water conflicts in South Asia have been mediated through a combination of treaties and international arbitration. These agreements govern water allocation between India and its neighbours and also develop a protocol for hydrological construction projects. Foremost among these accords is the Indus Waters Treaty (IWT), which has been a successful tool for addressing water-sharing issues between India and Pakistan since 1960. A brief account of the history and status of water disputes in South Asia is summarized below.

India–Pakistan

The longstanding Indus Water Treaty (IWT) has been the basis of river water-sharing arrangements between India and Pakistan. The treaty in 1960 brought to an end a 13-year-long conflict between India and Pakistan after a decade-long negotiation process that was mediated by the World Bank. India and Pakistan agreed on the distribution of Indus river water (20:80) as per the Treaty. The IWT provided for the division such that India was given complete usage of the three eastern rivers – that is, Sutlej, Beas and Ravi – and Pakistan of the three western rivers – the Indus, Jhelum and Chenab.[2] The treaty provided for the setting up of an Indo-Pakistani Permanent Commission with the provision for arbitration of disputes with respect to the treaty. Mechanisms for cooperation, consultations, data exchange and inspections were created for the purpose. While both countries have seen it useful to abide by the Agreement, some elements of the treaty continue to act as the basis of ongoing disputes between India and Pakistan. The disputes are invariably based on complaints by Pakistan on water flow being restricted by India given its upstream status. This derives significance from the fact that the Indus and its tributaries represent the only source of surface waters for Pakistan, including its prominent agricultural sector. Other disputes relate to the technical interpretation of the treaty, particularly with regard to dam-building projects by India, which it is considered divert or store water flowing to Pakistan. That the Indus, Jhelum, and Chenab all flow through Jammu and Kashmir, which has been the site of the decades-long territorial dispute between India and Pakistan, further aggravates the situation. Some of the persistent disputes in this context relate to the Baglihar Dam, Tulbul navigation/Wular Barrage, Kishenganga Dam and Indian retention of the waters of Beas, Ravi and Sutlej. These are briefly discussed below.

BAGLIHAR DAM

Under dispute since its conception in 1992, the Baglihar Dam on the Chenab River was completed in 2008. The Chenab river runs from India directly through the disputed territory of Jammu and Kashmir and then into Pakistan. The project entails a 144.5-metre concrete gravity dam with a 450-megawatt hydroelectric plant, with potential to expand to 900 megawatts, and also includes substantial storage capacity and gated spillways that would allow for flood-control and reduction of sedimentation for the greater region. Pakistan opposed the hydroelectric plant's construction, arguing that its design violates the Indus Water Treaty because of its potential to store or divert waters destined for Pakistan.[3] Formal talks between the two nations began in 2000 to address India's resolve to move forward with the Baglihar hydroelectric plant. As the talks did not lead to any resolution, on Pakistan's appeal a neutral arbitrator was appointed by the World Bank. The final verdict of the neutral expert was declared in 2007 upholding some of Pakistan's concerns, but rejecting their objections on gated control on spillway as well as the key issue that any dam constructed by India should be run of the river. The two countries agreed to abide by the final verdict. In 2010 India and Pakistan resolved the issue of initial filling of the Baglihar dam in Jammu and Kashmir with the neighbouring country deciding not to raise the issue further.

TULBUL NAVIGATION/WULAR BARRAGE

Dating back to the 1980s, the dispute regarding the Tulbul Navigation/Wular Barrage remains unresolved. India's construction of a barrier along the Jhelum River aims to improve water flow and, thus, navigation of a 20-kilometre stretch between the Sopore and Baramulla districts of Jammu and Kashmir. Though construction began in 1984, it was halted in 1987 due to Pakistani opposition stating violation of the IWT's provision restraining India from construction of storage facilities. Construction was halted even though India pointed out that the construction was not meant for storage and will in fact regulate the flow so as to benefit both the nations.

KISHENGANGA DAM

The dispute over the proposed Kishenganga Dam also remains unresolved. Under the plan, India seeks to build a 330-megawatt hydroelectric plant on the Jhelum River in the Jammu and Kashmir region. As with the Baglihar and Tulbul project, Pakistan claims the project violates the IWT because of its downstream effects.

India–Nepal

Water is Nepal's major natural resource. Unlike Pakistan and Bangladesh, Nepal is an upper riparian state for four major rivers, that is, Mahakali, Gandak, Karnali and Kosi. The five minor tributaries of these rivers provide water to both Bihar and UP in India during the dry season and also cause flooding in the monsoon. Regulation of the river waters is therefore an important issue for both countries. Disputes about Indian and Nepali water resources have related primarily to flood control and potential dam projects. There have been various disputes over the Kosi Agreement[4] on account of floods in the Kosi region. The 1954 Kosi agreement and 1959 Gandak agreement primarily established schemes of diverting water for irrigation. A general feeling in Nepal was that while both projects involved substantial submergence of scarce agricultural land with corresponding social and economic costs, the benefits to Nepal in terms of irrigation, flood protection and power were only marginal. The Indian view was that Nepal had received all the benefits without any investment.[5] Later revisions of 1966 and 1964 respectively granted Nepal the exclusive right to withdraw water for irrigation or any other purpose as needed from the river or its tributaries. The ineffectiveness of the barrage and embankments constructed for flood control around the Kosi basin, particularly in the 2008 floods, have been cause for both countries to blame each other. Compensation from India for land acquisition for the construction of the barrage has been the other issue of dissatisfaction on the Nepalese side, which claims to have been given less than a fair deal. India's control and management of the barrage is further considered as an infringement of the territorial sovereignty of Nepal. In fact Nepal's perception of unfair treaties holds true also of the Tanakpur agreement (1991) and the Mahakali Agreement (1996). In the case of India and Nepal, water relations have invariably been a reflection of the bilateral political relations at any point in time.

India–Bangladesh

India shares 54 trans-boundary rivers with Bangladesh, including the major ones: Ganga, Brahmaputra and Meghna. Water management is thus a major bilateral issue between the two countries. Bangladesh is prone to flooding during monsoon on account of its low elevation and to drought during the dry season of January to May. The dispute between India and Bangladesh over sharing of the Ganges water is known as the Farakka dispute, from the construction by India of a large barrage across the Ganges at the small town of Farakka, 11 miles upstream of the Indian border with Bangladesh. This was opposed by Bangladesh as it was seen to have serious implications for Bangladesh in terms of reduced dry season flow. This has continued to influence the river water policy between the two nations, even while the dispute seems to have evolved to insufficiency of the dry season water flow to fulfil the water requirements of the two nations, apparently because of the increasing needs of the Indian irrigation requirements. The dispute that centred on differing views about the negative effect of the barrage on farming, fisheries and industry in Bangladesh, and ways of boosting the lean season flow of the Ganges at Farakka was resolved when a comprehensive bilateral treaty on sharing the Ganges water was signed in 1997.

Water-sharing issues have also been at the heart of the Teesta river water management for the benefit of India and Bangladesh. In her three-day visit to India on January 10, 2010, Sheikh Hasina exchanged draft agreements on the Teesta water sharing issue with India, after a two-day ministerial-level meeting of the Joint River Commission was held. While Bangladesh presented a draft on an interim agreement, India presented a draft of a Statement of Principles on the sharing of river water during the dry season. The immediate achievement of this meeting was the decision that, within a year, an agreement over the Teesta river water sharing to provide key support to agricultural production in the northwest region of Bangladesh would be signed. However, the much-anticipated agreement in 2011 did not happen on account of a lack of coordination between the Central and West Bengal state government in India.

Cross-border terrorism/immigration/refugee settlement

Cross-border terrorism is rampant in South Asia and has on several occasions led to a perpetuation of bilateral conflict in the region. Relations between India and Pakistan have long been subject to either country's perception of the role of the other in sponsoring terrorism on its soil. India has accused Pakistan of sponsoring terrorism in Jammu and Kashmir, North East and Punjab, while Pakistan is similarly suspicious of India with regard to the ethnic and separatist movements in the country. Apart from this, India has constantly blamed Bangladesh and Nepal of their alleged 'help' to militants from India's north-east. There have also been reports of anti-terror camps in Bangladesh assisting Pakistani terrorist outfits against India. In a similar fashion, there have also been reports of anti-Bangladesh support by India to chakma insurgents. Sri Lankans have had problems with India in allegedly extending help to Tamil terrorist groups from Sri Lanka.[6] Terrorism in South Asia has acquired an almost regional character with a systematic networking between different cooperating groups across borders. The nature of the border configuration affords an easy opportunity to the infiltrators and smugglers to cross over to India. The crossing is further facilitated because the border is porous and adjoining regions are thickly populated.

Unabated illegal immigration also has serious long-term implications in terms of economic, political, social and security implications. Immigration and refugee problems prevail across the India–Bangladesh, Afghanistan–Pakistan and Nepal–Bhutan borders in South Asia. Immigrants from Bangladesh have settled in and around the border areas, including all the north-eastern states of India and also as far away as Delhi, Mumbai and other parts. Increase in the population of the north-eastern states is reflected in the census figures of 1991 and 2001 and provides evidence that India is facing the brunt of the demographic explosion taking place in the world's most densely populated country of Bangladesh. Such shifts in the local demographic balance pose an increased risk of violent conflicts between communities, and it is probability even higher in the north-eastern region, where resources are scarce.

Intra-state conflicts with inter-state effects

As South Asia is characterized by cross-border ethnic, cultural and religious contiguity and intra-border diversity, intra-state conflicts have often been transmitted to neighbouring states through these links. A brief mention of intra-state conflicts that have had spillover effects as inter-state conflicts[7] is made here to take cognizance of this phenomenon in the region. The emphasis of our analysis remains on inter-state conflicts only. Predominant among such conflicts have been the secessionist movements, such as Kashmir in India, which has been the major cause for India–Pakistan frictions, the Tamil separatist movement in Sri Lanka, which led to India–Sri Lanka bilateral tensions, and the Balochistan movement in Pakistan and Punjab in the 1980s in India, which have contributed to terrorist activities in and across the two countries. Other internal conflicts with cross-border dimensions include Pakistan's support to the Taliban in Afghanistan, which has in fact had larger regional implications, and Maoists in Nepal, who have established close links with Maoists in India and separatist groups in India's north-eastern states, with an established base in Bangladesh.[8]

Economic conflicts

Some economic issues have also been reasons for bilateral frictions in South Asia. Among these, transit rights across Bangladesh (for India's north-eastern states) and across Pakistan (for Afghanistan and India) are significant in contributing to lower intra-regional trade on a formal basis and simultaneously flourishing illegal trade in the region. India's trade deficit with the smaller economies in South Asia has been a bilateral irritant, except in case of Sri Lanka, where the FTA has helped ease the situation. In Bhutan, India's developmental aid has contributed to construction of hydro-power projects and power exports to India, resulting in bilateral trade in favour of Bhutan. In Bangladesh political hostilities have prevented the country from converting their trade deficit to a surplus by not allowing Indian capital to invest in their gas reserves, which could in turn have led to power exports back to India. Pakistan has similarly avoided giving India the MFN status, stating a large bilateral deficit to be one of the reasons. The transit between India and Bangladesh has now been facilitated by the 2010/11 agreement and the MFN status to India has been proposed, though for a third time, by Pakistan in 2011.

Chronological sequence of conflict events[9] and CBMs in South Asia

A chronological presentation of major events of inter-state conflict is given below, along with some of the confidence-building measures (CBMs)[10] that have also been established from time to time in the region over the reference period of this study.

India–Pakistan

1948–49: The first full-scale conflict between the two countries happened over Kashmir within a year after the two countries gained independence. The war began in 1947 and ended in December 1948. A UN-brokered ceasefire went into effect on January 1, 1949.

1965: The two countries clashed again in 1965 over Kashmir. The war began in August 5, 1965, and ended in September 22, 1965, by which time it had reached a stalemate and the two sides agreed to a UN-mandated ceasefire.

1971: India and Pakistan fought a conventional war that resulted in Pakistan being divided to create the new state of Bangladesh.

The decade of the 1980s: The covert war since the early 1980s, which began with the battle for Siachen, continues. Relations deteriorated in late 1980s when the Kashmiri separatist movement gained momentum. Pakistan escalated its covert war in 1988 after acquisition of nuclear weapons in 1987.

1987: India conducted an aggressive military exercise 'Brasstacks' on the Pakistani border.

The decade of the 1990s: India and Pakistan were in a state of conflict throughout the decade of the nineties. The early 1990s were marked by latent conflict and increased insurgency and terrorist activities in Kashmir and Pakistan's support to these activities.

1990: India's military exercise 'Mahajan' fuelled mistrust in Pakistan. Pakistan responded with another military exercise 'Zarb-e-momin'. Tensions escalated as India linked the exercise to surging violence in Kashmir.

1998: India and Pakistan conducted nuclear tests.

1999: Pakistan and India were involved in a limited conflict in Kargil. Ceasefire on July 26, 1999.

2001–02: Terrorist attack on Indian Parliament in December 2001, allegedly by Pakistan-trained Kashmiri terrorists. Forces were mobilized at the international border and a ten-month confrontation followed.

2008: India calls off talks after the 2008 Mumbai attacks.

CBMs[11]

The goodwill gestures and CBMs have been initiated between India and Pakistan since 1947 and sometimes they have covered some distance too in terms of ameliorating the conflict, but only temporarily so.[12]

1950: Liaquat-Nehru Pact, according to which India agreed to accept all immigrants who crossed over to the country by December 31, 1950. The pact sought to guarantee rights of minorities in both countries after the partition.

1960: Indus Water Treaty aimed at sharing the water of the Indus basin was signed.
1966: Tashkent Agreement in January 1966 formally concluded the 1965 Indo-Pak war. It stipulated that'relations between India and Pakistan shall be based on the principles of non-interference in internal affairs of the other'. India and Pakistan reaffirmed their resolve not to have recourse to force and to settle disputes by peaceful means.
1968: Rann of Kutch Agreement, according a peaceful resolution to a territorial dispute by determining a boundary which recognized about 90 per cent of the disputed territory to be Indian and upheld Pakistan's sovereignty over the balance.[13]
1970s: Post-1971 war, Pakistan's stand on Kashmir was more muted. This allowed the two countries to address economic and trade issues.
1971: Following the 1971 war a dedicated communication line, or hotline, between the Indian and Pakistani directors general of military operations was established.[14]
1972: Simla Agreement was signed between India and Pakistan after the 1971 war between the two countries that led to the independence of East Pakistan as Bangladesh. The agreement laid down the principles that should govern their future relations. Both countries agreed to respect the LoC in Kashmir and not to unilaterally alter the situation.
1975: Protocol of Resumption of Trade is signed by India and Pakistan, stating that trade will be conducted on the basis of Most Favoured Nation (MFN) rules. However, Pakistan does not extend official MFN status to India, while India only does so in 1994–95.
1978: Salal Dam Agreement that brought to an end, through bilateral negotiations, the 30-year-old dispute by giving India the rights to build the Salal Dam and a power project on the Chenab river in Jammu and Kashmir, and in return India agreed to respect some of the Pakistani views on changes in the design and nature of the project.
1980s: CBMs were more military in nature but not to the exclusion of non-military initiatives. The latter in fact included declaratory measures like Zia's idea of no war pact and Indira Gandhi's treaty of peace and friendship. This was followed by a meeting of the two leaders that resulted in two decisions, one of a continuation of the discussion of their peace proposals and two, the more significant one of establishing the joint commission, as follows.[15]
1982: Formation of the Indo-Pak Joint Commission to discuss trade, tourism and communication.
1988: As an outcome of the first meeting between Pakistan Prime Minister Benazir Bhutto and Rajiv Gandhi, when the latter had gone to Islamabad to attend the SAARC summit, three bilateral agreements were signed, as follows.

- No to double taxation from international air transport.
- Agreement on non-attack of nuclear sites and exchange of information on nuclear installations.
- Agreement on cultural cooperation.

1990: At the Male SAARC Summit the Indian Prime Minister Chandrashekhar and Pakistan PM Nawaz Sharif met and decided to start an additional hotline between the two leaders.

1990: In December, India and Pakistan agreed to re-establish the DGMO hotline and to use it on a weekly basis if only to exchange routine information.

1990: At the foreign-secretary-level talks in December it was agreed to evolve 'Code of conduct' for treating diplomatic personnel/staff.

1991: Agreement not to violate each other's air space, to provide advance notifications of air exercises and to follow agreed procedures for military flights within five to ten kilometres of the border.

1991: Start of a track II dialogue process called the Neemrana initiative.

1991, 1992: Military CBMs: A joint declaration on complete prohibition of chemical weapons was concluded, ratification and implementation of the agreement on the non-attack of nuclear facilities, which was signed in 1988. The DGMO hotline, which had been so far used intermittently, was now reactivated.

1993: Joint declaration on prohibition of production and deployment of chemical weapons. Establishment of a hotline between the air forces of India and Pakistan and between military commanders on both sides of the LoC, Naval communication agreement and various other military goodwill measures

1994–95: India grants Most Favoured Nation (MFN) status to Pakistan.

1997: In August, India and Pakistan sign an agreement for the sale of tea, to be imported into Pakistan from India, following India's liberalization of its tea industry in 1994–95.

1997: Initiation of the comprehensive dialogue, also called the composite dialogue.[16] The talks were to cover all issues, including terrorism, security, peace in South Asia and Kashmir.

Indian PM Gujral and Pak PM Sharif decided to reinstate the hotline.

1999: Lahore Declaration in February. Both sides decided to resolve all issues, including Jammu and Kashmir, agreed to refrain from intervention and interference in eachother's internal affairs, and to intensify their composite dialogue process for an early and positive outcome of the bilateral agenda.

1999: Several nuclear CBMs were introduced and included in the Memorandum of understanding accompanying the Lahore Declaration:

- February 20, 1999: Bus service between New Delhi and Lahore initiated by Indian PM Vajpayee.
- April 10, 1999: India and Pakistan sign a memorandum of understanding in New Delhi to set up the India–Pakistan Chamber of Commerce.

2003: India announces resumption of Delhi–Lahore bus service (May).

2003: Musharraf calls for a ceasefire along the line of control (LoC) at the UN General assembly in New York (September).

2003: India and Pakistan implement a formal ceasefire along the international border and the Actual Ground Position Line in Jammu and Kashmir.

2004: Air links between the two countries resume.

2004: During the 12th SAARC summit in January, Pakistani leaders state their commitment to move towards granting MFN status to India in the future.
2004: India announces it will ease visa rules for visiting Pakistani journalists, doctors and academics.
2005: First bus service from Srinagar to Muzaffarabad flagged off.
2005: Talks on nuclear confidence-building measures commence.
2005: Agreement on advance notification of ballistic missile tests signed.
2005: Agreement reached on the establishment of hotline between their maritime security agencies to facilitate early exchange of information regarding apprehended fishermen who inadvertently stray on the other side's territorial waters.
2006: Bus service from Amritsar to Lahore launched.
2006 Pakistan and India agree to open rail links between Munnabao in Rajasthan and Khokhrapar in Sind.
2006: India and Pakistan resume train service after 40 years and agree in principle to expand airline service between the two nations.
2006: Fibre optic link between Amritsar and Lahore becomes operational.
2006: Amritsar–Nankana Sahib bus service is flagged off.
2006: India and Pakistan agree to revive trade in Kashmir; formally agree to trade raw products between divided regions of Jammu and Kashmir.
2007: MoU signed between India's University of Mumbai and Pakistan's University of Sindh for exchange of faculty, scholars and students.
2007: The first overland truck route is opened at the Wagah crossing.
2008: India and Pakistan sign an agreement allowing regular contact between India's Institute for Defence Studies and Anlaysis (IDSA) and Pakistan's state-run Institute for Strategic Studies (ISS).
2008: India joins a framework agreement on a gas pipeline from Turkmenistan-Afghanistan-Pakistan to India.[17]
2008: Formal announcement for opening of several trade routes between India and Pakistan. These are the Wagah–Attari road link and the Khokrapar–Munnabao road, Uri-Muzaffarabad and Poonch–Rawalakot roads.
2008: Trade across the LoC commences as the first trucks cross the line that divides Kashmir. Trade is limited to 21 items and two days a week.[18]
2008: A second trade route across the LoC connecting the cities of Rawalkot and Poonch is opened.
2010: India offers flood aid to Pakistan (US$5 million followed by US$20 million).
2011: Foreign secretaries agree to resume structured dialogue.
2011: India and Pakistan announced a plan to 'normalize' bilateral trade.
2011: Foreign minister says that Pakistan has made a principled decision to grant MFN status to India.
2011: Pakistan cabinet approves MFN status for India.[19]

It is interesting to observe that the maximum number of CBMs were initiated over the decade of the 1980s and 1990s, which are also decades of maximum tensions reflected in both overt and covert conflictual events between the two nations.

India–Nepal

As regards to India–Nepal bilateral relations, the economic factors have clearly played a predominant role, as Nepal's economy is inextricably linked with India's. India is Nepal's major trading partner and remittances from Nepalese migrants in India are a major source of capital flows and savings for the country. India and Nepal have signed many treaties on trade and commerce that have benefitted both through more open trade and investment. Treaties on natural-resource-sharing have been other modes of trust and cooperation between India and Nepal. Conflict has not been major or explicitly manifest between these two countries. On a few occasions there have been reasons for interference with economic exchange by both sides like in 2002 when the trade treaty of 1997 was revised with stricter RoOs. A delineation of conflict and CBMs may therefore not be appropriate in this case. The treaties of cooperation and trade are presented below in a chronological order.

1950: Indo-Nepal Treaty of Friendship as also India's first Treaty of Trade and Commerce with Nepal was signed on July 31, 1950. The treaty envisaged a customs union between the two countries.
1954: Kosi agreement to regulate the flow of the river and ensure flood management.
1959: Agreement towards Gandak irrigation and power project.
1960: The trade treaty of September 1960 removed the requirement of a customs union, enabling Nepal to adopt its own tariff and trade policy, which led to its trade diversification with third countries.
1971: The trade treaty signed in August 1971 permitted mutual bilateral exports of primary products free of basic customs duties. Other concessions were also extended in accordance with the value-addition taking place in Nepal.
1978: In August 1978 India agreed to sign two separate treaties, a treaty on trade and a treaty on transit, fulfilling a long-standing Nepalese demand. In addition, the Indian demand to prevent deflection of unauthorized trade was also satisfied with the signing of an Agreement on Cooperation to Control Unauthorized Trade. After the expiry of this treaty in 1988, a trade deadlock ensued between the two countries until a democratic government was set up in Nepal in 1990.
1991: The High Level Task Force was set up to identify areas of economic cooperation.
1991: Following this, a new agreement was signed in December 1991, which was renewed in December 1996.
1992: In October, India agreed to improve and simplify the rules for export of goods from Nepal. India agreed to extend stand-by credit facility to Nepal from (IC) Rs.35 crore to Rs.50 crore. Nepal's private vehicles were allowed to move from its border to Calcutta and Haldia ports and back, provided the vehicles were authorized by the Nepal Transit and Warehousing Company Ltd or Nepal Transport Corporation. This was agreed to facilitate Nepal's exports to India. Movement of vehicles from Nepal to Nepal via Indian territory was allowed without any bond or cash deposit. Nepal was also allowed to import goods from India in convertible currency.

1996: Mahakali Treaty envisioned joint development of the Mahakali river. The treaty provided for the building of the Sarrada and Tanakpur barrages and the creation of the Pancheshwar project, a 315-metre multipurpose dam. Much of the work on these projects is not complete, so the full implications of their construction remain unknown.

1997: Treaty on Integrated Development of the Mahakali Basin was signed in February.

1997: In June a power agreement was signed to encourage private and semi-government investment in Nepal

India–Bangladesh

1972: India and Bangladesh signed a Treaty of Friendship, Cooperation and Peace to promote goodwill and support for common ideals. The treaty supported joint action in managing shared water resources and remained in force until its expiration in 1997.

1974: Indo-Bangladesh Border Agreement. After the emergence of Bangladesh an Agreement listing in detail the modalities to deal with each of the outstanding border concerns, including enclaves and un-demarcated boundaries, was signed between Indian Prime Minister Indira Gandhi and Bangladesh Prime Minister Sheikh Mujibur Rehman. The Agreement was subject to ratification by the two governments. While Bangladesh ratified it in November 1974, India did not ratify it. The issue was resolved in 2011.

1977–82: The Ganges water Agreement of 1977[20] was signed and implemented. Treaty was not renewed despite provisions to do so.

1983–87: Independent national river development.

1996: Ganges River Water Treaty. A comprehensive bilateral treaty was signed by the Indian Prime Minister H. D. Deve Gowda and his Bangladeshi counterpart Sheikh Hasina Wajed on December 12, 1996. This treaty fills the gap after the lapse of the 1977 treaty. The treaty gives a new formula for the sharing of water in the dry season (1 January to 31 May), providing also that below Farakka the waters are not to be reduced further except for 'reasonable use' in a limited amount.[21] This treaty established a thirty-year water-sharing arrangement with guaranteed minimum quantities of water supply for Bangladesh, whose rights as a lower riparian country were recognized.

1989: Border Fencing. As initiated by the government of India, the first phase of the project started in 1989. The second phase of the project was approved by the Government in June 2000 and comprises a far greater component of fencing (2,429km), roads (797km) and bridges (4,062m) in different states.

1985: Border skirmishes over Muhurichar island.

1990: Dispute over the Farakka Barrage.

2001: Minor Border confrontation regarding the disputed border territory near Pyrdiwah village. The boundary dispute between India and Bangladesh in April 2001 worsened relations.

2011: The two countries signed a historic agreement on the demarcation of land boundaries and resolved the status of enclaves and adversely possessed areas.

India–Sri Lanka

The 1980s were marked by an escalating level of tension between India and Sri Lanka owing to India's initial intervention in Sri Lanka's domestic ethnic conflict.

1983: India's attempt at mediation in Sri Lanka's domestic conflict.

1987: India intervened directly for the first time after Sri Lankan government's attempt to regain control of northern Jaffna through blockade of Northern Sri Lanka. India came to the blockaded areas' rescue by supplying food and medicine through air and sea routes.

1987: India and Sri Lanka Peace Accord was signed in June. The Accord was to resolve the ongoing Sri Lankan Civil War.

1987: India sent the peacekeeping force, the IPKF, to oversee the implementation of the Accord.

1987–90: The events that unfolded between 1987 and 1990 imparted a new dimension to bilateral ties and these were the most troubled and, by and large, conflictual years in the India–Sri Lanka relationship. India's intervention in the island state had embittered both the government and people of Sri Lanka. Keeping in view New Delhi's changing foreign policy perceptions and India's earlier experience of the Indo-Sri Lanka Agreement of July 29, 1987, and subsequent mission of the IPKF from 1987 to 1990, and particularly after the assassination of former Prime Minister Rajiv Gandhi by the Liberation Tigers of Tamil Elam (LTTE), India has resisted the option of mediation or intervention in the ethnic conflict of Sri Lanka.

1991: Indian Prime Minister Rajiv Gandhi was assassinated and LTTE was named as the alleged perpetrator.

1991: An Agreement was signed between India and Sri Lanka in July 1991 to establish an Indo-Sri Lanka Joint Commission. Its sub-commissions included those on trade, investment and finance, and science and technology. This is after the coming into power of the new congress government led by P.V. Narsimha Rao in India and his declared policy of not interfering in Sri Lanka's internal problems. The new government in Sri Lanka led by Premadasa was of help too.

1998: The India–Sri Lanka Free Trade Agreement (ISFTA) was signed at the highest political level on December 28, 1998, with the overall objective of enhancing trade and economic relations between the two countries. The FTA Agreement entered into force from March 1, 2000.

After 2009: In the post-LTTE era/post-2009, a frictional chapter in India–Sri Lankan history has come to an end.

Regional CBMs

1985: The South Asian Association for Regional Cooperation (SAARC) comes into being on December 7, 1985, with the following member countries: Bangladesh, Bhutan, India, Maldives, Nepal, Pakistan, and Sri Lanka.

1993: The South Asian Preferential Trade Agreement (SAPTA) is signed by the countries of SAARC, with plans to eventually create a South Asian Free Trade Area (SAFTA).

2004: A Framework Agreement on the SAFTA is signed at the Islamabad SAARC summit.

2006: SAFTA was implemented. All signatories to the Agreement start with a negative-list approach while Pakistan continues to have a positive list specified for goods to be traded with India. The matter is now under review of the Pakistan cabinet.

Conflict between India and Pakistan thus shows an element of *continuity* that has persisted even when there have been attempts to establish CBMs. In fact through all the decades significant and landmark CBMs have been introduced, only to be interrupted or stalled by major conflicts. This is apparent in the 1960s, which saw the IWT and Tashkent agreement but were interspersed by the 1965 war and followed by the 1971 war at the beginning of the next decade. The 1980s were marked by both military and non-military CBMs, like the formation of the Joint Indo-Pak Commission, but were accompanied by covert war and skirmishes over the Siachen glacier almost throughout the decade. The 1990s were tense, marked by latent conflict in the early years and overt violent conflict in 1999. At the same time, the 1990s saw some significant peace initiatives, like the initiation of the composite dialogue process, the Lahore declaration and, at the regional level, the SAPTA, which was later subverted on account of the India–Pakistan bilateral hostilities. For India and Pakistan, therefore, it would not be inappropriate to say that the two countries have a relationship of persistent conflict and no matter what the strength of a peace initiative it has rarely been allowed to succeed. Conflict has clearly not allowed the CBMs to be used or maximized to their full potential and this creates an atmosphere that anticipates further proliferation and perpetuation of disputes in the future rather than their isolation in favour of resolution

The persistence and hence the reason for anticipation of continued conflict – latent or overt – does not, however, characterize the other dyads in South Asia. For India and Nepal the conflicts have been in the nature of largely economic frictions that have sometimes taken a political colour or been a reflection of some political opposition, but these have been overcome in relatively short periods of time and without a significant adverse impact on bilateral economic exchange in the long run. India and Sri Lanka experienced an intensely tense period in the late 1980s to early 1990s, but this was overcome by the ISLFTA and permanently in the post-LTTE era and conflict resolution in Sri Lanka. India and Bangladesh, while not like Pakistan, have been conflictual and cordial more as a function of a pro-India or anti-India political regimes in Bangladesh. The permanence of conflict is true only of the India–Pakistan dyad in south Asia.

Impact of conflict on bilateral trade: visual impressions

As a preliminary to the formal econometric estimation of the cost of conflict in chapter 7, a graphical analysis is undertaken in this section to draw some initial impressions on the relationship between conflict events and intensity and the trends in bilateral trade observed in the region. The exercise is expected to provide some useful indications of how trade has been impacted by conflict – specifically, that is, major events, or more generally, through regional instability. The exercise is undertaken with India as the reporter country[22] with the four partner countries with which conflict has been experienced in some form (armed/violent or otherwise) either as a continuum or in an episodic fashion. The analysis is for the period 1988–2008, when trade became an integral part of South Asian economies.

Our analysis in the preceding sections has shown that for India–Nepal and India–Bangladesh conflictual relations have been interspersed with cordial relations. With Sri Lanka conflict was intense in and after 1987 upto the time that the two countries signed the bilateral FTA in 1998. The 2000s have been marked by improvement in bilateral relations owing largely to the mutually beneficial trade deal. For India–Pakistan conflict has been a continuum and the predominant influence in comparison with CBMs. The persistent tensions have periodically erupted in the form of more severe and sometimes violent/armed conflict, as in 1999. Bilateral trade trends are observed to follow conflict and cordiality in bilateral relations.

For India–Pakistan bilateral trade is seen to be at low levels until the early 2000s. Every dip in exports from India to Pakistan coincides with a major conflict event. The graph in Figure 5.1 shows a dip in 1999 and 2002, the first coinciding with Kargil and second in 2002 immediately following the terrorist attack on the Indian parliament. The increase in bilateral trade, though observed for a year after 1995, probably on account of economic CBMs like India granting Pakistan the MFN status, agreement on sale of tea, and initiation of the comprehensive dialogue, starts to dip again after 1997 up until 2002–03, coinciding with rising tensions following the nuclear tests and change in political regime in Pakistan. Trade again improves in 2003 as political relations improve, signalled by the call for a ceasefire along the LoC and resumption of the Delhi–Lahore bus service, but the steep and relatively more sustainable increase is observed only after 2005, clearly coinciding with improved relations as apparent from the resumption of the India–Pakistan comprehensive economic dialogue in 2004. For India–Nepal the trade pattern is a reflection of the revisions in the trade treaty. India's imports from Nepal increase and exports decline following the more favourable trade terms offered to Nepal as per the 1996 revision in the treaty. Subsequent complaints by Indian producers (with respect to some commodities, for example vanaspati, and trade deflection) that led to a revision in 2002 with stricter provisions, particularly with regard to the RoOs, led to the trade balance reversing back in favour of India. Bilateral trade between India and Sri Lanka registers a change in 2000, the year of implementation of the FTA, with a steep upward rise in imports and exports.

92 Conflict in South Asia

The trade data is thus revealing. India–Pakistan is the only country pair for which trade follows conflict. Economics is overpowered by political events and bilateral trade does not appear to move independently of the political scenario. For the other country-pairs bilateral trade appears to be influenced predominantly by economic events.

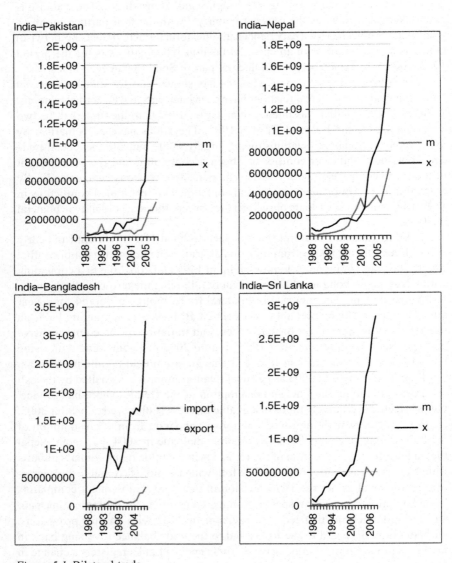

Figure 5.1 Bilateral trade

Source: UNCOMTRADE, x: exports and m: imports.

Regional intensity of conflict and trade

Taking the analysis a step forward, an attempt is made to analyze the relationship between trade and the intensity of conflict at the regional level. We also take into account civil conflict intensity to assess how trade between any two countries in a region is impacted by domestic instability in the partner country. Again all analysis is undertaken with India as the reference reporter country. The analysis is limited to the period 1988 to the latest year for which data is available. It is interesting to note that to a large extent regional instability is a reflection of the India–Pakistan conflict and tensions. This is evident from the fact that regional conflict intensity reached a peak level in the year 1999, which coincides with sequential nuclear tests by India and Pakistan, regime change in Pakistan led by the army coup and the ensuing years of declining democratic characteristics of Pakistan polity and increasing India–Pakistan bilateral tensions. It is also observed that the rising tensions peak again at a higher-than-previous level around 2001, again a year of highly strained India–Pakistan relations. Thereafter, though, no new peak is observed, tension settles at a level higher than the 1990s, though less than that in the late 1980s.

India's trade with Pakistan

India's trade with Pakistan appears to be relatively less influenced by domestic conflict in comparison with regional conflict. Maximum regional instability during the late 1980s coincides with the lowest levels of bilateral trade, export and import. Bilateral trade increases upto 1992–93, which are the years of democracy in Pakistan, but again dips and remains stagnant through the 1990s, which is the decade of increasing strife between the two countries and regional instability that is to a large extent a reflection of the India–Pakistan strife. Regional instability peaks in 1999 and bilateral trade sees a dip in the same year. India–Pakistan trade has registered rapid increase since 2003 with improved bilateral relations. During this period regional stability, although not at its lowest level, is stable over a relatively long period and this perhaps lends an element of predictability to the regional environment, with the later years of 2000s also coinciding with the return of democracy in Pakistan. It may, however, be that even while the constant/stabilized conflict intensity is observed to not adversely impact trade, as there are no decline/dips in bilateral trade, the impact may be in terms of lowering the trade level to below potential. The conflict intensity may have been factored into trade calculations such that traders do not trade much and thereby keep their risks of loss low. This may be more evident when we undertake our formal estimation using a variable for expected risk owing to a prevailing threshold level of conflict. Interestingly during this time domestic civil strife in Pakistan was increasing but it seems to have no influence on Indian exports to Pakistan as well as imports from Pakistan, even though the latter are at relatively lower levels. It may also be noteworthy that in this period of political tensions in the 1980s and 1990s many CBMs were initiated, with some significant non-military ones, including the setting

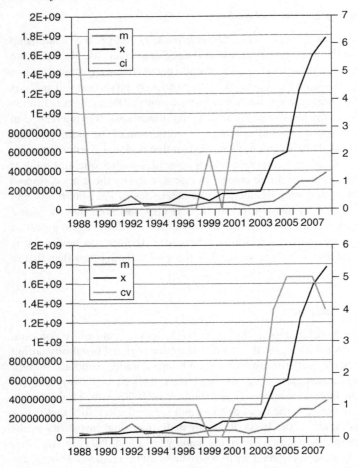

Figure 5.2 Impact of regional and civil conflict on bilateral trade: India–Pakistan

ci: regional conflict intensity; cv: civil conflict intensity; m: imports; x: exports. Source: MEPV Database, Polity IV.

up of the joint commission to discuss, among others, trade issues and India granting the MFN status to Pakistan.

India's trade with Bangladesh

India's trade with Bangladesh appears independent of regional or domestic conflict. India's imports from Bangladesh are very small, exports relatively are much larger. Regional instability coincident with India's worsening relations with Pakistan and the nuclear test seems to impact India's exports to Bangladesh but trade appears largely independent of regional conflict. Political regimes per se do not impact trade. In fact the onset of democracy in 1991 does not reveal favourable bilateral trends. To some extent it may have been on account of the quasi-democratic character of the political regime. Also the alternating parties in rule, that is, the Awami League party, which has been more inclined to maintain favourable relations with India, and the Bangladeshi Nationalist party, which is more distant regarding its approach to India, have made the environment less certain and not very trade friendly. Political power in Bangladesh has frequently changed among the Awami League, the military and the Bangladesh Nationalist Party (BNP). India signed some of its major treaties and agreements that had implications on border management during the rule of Awami League, like the Trade Agreement between India and Bangladesh in 1972 and 1973, the Indo-Bangladesh Border Agreement in 1974, and the Indo-Bangladesh Water Sharing Treaty in 1996. During military rule and the BNP era, however, only minor protocols or agreements could be signed, despite India providing the Tin Bigha corridor to Bangladesh.

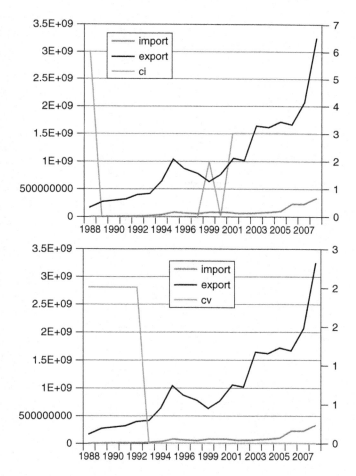

Figure 5.3 Impact of regional and civil conflict on bilateral trade: India–Bangladesh
ci: regional conflict intensity; cv: civil conflict intensity. Source: MEPV Database, Polity IV.

India's trade with Nepal

Conflict – regional, bilateral or domestic – appears to have had no influence on India–Nepal trade. There is a steady increase in trade that is observed for the two nations with the first dip seen in 2002 when India introduced stricter RoOs in the trade treaty. The economics that dominates the India–Nepal relationship appears least political in character in South Asia. Political regimes have been authoritative, with democracy being only episodic, but this does not seem to have influenced trade relations between the two nations either.

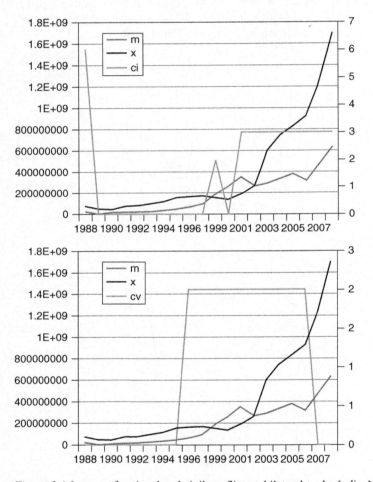

Figure 5.4 Impact of regional and civil conflict on bilateral trade: India–Nepal

ci: regional conflict intensity; cv: civil conflict intensity; m: imports; x: exports. Source: MEPV Database, Polity IV.

India's trade with Sri Lanka

Sri Lanka is another example of an economy with which India's trade relations have consistently improved since the signing of the India–Sri Lanka FTA in 1998. Regional, bilateral or domestic civil strife in Sri Lanka have had almost no affect on bilateral trade. Domestic civil conflict, which has been constant but at a high level (conflict intensity of 5 through the 1990s until 2008), shows almost no reflection in the bilateral trade volumes. Trade has been increasing almost throughout the reference period with a major and steep rise observed since 2000 when the India–Sri Lanka bilateral FTA was implemented. Sri Lanka, like India, has been the longest-running democracy in South Asia.

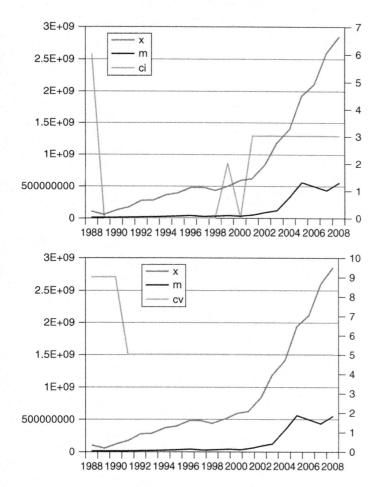

Figure 5.5 Impact of regional and civil conflict on bilateral trade: India–Sri Lanka

ci: regional conflict intensity; cv: civil conflict intensity; m: imports; x: exports. Source: MEPV Database, Polity IV.

Democratic peace and trade in South Asia

In South Asia the democratic peace theory may not be subject to validation. For Nepal and Sri Lanka – where political regimes are at the extreme opposites – with monarchy in Nepal and democracy in Sri Lanka, the political regimes have had no direct implications for an otherwise largely frictionless trade relationship with India. Trade has been disrupted or accelerated on account of economic events and not political regimes or changes therein. India–Pakistan may have seen more CBMs during democratic regimes but with limited durability of democracy the impact of these CBMs has not been durable either. Bangladesh, which has seen longer periods of democracy, has however had party leanings for and against India such that all democratic regimes have not followed an equally friendly India policy. A generalization of democracy–peace–trade theory, therefore, may not be a correct conclusion in the South Asian case.

6 Theoretical foundations of the economic integration and conflict relationship in South Asia

This chapter presents the theoretical foundations of the relationship between economic integration and conflict. At the outset, it needs to be stated that the theoretical foundations of the trade-conflict relationship in this chapter are presented with twin perspectives of economic analysis and the South Asian context. The need for this clarification has arisen on account of the differential emphasis that is laid upon the causality of direction in the conflict-trade relationship by the two disciplines of economics and political science. The latter continues to debate on whether conflict is positively or negatively impacted by trade, even while including studies that delve into the possible duality of causality in this relationship. The former is, however, exclusively focused on the conflict-reduces-trade aspect of the relationship. The chapter, while taking note of the possible bi-directional causality in the trade-conflict relationship, establishes the appropriateness of a unidirectional view in the South Asian context. Given the fact that the ongoing preferential trade agreements among the South Asian countries at all levels – regional, sub-regional, bilateral – do not as yet cover or are only as yet negotiating to incorporate investment liberalization, the trade-conflict framework is the mainstay of our analysis.

The South Asian experience of economic integration has been unique. As discussed in the preceding chapters, the South Asian Association for Regional Cooperation (SAARC) was established in 1985 comprising seven nations, all having come to the initiation of the forum with differing expectations and in an adversarial mode. As evident from the analysis in the preceding chapters, intra-regional trade in South Asia is low and has undergone little change since the inception of the regional organization over 25 years ago. Progress of SAPTA and SAFTA, the two attempts at regional preferential trade agreements, has been repeatedly stalled by both economic and political barriers. History and hostility have evidently played an overwhelming role in South Asia and the adversarial stance of the member countries has prevented them from lowering trade barriers in the region. It is often suspected that benefits that are likely to accrue from regional economic integration in the form of increased income and welfare will only go towards strengthening the adversary, maybe even in terms of increased defence expenditure. The experience of regionalism in the case of the EU, ASEAN, NAFTA and others has been different and positive, in terms of achievement of both peace and economic gains.[1] As such, therefore, it is imperative for South Asia to understand the possible gains of regional economic integration in terms of increased trade and welfare that are being sacrificed on account of protracted conflict. As the trend for regional economic integration intensifies globally, the quantification of the role of conflict in inhibiting trade and economic integration in South Asia acquires even more significance. While the formal econometric estimation is undertaken in the following chapter, we focus here on the suitability of theoretical frameworks for the South Asian context, in the process identifying some of the variables that will define the estimable econometric framework.

The empirical analysis undertaken in the next chapter is based on the premise that bilateral trade is influenced by both economic and political factors. In the tradition of research on applied economics of international trade, which is undertaken to explain, theoretically and empirically, the relation between bilateral trade and measures of joint economic activity and costs of trade, the empirical framework for estimation will be the trade gravity model. We undertake to augment the basic gravity equation[2] by incorporating variables that are representative of the economic and political environment of trading country pairs with the aim of quantification of the cost of conflict in terms of trade loss in South Asia. While many have undertaken to estimate bilateral trade potential using this equation, few have used it to understand the implications of political environment on bilateral trade in general and none in case of South Asia. In fact, most studies in the economic literature on international trade do not include political factors as explanatory variables in their models. Our approach differs from the earlier studies in that it amalgamates the most pertinent features of the two perspectives such that they provide the theoretical foundations for our empirical analysis of the impact of conflict on trade in South Asia. As discussed by Pollins (1989a, b), any technical analysis wherein trade behaviour, patterns and volumes takes account of political factors in addition to the economic factors is likely to outperform trade theoretical modelling that excludes the political influence. This is certainly true in the case of South Asia, where political environment has overwhelmingly overshadowed economic rationale.

Below we present the broad contours of the theoretical perspectives of the trade-conflict relationship as discussed in the economics and political science literature. This is followed by specific aspects from each of these perspectives that best characterize and help formalize the trade-conflict relationship in the South Asian region.

Theoretical foundations

The conflict-trade inter-linkage debate can be viewed as first having been between political scientists and international economists. In the economic literature for a long time the contribution of political events and regimes to bilateral trade received little attention and focus. The subject was considered to lie in the domain of political science research. However, even among political scientists the focus has been on examining the impact of international trade and some political features on bilateral/dyadic conflict. Few studies have attempted to quantify the impact of conflict on bilateral trade. Since the 1990s the nature of discussion has been in terms of opposing views held by liberals and realists. The former insist on the pacifying role of trade, while the latter, subject to several qualifications, hold trade responsible for conflict.[3] More recent research has focused on situations where the liberal claim may not hold. While emphasizing the reciprocal nature of the relationship, some recent studies provide evidence that more strongly establishes that conflict reduces trade rather than the other way round. Economic analysis has incorporated the political relations variables in the gravity model, which in turn has been used by many political scientists for the trade-conflict analysis.

Economics perspective

In economic trade theory it is generally assumed that international political considerations are 'transient and random in nature' and therefore safely ignored relative to long-run market factors.[4] Relatively few studies have been undertaken to estimate the trade costs of conflict in comparison with the large number of studies undertaken to calculate the trade benefits associated with tariff reduction and non-tariff barrier elimination. However, as countries are getting more and more globally integrated, politics and political variables are seen to influence economic relations, international trade patterns and volumes to a large extent. This is also relevant for South Asia, which in recent years has registered one of the fastest growth rates of trade in the world[5] but has the lowest levels of intra-regional trade and some of the most persistent and long-standing conflicts among its member economies.

Available studies have focused on two channels of transmission of the costs of conflict. These are domestic and globalization, or what is referred to as global integration. While the domestic channel is seen to operate through the crowding-out effect of conflict-induced increased defence spending by the government, the latter operates through trade. Recent research in this context has been undertaken by Blomberg and Hess (2006) and Glick and Taylor (2005), among others. The arguments presented suggest that conflict impacts economic activity like any other trade cost. Inter-state conflict, or a regional terrorist attack, or even increased terrorist activity within a country, or bilateral instances of terrorism all imply that the cost of doing business with the region/country will increase. Economic activity and trade will be directed away from that country, thus replicating the effects of trade-distorting tax/tariff that limits the benefits of free trade. The focus of the economic analysis is thus on the cost that conflict[6] imposes on a nation in terms of loss of trade and consequently economic welfare. Costs of conflict can be both direct and indirect. These are discussed below along with their relevance to the South Asian context.

Costs of Conflict

Traditional definitions of conflict are presented in terms of direct costs as measured by loss of life and resources used to wage war, with occasional additions in the form of lost and damaged property as well as the expenditure towards conflict mitigation. It is also accepted that political contests result in a negative externality that is reflected in the form of enhanced insecurity and risk. Any kind of conflict will therefore, in general, imply additional transaction costs for private agents by increasing the element of uncertainty related to the transaction. In addition, risk would also entail more expensive methods of protection to provide security for trade, and this would further add to costs.

There are also some costs that are indirectly incurred by warring nations. Glick and Taylor (2005) have examined the impact of the indirect costs of conflict on the volume of international trade. They find that while the impact of war on trade is very strong, the costs of war are further exacerbated as the impact of conflict is persistent and invariably lasts beyond the actual years of the event. Further, they also highlight the fact that the destructive and damaging costs of conflict extend beyond the conflicting states, to neutral partners. Indirect costs upon trade are also inflicted through policy changes that would inhibit trade between two countries that are in conflict situations. Long (2009) emphasizes economic policy changes like embargoes, sanctions, and so on, in this respect.

This is a relevant aspect for the South Asian case where conflict has been long standing and persistent well beyond the years of wars in the region. Conflict-induced costs on the level and pattern of trade in South Asia are multifaceted and all too evident. Conflict and political events have led to policy changes, such as thickening or hardening of the border, that may in turn have raised the costs of trade and reduced the volume of cross-border commercial transactions in the region. Non-tariff barriers imposed in the form of excessive and time-consuming checks and heavy deployment of security forces at the border are examples in this respect. The obverse has been observed when during relatively peaceful periods border trade is opened and free flow of people and goods is allowed. The opening of the border trade along the Srinagar-Muzaffarabad road in 2008 is in the nature of initiating greater confidence through opening the border for commercial exchange. Border trade at this point, when bilateral relations were not strained, was opened up for the first time in 61 years.[7] That trade and commercial activity in general has been held hostage by conflict is also amply reflected in the unsuccessful attempts at resolving the issue of construction of the Iran-Pakistan-India gas pipeline. Negotiations between India and Pakistan during different political regimes in Pakistan and India's withdrawal from this joint framework show how the uncertainty and distrust inherent in a region suffering from prolonged conflict and hostilities engenders decisions that may go against the welfare of the nations involved. The issues relating to investment in energy infrastructure between India and Bangladesh, despite the advantages of a cooperative initiative in terms of ensuring energy security in the region and introducing the possibility of a reduction in Bangladesh's trade deficit through export of gas to India, did not see the light of the day for purely political reasons based on hostilities. Refusal of countries in South Asia to provide transit rights to facilitate cross-border trade is evidence of how politics has been allowed to suppress economics even when it could have meant gains for many of the smaller nations of the region. Embargoes or sanctions, on the other hand, don't mean much and provide little scope for being used as hostile policy instruments in the South Asian context as the intra-regional trade and commercial exchange has been low, having been pre-empted by constant conflict. Additionally, trade transactions in crucial raw materials/natural resources in the region that could become the basis of imposing sanctions or the restricted supply of which could be a potential constraint on a country's growth process are not relevant for a region where the movement of available natural resources has, as it is, been restricted by conflict and hostile relations (for example, water flows across borders that can be harnessed for power generation/trade).

Globalization/multilateral trade openness and bilateral conflict

A high degree of multilateral trade openness reduces bilateral dependence on account of the multiplicity of trade partners and the options thereby to import from/export to alternative sources/destinations. The multiple options offered by increased multilateral openness weaken the incentive to make concessions to a feuding bilateral trade partner to prevent the escalation of a dispute. Reduced bilateral trade could then be a likely negative fallout of this sequence of events. Multilateral trade, though, remains unaffected in this situation.

It is to be noted, however, that in theory the propensity of multilateral trade, to Martin, Mayer and Thoening (2007), show how increasing global integration may reduce the peace prospect between a trading pair of countries that are in dispute. If the bilateral or regional dispute does not significantly impact a country's trade with the rest of the world, multilateral openness reduces the opportunity cost of a bilateral dispute. From their analysis it can also be inferred that even when it is accepted that trade increases welfare and war is pareto dominated by peace, the intuition that trade promotes peace may only be partially correct, as even while bilateral trade may act as a deterrent to war, multilateral trade liberalization by providing multiple options of supply may actually introduce a counter effect. The need to offer concessions and make peace with your neighbour in dispute to resolve negotiations is diluted on account of multilateral opening that would result in lowering the opportunity costs or gains at stake from bilateral trade. According to Martin *et al.* (2007) this is especially true for countries with a high probability of dispute linked to local dimensions (borders, resources and minorities). The argument holds true of South Asia – where inter-state disputes are all on local dimensions and trade is more with partners outside the region than within, even though the latter is more prudent in economic terms. As stated earlier,[8] it may be wise for many South Asian countries to trade with India and consequently reduce their trade deficit with the rest of the world. However, what probably makes multilateral trade opening a preferred option for these smaller South Asian economies is the conflict-induced high risk that is entailed with every such trade transaction in the region. It is therefore imperative that the cost of conflict is measured and reflected upon in terms of the trade loss to the region. While the most obvious interpretation of regional and multilateral trade integration of the South Asian economies appears to contradict and challenge economic logic, it is the not-so-obvious (at least not in measurable terms so far) costs of conflict and the attached risks that make trade within the region costlier. Actual trade is in all likelihood therefore lower than the potential in South Asia. Measurement of the costs of conflict and potential trade lost on account of conflict must be taken up and serious consideration ought to be given to reducing these costs and raising trade to potential possibilities. Possibility of bilateral conflict is a function of many factors, including the cost of multilateral trade. If the latter is higher and can be substituted by bilateral trade, the cost of bilateral conflict in terms of bilateral trade costs or losses would be much greater. For South Asia this seems to be true too, and particularly with reference to India–Pakistan trade patterns. Even though Pakistan can import many commodities, essential and otherwise, from India, it chooses to import these at much higher costs from other countries, with expensive implications for its trade balance with the rest of the world.[9] This reveals the extraordinary role that conflict plays in South Asian trade patterns and volumes and provides the imperatives for our analysis. The cost of conflict is to be understood in terms of lower trade levels (vis-à-vis the potential) as well as higher costs entailed in finding new trade partners. The greater the potential for bilateral trade, the greater the conflict-imposed trade losses. What brings this theoretical precept even closer to the regional scenario in South Asia is the fact that geographically and culturally proximate countries are more likely candidates for such an outcome.

Anticipatory effects of conflict

Another cost of conflict is the building up of expectations of future conflict. According to Long (2009) the 'shadow of war' or anticipated conflict may also have a role to play in the volume and direction of trade. While actual conflict definitely endangers trade transactions, expectation of a conflict also increases the element of risk in the transaction undertaken with a conflict-prone region or country. Expected conflict may lead to higher transaction costs through increased possibilities of currency instability, breach of contract, low institutional credibility, increased government restrictions (e.g. through tariffs), and thus reduce the scope for profitable trade. According to Morrow, Siverson and Tabares (1998, 1999) there will be ex ante reduction in trade where firms anticipate conflict owing to a state's violent relations with its neighbours, that is, where risk of conflict is greatest. In such cases the expected return on capital and other commercial transactions adjusted for risk would be much lower than potentially possible. Trading enterprises/ economic actors factor in the risks of a political conflict, existing and future, and make their profit calculations accordingly. In such situations, therefore, the traders are likely to undertake transactions much lower in number than they would if peace was the norm between two countries.

Furthermore, expected conflict and the associated uncertain bilateral political environment not only reduces trade but also diverts it away from conflict prone to 'safer' sources. Sometimes this may entail not just production, transport and transaction costs but, in a more fundamental sense, direct trade away from more-efficient to less-efficient producers. Profits would take a hit on this count as well, but additionally there would be an impact on national welfare as well as global efficiency.

In an interesting analysis, Long (2009) explores the conflict-trade relationship in a gravity model framework. According to Long the possibility of conflict, independent of actual conflict, reduces bilateral trade as expectations of a possible conflict raise the production, transaction and transportation costs for the producer and thus the expected profit of the producer, making him wary of trading with a country/region that is conflict prone. Long translates the economic agent's expectations of conflict in a rational expectation framework[10] that, when incorporated in the empirical analysis, shows that trade between a pair of countries doubles when the risk of inter-state conflict is reduced from its highest to lowest levels.

Even though the rational expectations-based modelling of anticipated conflict may not be fully justifiable – after all, even political leaders may not be exactly sure of the date of a conflict event – anticipation of conflict is an important variable for inclusion in the empirical estimation in the South Asian context. Conflict in South Asia has often been interspersed by periods of peace and diplomatic initiatives. These periods, however, do not necessarily coincide with an upsurge in trade levels.[11] One reason for the unchanging level of trade over a long period of time in South Asia could be that traders do not increase trade during peace time or increase it only marginally so as not to risk their business as they 'anticipate' future conflict. In recent times when conflict in South Asia has been more in the nature of ongoing hostilities rather an overt war this may be even more true. In fact the limited impact of the regional FTA can be partially attributed to the effect of anticipated conflict, as the earlier attempt was sabotaged by heightened tensions between India and Pakistan. The hostilities have rendered people wary and in a constant mode of expecting increased intensity of conflict as the confidence-building measures that have interspersed hostile times have not been able to sustain peace or trust among the two countries over the medium or long term. Both, the expectation and actual occurrence of conflict are thus relevant in the South Asian context,which has been witness to actual wars, minor wars and perpetual hostilities.

Political science perspective

The political science literature on the subject is vast. Below we present the broad political science perspective highlighting the studies that have shown that the trade to conflict causality is weak and that it has to have a precondition in the form of peaceful relations leading to more trade that is then feared to be lost if a conflict event happens. Additionally, some features derived from the political science literature are reinterpreted in economic terms as relevant to South Asia.

Theoretical and empirical studies in the political science literature[12] have addressed the issue of conflict among nations being a function of economic interdependence including bilateral trade, in addition to other factors. The focus has largely been on the direction of causality that runs from trade to the likelihood of conflict. Broadly the political science literature can be studied under the following categories, the liberal proposition that trade promotes peace; neo-Marxist and others who say that symmetric trade leads to peace whereas asymmetric economic interdependence is more liable to lead to conflict; that trade increases conflict; and last, that trade is irrelevant to peace or political relations.

Polachek (1980) and Arad and Hirsch (1981, 1983) provide theoretical foundations for trade-conflict relationship, while Polachek (1980) and Gasiorowski and Polachek (1982) present the empirical support for the liberal hypothesis. Polachek proposes in his exposition that trade patterns are a consequence of the heterogeneous factor endowments-based differential comparative advantage of nations. Trade has many benefits like diversified consumer choice, increased income and welfare. These benefits of trade influence a nation's foreign policy, as the state, being a welfare maximizing rational economic agent, aims at maximizing these benefits and consequently national welfare. In a nation's expected utility calculus, conflict would entail costs in the form of lost potential trade and the consequent loss of associated welfare gains.[13] It would hence be natural to expect that national leaders would hesitate to initiate or persevere with conflict situations with important trade partners. The concept of supply and demand elasticities has also been incorporated in this analysis to bring forth the commodity-specific relevance of this proposition. Normally, therefore, trade should lead to deterrence or cessation of conflict.

Neo-Marxists analyze the trade-peace relationship not in terms of interdependence, but dependence. The emphasis of this view is on the unequal nature of the trade ties, with the weaker partner having to bear the costs of economic manipulation and coercion by the stronger power in the exchange process. In addition they also argue that the process of bilateral exchange itself does not benefit the trading partners in an equal measure if the two are not, a priori, politically and economically equal partners. While the argument has been questioned by many, the significant aspect is that unequal exchange, while not being the sole reason for conflict, does make its perpetuation more likely. Barbieri (1996, 2002) projects a positive relationship between economic interdependence and conflict in cases of asymmetric interdependence.

The theoretical argument for the proposition that trade leads to conflict rests on the resource-scarcity-induced state interventionism and protectionist policies that eventually result in hegemonic wars.[14]

One strand of the literature also proposes that economic factors such as trade are important only at the margins. This follows from the view that strategic interests are the primary causes of war and fits with the argument that economic considerations are sacrificed for security interests at times of serious conflict. McMillan (1997) has pointed out that the interaction between economic and political factors needs to be further researched and in particular we need to identify the situations where strategic objectives override domestic interests in economic cooperation.

Some specific aspects of the political science debate as suited to the South Asian context and our analytical framework are discussed below.

Asymmetry

As mentioned above, Barbieri (1996) considers the proposition that the trade-peace relationship is contingent upon the nature and context of economic linkages. In particular symmetrical trade relations may foster peace, while asymmetrical dependence creates tensions that tend to manifest themselves in conflict interactions. Historically, this can be traced back to the mercantilist thinking whereby international trade and capital flows are used to push forward national foreign policy interests. In this case the economic policies are used as instruments of statecraft/ diplomacy or, simply put, for compliance by the weaker power.

While this is a thought that we neither follow nor test in our empirical analysis, we do take account of the impact of an inherent asymmetry, economic and geographic, in South Asia that places India in an economically stronger position vis-à-vis the other nations in the region. This asymmetry has led to a sense of insecurity among the South Asian nations, and has in fact become one of the causes of the reluctance of the smaller nations in South Asia to adhere to the concept of regional economic integration. They fear that economic integration and increased Indian access to their markets will further strengthen India's position in the region and simultaneously destroy their industry by flooding their markets with cheaper goods. While this argument may not find support in economic logic, the history and nature of conflict in the region contributes to this fear psychosis.[15]

Distinction also needs to be drawn between asymmetry as interpreted by political scientists and as by economists. Asymmetry for the latter is interpreted in terms of economic strength and the former in terms of power. In South Asia asymmetry is evident with respect to differential economic development and dynamism of the member economies. Conflict is, however, not an outcome of the economic leverage of the larger country vis-à-vis the smaller. Instead conflict has its roots in the history of the region and has over the years acquired varying forms. While asymmetry has added to apprehensions of the smaller nations vis-à-vis India, it is not necessarily to be viewed as economic strength translated into political or military strength. Further, it is the distribution of gains from trade, that is, relative gains, that in the political science literature is considered as an outcome of asymmetry and a reason for conflict.[16] In South Asia this aspect is visible but needs to be seen in the correct perspective. India, the country that is largest in size, is expected to be the highest gainer even though this has not found sufficient proof in the empirical literature. More empirical work needs to be undertaken to counter this economic fallacy. The smaller nations are bound to benefit through the integrated supply chains that could be a consequence if regional economic integration is promoted in a judicious manner.

Finally, even though the South Asian region is characterized by India-centricity in many respects, particularly economic, this does not by any chance give India the hegemonic status that is theoretically assumed by the larger nation. The majority of the smaller states in South Asia are hyper-sensitive about sovereignty and are hence unwilling to accept its economic leadership or its model of a secular, democratic, economically viable nation.[17]

Political Regimes

The nature of a political regime is an important determinant of a country's trade policy. Policy preferences of the relevant political agents are reflected in the national trade policy after the due process is undertaken by political institutions. Governments are more likely to initiate and promote trade with countries that have similar political alignments. Traders on either side would be reluctant to establish relations with their counterparts in a hostile country as reversal of foreign policy posture may abruptly lead to severing of commercial ties.

In this respect, it is considered that democracies are capable of initiating and sustaining economic relationships to a greater extent. Democracies commit themselves more credibly than non-democratic regimes to protect property rights and respect the rule of law – all factors that reduce the risk element in bilateral trade. Therefore, economic actors are more assured that their interests will be protected from government fiat when trading with a democracy. Furthermore, welfare of the public at large is at the heart of a democratic regime and this is promoted by freer trade, in contrast with autocracies/military dictatorships, where the perpetuation of the power base reigns as the supreme objective. Democracies are therefore presumed to be interested in lowering trade barriers in the interest of national welfare.

The political science literature has, however, stressed upon the peace-promoting characteristic of democracy and many studies have reported that joint democracies are more peaceful.[18] The relationship in some cases is analyzed as being based on the intermediate positive relationship between democracy and trade.[19] Bliss and Russett's (1998) analysis with annual regressions for the period 1962–89 broadly supports the proposition that bilateral trade increases as the least democratic of the two trading partners becomes more democratic.

This is a significant aspect that needs to be factored in in all its dimensions as evident in the South Asian context. The present period is for the first time witnessing simultaneous democratic regimes in all the South Asian countries. However, South Asia is experiencing only an evolution of democracy across all nations, except India and Sri Lanka, where it has been thriving for a long time now. The other countries have not experienced durable democracy and have often lapsed back to military rule/dictatorship. Long (2009) has discussed stability of political institutions as an important contributory factor in ensuring successful fulfilment of contractual obligations. The extent to which democracies can be effective in containing conflict and promoting economic exchange is a function of the citizens' abilities to express their preferences to country leaders, checks and balances on the executive branch of the government, and the degree to which civil liberties are protected – that is, the successful establishment of institutionalized democracy. In South Asia transition to democracy has sometimes been accompanied by improved bilateral relations reflected in the opening up of border trade and signing of trade agreements. Many of these agreements, though, are rendered ineffective and end up as only rhetoric after the reversal of political regimes in these countries. At other times democracies may not have been in favour of trade pacts or increased trade with hostile nations.

As an example, policies –economic or otherwise – in Bangladesh with respect to India have varied depending on the Awami League or Bangladesh Nationalist Party being in power.[20] Even for India, where the tradition of democracy has been maintained since its independence, the current coalition form of government imposes its own compulsions depending on its composition. This was evident to some extent in the negotiation process of the India-ASEAN free trade area agreement (FTA) that took place for over six years before the deal was signed in 2009. The long period of negotiations between India and the ASEAN amply reflects the limited abilities of the United Progressive Alliance (UPA) I and II government to take forward a process that had been initiated in 2003 by the Bharatiya Janata Party (BJP)-led National Democratic Alliance coalition in India. Clearly, political rulers of strong ruling coalitions are both more willing and capable of carrying forward the idea of regional integration and attendant trade policies. Transiting democracies, durability of regimes and alternative political regimes are therefore all relevant from the South Asian perspective and need to be suitably included and interpreted in the estimation process.

Interestingly theoretical arguments have also proposed an interaction effect for political and economic regimes. Supported by the Hecksher-Ohlin and the Stolper Samuelson Theorem, Milner and Kubota (2005, p. 116) argue that democratization will enfranchise a new group of voters that have a preference for lower levels of protectionism. In autocracies those with voting rights benefit the most from high levels of protection. In the South Asian case, additionally, it may be appropriate to consider the economic regimes for their independent effect as well, as the region has undergone a transition from inward-looking, almost autarkic economies to more liberalized and open economies in the 1990s.

Economic regimes

The South Asian economies have been distinctly inward looking following an import-substitution industrialization growth strategy until the beginning of 1990s. The growth strategy impacted on restricting trade directly and indirectly by making trade less relevant to the economy. This is pertinent in the context of the observation made by Long (2009) that countries that follow the 'trade as an engine for growth' model are more likely to achieve prosperity through peace. In this sense the economic regime in South Asia may have contributed in a way to protracted conflict and the notion of deriving benefits from maintaining internal and external peace, may not have figured in the South Asian psyche or the economic costs of conflict, and may not have been obvious to the region. This position is likely to have changed since 1991 as the South Asian economies have adopted more open economic regimes and are consequently experiencing economic dynamism and rapid trade integration with the global economy. This, it is considered, would make apparent the imperatives of regional stability for the region.

Common-border and territorial disputes

In contrast with the economic connotation of a common border as a trade facilitator, the political science literature sometimes attributes conflict to shared borders. The focus in case of the latter is on unresolved border and territorial issues. As discussed in Chapter 5, the issue of territory has long been responsible for conflict in South Asia. Around the world it is observed that systems/regions where all the major states have reached agreements with their neighbours on issues of boundary/territory are more peaceful than those that have not. North America, for example, has been more peaceful than Europe. The presence of a major state has facilitated the process of conflict resolution in the North American region. South Asia, though, is different and this needs to be incorporated in our analysis. There is also the notion, (not necessarily proved though) that conflict will be greater, the greater the number of countries with which borders are shared, and this appears to reflect the South Asian situation, where almost all border/boundary/territorial conflict is with India, the only country that has a shared border with all other economies in the region. Therefore, it may just be natural that inter-state conflicts in South Asia revolve around India. This duality in the border issue needs to be appropriately incorporated and interpreted in the South Asian context.

Regional trading arrangements (RTAs)

The regional trading arrangements (RTAs) have been discussed in both the economics and political science literature. RTAs impact on trade as instruments of accelerating trade liberalization and economic integration. Political benefits like peace and stability are perceived as outcomes of successful economic integration through RTAs, sometimes larger and more desirable than simple material gains.

Many analysts have stressed the diplomatic role that RTAs can perform, saying that these arrangements, especially those aiming at deeper integration, can be used as instruments of rapprochement between antagonistic states and assist the process of peace building in a regional context. Negotiations that are part of the RTA process inevitably involve an element of trust among the members and enable individual countries to recognize each other's sensitivities as the outcomes are based on consensus. Many examples have been cited in the literature – EU, APEC, CACM, ASEAN – all regional groupings that were primarily motivated by potential political gains in terms of reduction in bilateral tensions among the members. The security externalities are cited in the case of the ECSC (1951) and the EEC (1957), where in both cases the underlying motivation lay in the reduction of the threat of war in Europe, in ASEAN to reduce tensions between Malaysia and Indonesia and in Mercosur to reduce tensions between Argentina and Brazil.[21]

A significant reality that needs to be recognized in this context is that regional groupings that have achieved peace through trade policies are the ones where pacific aims were the underlying motivations and hence the success. This, though, may not always hold true. In many cases the differential economic and geographic size of member countries matters and the pacific effects of regional economic integration are possible only when the gains from economic integration are attained and distributed in a balanced and equitable fashion. In many cases where the economic outcomes are either unequal or the resultant income transfers lead to unequal gains, peace need not be a natural outcome of the integration process. The unequal gains may in fact make the region even more susceptible to increased security risks. South Asia, where the fears of unevenly distributed gains from trade integration have prevented these countries from coming together on the economic front, is an appropriate example in the second category. The economic asymmetry in the region, which is part inherited and now also a consequence of India's exceptional economic dynamism, has created insecurities among other countries in the region. The unequal gains of economic integration are, however, more perceived than real. Not only has this perception of asymmetric gains not allowed SAARC to progress, it has also combined with persistent hostilities to prevent any major technical analysis to prove otherwise. Since its inception, SAARC has had to grapple with bilateral conflicts even while the stated objective of the organization is non-interference in internal matters/disputes and bilateral issues to remain outside the purview of the forum. The underlying theme for regional economic integration and regional cooperation under the aegis of SAARC in South Asia was not peace building and reconciliation. In fact, when SAARC was set up, all the regional leaders joined the initiative with great trepidation. On the one hand, there was fear in India's mind that this forum would be used by smaller countries to gang up against India, and on the other hand Pakistan thought that this was an attempt by India to unite the smaller countries against it. Many SAARC summits as well as summit agendas have been held hostage to the bilateral conflicts in the region. Even when the organization has initiated the process of FTA formation, progress has been stalled by the ongoing India–Pakistan conflict that is reflected in the latter's stubborn and unreasonable stance of not granting India the most favoured nation (MFN) status, which it is mandatorily required to grant as a WTO member, and adamantly trading with India on a positive-list basis, even while it is a signatory to the SAFTA provision of a negative-list approach to preferential trade for over six years of the Agreement's implementation process. In South Asia, therefore, conflict is quite obviously a prior and a constant that limits the regional organization in its developmental and cooperative efforts. Our empirical analysis will undertake a detailed representation of the RTA variable to highlight its potential contribution to intra-regional trade as well as quantify the extent to which this potential is constrained by conflict.

Empirical analysis and bi-directional causality

Apart from the fact that the South Asian context and experience clearly justify the unidirectional analysis of the impact of conflict on trade, the political science literature itself reflects upon this issue with many empirical analyses providing sufficient evidence to emphasize the strength of direction of causality from conflict to trade. A brief account of the literature in this context is given below.

After Polachek's (1980) seminal work on modelling the theoretical foundations of the proposition that trade leads to peace, the trade-conflict debate has been largely empirical in nature.[22] Formal testing of the strength of causality in either direction has been undertaken, but with many methodological issues being raised simultaneously the results have not been unambiguous. Most empirical analyses have assumed contextual causality with no formal tests to support the same. Gasiorowski and Polachek (1982) test the causality using a granger test but for a single dyad and conclude that granger causality over short lag periods runs overwhelmingly from trade to conflict. Their conclusion has been criticised on methodological grounds. In a repeat analysis with 130 dyads, in which US is an actor, Gasiorowski (1986) finds that his results are only partially in agreement with the results of the earlier joint study. Reuveny and Kang (1996) have investigated the causality between these variables using Granger causality tests for 16 individual dyads over the period 1960 to the early 1990s, with the end date defined as the last reports of conflict/cooperation in the sample countries. The relationship has been examined in a dynamic context. While the results of the empirical analysis show that causality runs in both directions, the trade-conflict relationship with conflict as the dependent variable is dyad dependent. On the other hand, trade improves/decreases as conflict intensity increases or decreases in an unambiguous manner.

Barbieri and Levy (1999) have studied the impact of war on trade. After a formal analysis they arrive at the conclusion that the adverse impact of war on trade is small and not statistically significant and limited largely to the period of war with resumption of trade in the post-war period, even if not immediately so. They also aver to the illegal trade that takes place during wartime as being indicative of the absence of or limited depressive effect of war on trade. Their conclusion, though, is hard to generalize as conflict is to be understood beyond just the event of war. For South Asia this may certainly hold true. Barbieri and Levy's conclusion was later countered by Anderton and Carter (2001) in their analysis presenting evidence to show that war disrupts trade.

It also needs to be pointed out that in the discussion on causality some studies that have undertaken a joint simultaneous estimation of the conflict-to-trade and trade-to-conflict relationships have expressed in their results that while interstate disputes reduce bilateral trade, the reverse need not hold. In fact in these estimations the pacific effect of commerce is eliminated. This has been reported by Keshk, Pollins and Reuveny (2004) and Kim and Rousseau (2005). While methodological issues have been raised in the context of these studies by Hegre, Oneal and Russet (2009), the argument does provide a basis for the singular relationship testing, apart from the other reasons, as given earlier by Reuveny in support of what is otherwise justifiable in a contextual manner for South Asia. Keshk, Pollins and Reuveny (2004), in a simultaneous estimation model, establish the primacy of political variables in the trade-conflict relationship, implying thereby that, based on empirical evidence, conflict reduces trade is a more robust result than the liberal claim that trade reduces conflict. The latter, according to the authors, can be accounted for by simultaneity bias.

Pollins (1989) provides the formal theoretical analysis for the approach that nations with cooperative political environments will trade more. Pollins highlights the co-variation between political climate between nations and commerce while discussing the many effects of international politics on trade flows. These effects may range from economic power plays such as sanctions to those between diplomatic climate and commercial relations. In his analysis Pollins points out that that the empirical relationship as tested by Polachek and others goes against their theoretical framework. Elaborating, he says, in the long run the relationship between trade and conflict/cooperation may necessarily be viewed as reciprocal and that eventually increased trade will lead to more peaceful coexistence. However, this eventuality has a prior in the form of increased trade happening only after the improvement of bilateral political environment, often reflected in trade agreements. As mentioned by Pollins, such a multi-stage evolution of bilateral relations may not be easily testable and hence most empirical analyses stick to the view that trade is a consequence of bilateral conflict/cooperation climate. Interestingly, therefore, while the conflict model empirically tested by Polachek may not exactly form the basis of our analysis, the crucial assumption of his theoretical analysis – that the utility maximizing agents are conflict-averse *because* they realize that conflict inhibits commerce (italics as in Pollins) – provides appropriate basis for our analysis in the South Asia context, even though not as much for Polachek's own analysis.

It is clear from our discussion that conflict among the South Asian economies has not allowed the force of economic integration to impact the region. The South Asian psyche has been dominated by asymmetry – geographic and economic – so much so that consequences of economic integration in any mode or form are prejudged, often without economic rationale, to benefit the larger nation. It also cannot be disputed that the conflict between India and Pakistan has been the overriding factor limiting the effective implementation of the instruments of economic integration in South Asia. Other bilateral conflicts have only further perpetuated the situation. It may therefore be most appropriate to study the region in an independent perspective, exclusive to the region and while not negating the theoretical possibility of reverse causation, to focus our formal econometric analysis on the negative impact of conflict and the extent of economic benefits that are locked on account of this protracted conflict in the region.

In the South Asian context, therefore, the economics perspective of the direction of causality that explains trade as a function of conflict defines our estimation framework. Theoretical aspects of the political science literature that help analyze and characterize the conflict-trade relationship in the South Asian context are included to make the analysis complete, holistic and theoretically rigorous. These are suitably incorporated through representative variables in the formal estimation framework. Apart from conflict, costs of other barriers to trade in the region are also included in the empirical analysis. These costs will help identify the relative contribution of each barrier in restricting trade in South Asia. The estimation of trade losses will be undertaken using the gravity model. Some earlier versions of gravity models that have accounted for bilateral political relations have done so through the use of binary dummy variables representative of membership/non-membership of institutional economic/political cooperation mechanisms.[23] However, membership of regional organizations may not necessarily be a reflection of the absence of conflict or hostilities among nations. South Asian countries that are all members of SAARC have at one or another time been in conflict with each other. A more comprehensive representation of conflict is incorporated in the formal econometric estimation analysis of the impact of conflict on trade in South Asia, as undertaken in the following chapter.

7 Impact of conflict on intra-regional trade in South Asia
A gravity model analysis

This chapter presents quantitative estimates of cost of conflict in terms of trade foregone for the South Asian economies. The estimation is undertaken using the gravity model as in Batra (2004), which has been further augmented with a set of conflict and policy variables within an overall trade-conflict theoretical and analytical framework as considered appropriate to the South Asian context. The theoretical origins of the gravity model are discussed below, followed by the specification of the estimable equation for empirical analysis with the description and rationale for inclusion of the dependent and various independent variables. The results of the estimation process are analyzed in the following section.

The gravity model[1]

The gravity equation is a simple empirical model for analyzing bilateral trade flows between geographical entities. The gravity model for trade is analogous to the Newtonian physics function that describes the force of gravity. The model explains the flow of trade between a pair of countries as being proportional to their economic 'mass' (national income) and inversely proportional to the distance between them. The model has a lineage that goes back to Tinbergen (1962) and Poyhonen (1963), who specified the gravity model equation as follows:

$$\text{Trade}_{ij} = \beta \frac{\text{GDP}_i . \text{GDP}_j}{\text{Distance}_{ij}} \quad (1)$$

Where Trade_{ij} is the value of the bilateral trade between country i and j, GDP_i and GDP_j are country i and j's respective national incomes. Distance_{ij} is a measure of the bilateral distance between the two countries, and β is a constant of proportionality.

Taking logarithms of the gravity model equation as in (1) we get the linear form of the model and the corresponding estimable equation as:

$$\text{Log}(\text{Trade}_{ij}) = \beta + \beta_1 \log(\text{GDP}_i . \text{GDP}_j) + \beta_2 \log(\text{distance}_{ij}) + u_{ij} \quad (2)$$

Where β, β_1 and β_2 are the estimable coefficients of the model. The error term captures any other shocks and chance events that may affect bilateral trade between the two countries.

Equation (2) is the core gravity model equation where bilateral trade is predicted to be a positive function of income and negative function of distance.

Theoretical foundations

While the core gravity equation has been used for empirical analysis since the econometric studies of trade by Tinbergen (1962) and Poyhonen (1963), the theoretical foundations of the model are of more recent origin. The most classic and early application of the model to international trade was perhaps by Linnemann (1966). Trade theorists have found the model to be consistent with theories of trade based upon models of imperfect competition and with the Hecksher-Ohlin model. Frankel (1997) credits Helpman and Krugman (1985) for the standard gravity model. The derivation of a proportionate relationship between trade flows and country size as given by Helpman does not include a role for distance. There are several reasons, though, for the inclusion of distance as an explanatory variable. When correlated with the costs of searching for trading opportunities and the establishment of trust between potential trading partners distance may be a proxy for transport costs and/or transaction costs. This is particularly true when greater geographical distance is correlated with larger cultural differences. Distance may also be representative of synchronization costs in case of factories that combine multiple inputs, the timing of which needs to be synchronized so as to prevent emergence of bottlenecks. In such cases synchronization costs would be higher for increasing distance as an indicator of the time elapsed during shipment, particularly for perishable goods in which case the probability of surviving intact is a decreasing function of time in transit. Cultural differences can impede trade in many ways such as inhibiting communication, bringing clashes in negotiating styles, and so on.

Bergstrand's (1985) version of the imperfect substitutes theory incorporated a role for shipping costs, proxied in practice by distance. More recently, Deardorff (1995) has derived the gravity model from Hecksher-Ohlin (H-O) theory. Deardorff shows that the gravity model can be derived from two extreme cases of the classical framework of the Hecksher-Ohlin model. The first case is frictionless trade, in which the absence of all impediments to trade in homogenous products causes producers and consumers to be indifferent among trading partners. Resolving this indifference, randomly expected trade flows correspond exactly to the simple frictionless gravity equation if preferences are identical and homothetic or if demands are uncorrelated with supply and they depart from that equation systematically when there are such correlations. The second case is that different countries produce distinct goods, as in the H-O model, with complete specialization. Expression for bilateral trade are derived, first with Cobb-Douglas preferences and then with CES preferences. Distance is included in the second of the two models.

Trade theories based upon imperfect competition and the Hecksher-Ohlin model justify the inclusion of the core variables – income and distance. Most studies have, however, included additional variables to control for differences in geographic factors, historical ties and, at times, economic factors like the overall trade policy and exchange rate risk. The particular theoretical model that best describes the empirical findings of the gravity model is a matter of contention. The main point, however, is that it seems possible to derive the gravity model equation from a variety of leading theories.

The gravity model of international trade has a remarkably consistent history of success as an empirical tool. The elasticities of trade with respect to both income and distance are consistently high, signed correctly and statistically significant in an equation that explains a reasonable proportion of the cross-country variation in trade. It is to be noted, however, that, in analyzing trade between country A and B, the gravity model makes no provision for third-party effects, that is, the model does not take into account the conditions and opportunities that prevail between A and C and B and C.

The gravity model specification

Dependent variable

The estimation of trade costs is undertaken with bilateral trade as the dependent variable. As discussed in the preceding chapters this is in accordance with the trade-conflict relationship evident in the South Asian context. The analysis has been undertaken in various stages. The basic formulation for estimation is the gravity model of bilateral trade with global coverage. This is followed by alternative sub-sample estimations and analyses.

Independent variables

Trade costs are estimated in two categories – *non-policy variables*, which include bilateral distance, geographical features, adjacency, contiguity/border, similarity in language, and colonial links, and *policy-related costs*, as defined by trade agreements, economic regimes, political regimes and costs that are induced by inter-state political conflict – *monadic*, that is, inter-state conflict between a trade partner and a third party, and *dyadic*, as between the trading pair. Alternative measures have been used to specify the conflict variable to get as detailed and nuanced a measure as possible of the cost of persistent conflict and consequent instability within the neighbourhood and/or region. As some domestic conflicts may have spillover implications on inter-state relations and hence bilateral trade, civil conflict for neighbouring/bordering countries has also been included in the estimation process. The independent variables thus incorporated in the model are described as follows.

NON-POLICY VARIABLES

GNP (Y): There are two standard ways of measuring the size of countries in the gravity model: GNP (output) or population. The focus is on GNP as a measure of size and self- sufficiency with an alternative test undertaken using population to ensure robustness.[2]

As regards GNP, the model is estimated using GNP in US dollars and also GNP in terms of purchasing power parity (PPP). The main assumption is that trade usually happens at international prices, and so GNP at PPP has no bearing on trade levels. At the same time, given the strong under-valuation of certain countries' GNP, importantly for India, it is tempting to estimate the model with GNP at PPP and observe if the corresponding coefficients change in any significant fashion.[3,4]

Distance: D is the distance between country i and country j measured 'as the crow flies' – technically called the great-circle distance measured between the two latitude-longitude combinations. A major proportion of trade today goes by air (and not by sea or land) and therefore the air routes provide the most convenient justification for using the straight-line or great-circle measure of distance. The ultimate justification is of course given by the fact that this measure seems to be a reasonable measure of averaging across different modes of transportation and works well in practice.

Contiguity: Contiguity is defined as a variable that takes account of both land and water contiguity While the former is defined as an intersection of the homeland territory of the two states in the dyad either through land boundary or water (river), the latter is based on whether a straight line of no more than a certain distance can be drawn between a point on the border of one state, across open water, uninterrupted by the territory of a third state, to the closest point on the homeland territory of the other state in the dyad.[5] Only the closest form of contiguity is recorded for each year. The variable is represented by a dummy variable that assumes a value of one for contiguous nations and zero otherwise.

Border: Apart from contiguity, we also include border as a variable in the estimable equation. The variable helps understand the impact of adjacency among country pairs. This variable is also in addition to the inclusion of the distance variable so as to account for the possibility of centre-to-centre distance overstating the effective distance between neighbouring countries that may often engage in large volumes of border trade.

In case of South Asia another additional aspect of border in terms of the associated territorial disputes holds relevance for estimation and analysis. As evident from the analysis on the nature of conflict in South Asia, shared borders are a cause for many territorial as well as related disputes and conflicts in the region. For this reason it has been observed that sharing borders has not necessarily been advantageous for South Asian countries, not just because some of the regional conflicts flow out of and because of a common border, border disputes, or territorial sovereignty, but because conflict prevents borders from facilitating trade in the region. In South Asia border trade routes have long been closed, heavily manned by armed forces or have simply fallen out of use, and terrain difficulties have not been worked upon to establish connectivity. Therefore, trade flows that could have been eased and encouraged across shared borders have on the contrary been restricted. The inclusion of border as an independent variable in addition to contiguity and distance thus allows for an understanding of its implications and dual connotation in the region.

Border or adjacency is defined as a dummy variable that is unity if countries i and j share a common border and 0 when they do not.

Number of border countries: nborder: A unique characteristic of South Asia is that India shares a border with all other countries of the region, while the reverse is not true. In fact India's centrality in the many territorial and other resource conflicts in the region is often on account of its common border with all other countries of the region. In order to account for this feature and the related aspect of conflict, we add another variable (in addition to border and contiguity) to the estimable equation that represents the number of neighbouring countries sharing a border with member countries in a trading pair. The variable is indicated by 'nborder'.

To capture the impact of geographical factors and historical ties between countries on bilateral trade, we include dummy variables. These are explained as follows:

- *Common language*: Langij: is equal to one when two countries share a common language (official or commercial). Common language is expected to reduce transaction costs, as speaking the same language helps facilitate trade negotiations.
- *Colonial links*: Shared history is expected to reduce transaction costs caused by cultural differences.
- *Comcol.:* is equal to one if i and j were colonies after 1945 with the same colonizer.
- *Col.:* is equal to one if i colonized j or vice versa.

Landlocked: number of landlocked countries in the pair
Island: number of countries in the pair that are islands

POLICY-RELATED VARIABLES

The conventional gravity model and estimable equation noticeably ignores the political context in which trade between any two economies takes place. The gravity model, as we estimate, includes political controls, as these are likely to influence conflict occurrence. These include the political regimes and their durability. The democratic peace hypothesis analyzed by both political scientists and economists (Levy and Razin, 2004) states that democratic countries are less prone to enter into a conflict and more inclined to trade. The variable is relevant in the South Asian case as democracy has not been the norm in all countries over the entire reference period. The democratic process has in fact been episodic in South Asia, except in case of India and Sri Lanka. The differential implications of this variable in the global and South Asia sample would therefore be revealing in this context.

Political regimes: Representative variables are included in terms of democracy and/or autocracy. The variables are indicated as an additive eleven-point scale (0–10) as defined in the Polity IV database (www.systemicpeace.org/polity/polity4.htm). Apart from country-specific political regime variable we have also included a country-pair specific polity variable in order to understand if similar political regimes, and consequently greater familiarity with political features of the trading partner, in any way facilitate trade among economies.

In particular the joint democracy variable has been formulated to test for the hypothesis that democracies trade more, which is the notion as derived from the Kantian philosophy. Joint democracy is indicated as a binary dummy variable, which is 1 if both countries in the pair have a polity score of 6 or more and 0 otherwise. Alternative formulation using the Li and Sacko (2002) version of the joint democracy variable – which is (Democracy$_{it}$ – Autocracy$_{it}$ + 10) * (Democracy$_{jt}$ – Autocracy$_{jt}$ + 10), where the variable is the product of the difference of the two countries' Polity IV democracy and autocracy scores plus 10, yielding a range from 0 to 400[6] – has been included to ensure more robust results. Further, given the South Asian context, estimation has also been undertaken for mixed regimes with one country in the trading pair being autocratic while the other is characterized by a democratic polity.

Economic regimes: As discussed in the preceding chapters it is only after 1991 that the South Asian countries made a transition from closed inward-looking economies to more open economies with due emphasis on the external sector. Trade policy orientation towards greater integration with the world market, which was undertaken through a major reduction in tariffs, quantitative restrictions and other import controls, was also evident for other developing countries and transition economies around this time. The period since 1990 has coincided with trade policy reform the world over. According to the World Bank World Development Indicators, the average tariff rate in the world went down from 10.5 per cent in 1990 to 6 per cent in 2002, and the openness index (exports plus imports to GDP) increased from 75.2 per cent to 86.8 per cent over the same period.[7] The share of developing countries exports as a share of world exports doubled over 1991–2009, while that of developed countries only rose by 50 per cent. Given the extent of change that was experienced in world trade and the South Asian economic regimes,[8] from inward to outward orientation, it is imperative that this period be separately analyzed for trade costs. We therefore estimate the conflict augmented gravity specification for pre- and post-1991 for the full sample as well as the South Asia sub-sample.

Regional trading arrangements: Countries often enter into regional trading agreements with the intention of availing both economic and non-economic gains. A priori it may be difficult to predict as regional trading agreements may have both trade-creating as well as trade-diverting implications for the participating nations. Taking this possibility into account we structure the RTA variable in a manner so as to get an understanding of the differential implications of the RTA. The dummy variable is equal to one when both countries in a given pair belong to the same regional group, and 0 otherwise. The estimated coefficient will then tell us how much of the trade can be attributed to a special regional effect. On average it has been found that RTAs impact positively on trade with a study by Rose (2000a, b)[9] indicating a tripling of trade between partners on account of membership of RTAs.

RTAs are also considered to have non-economic benefits in terms of promoting peace based on the theory of interdependence among member economies. The impact of RTA on trade through its peace-promoting characteristic and potential to restrict conflict is observed in our analysis through an interaction term between conflict and RTA.

The RTAs included in the estimation include AFTA, NAFTA, MERCOSUR and SAPTA.[10]

Conflict: Conflict has been represented in the estimable equation using alternative databases and alternative variables from within the same dataset. We use the conflict dataset that is the Major Episodes of Political Violence dataset (MEPV, Polity IV) from the University of Maryland's Centre for Systemic Peace (www.systemic peace.org). The data measures the systematic and sustained use of lethal violence by organized groups that result in 500 directly related deaths over the course of the episode. The use of violence is coded for time span and eleven-point scale of 0–10; magnitude scores are then assigned to one of seven categories of armed conflict – international violence, international war, international independence war, civil violence, civil war, ethnic violence, and ethnic war. Our analysis is focused to include data on major episodes of political violence that are inter-state in order to gauge its impact on bilateral trade.[11] It may also be noted that inter-state conflict need not be limited to dyadic conflicts that occur between the trade partners themselves but also inter-state conflicts that go beyond the dyads to include the inter-state conflict of the dyad members with third parties that may be equally likely to affect trade between two countries. The dataset also makes available a precise description of the number and magnitude of the extent to which bordering states are involved in interstate and/or civil political violence, aspects that are relevant to our analysis in the South Asian context, as conflict in the region is manifested at several levels across borders and among neighbouring countries with significant spill-over consequences.

The *dyadic* conflict is incorporated in the estimable equation using the militarized inter-state dispute (MID) dataset as from the Correlates of War (COW) project at the University of Michigan.[12] We use Maoz's Dyadic MID Dataset (version 2.0), a revised version of the COW dataset compiled by Jones, Bremer and Singer (1996). A MID is defined as an international interaction involving the threat, display and use of military force, or war. The dataset codes the level of hostility reached in a given country's conflict with an opposing state as threat of force, display of force, use of force and war. In our analysis we do not distinguish between the nature of conflict, and irrespective of the level of hostility define a binary dummy variable, which is 1 if there is a dispute and 0 if there is no dispute in the particular year. We include all conflicts irrespective of the level of hostilities as our aim is to analyze the impact of long-standing/persistent conflict and hostilities among countries that need not necessarily have manifested itself in a violent/war-like event at a point in time. However, even when using a broader definition reflecting the level of hostility as less than war, the MID data restrict the sample size making it difficult to obtain robust estimates. In order to maintain an appropriate sample size and considering the persistent and multi-dimensional nature of conflict in South Asia, MID is used together with the MEPV database, which is more detailed and therefore more suitable for South Asia-specific analysis. The two databases and conflict descriptions are used in alternative estimates to draw context-specific conclusions.

Trade is expected to be lower for two conflicting rival nations and positive for allies. This construct of the conflict-trade analysis finds support in the competing theoretical arguments that have been proposed by different schools of thought. The liberal approach based on traditional security concerns implies trade is directed away from adversaries and towards friendly nations, while the realist approach views the security externality of gains from trade being used to enhance national security as the guiding force in determining trade patterns. In the empirical analysis, however, different authors have arrived at varying conclusions on how militarized inter-state disputes or wars impact bilateral trade. Some have found the relationship to be negative in general, or only for some years, or for some dyads (Barbieri and Levy, 1999; Gowa and Mansfield, 1993), or that MIDs have no significant impact on trade (Morrow, Siverson and Tabares, 1998, 1999). The many variations in the empirical analysis often reflect the differential database, time periods and/or hostility levels. In our case the conflict interpretation is at several levels and in all its dimensions-bordering states, violent or otherwise, civil and inter-state, wars and MIDs. It would be revealing, therefore, to observe the differential impact of conflict on bilateral trade. The conflict variables as incorporated in the gravity model specification are described as follows.

Inttot: Total of the summed magnitudes of all interstate MEPV (international violence and warfare involving that state in that year). The variable is representative of *monadic* conflict in our analysis.

Totint: Sum of all interstate MEPV magnitude scores for all neighbouring states.

Totciv: Sum of all societal (civil and ethnic) MEPV magnitude scores for all neighbouring states.

Nciv: Numbering of bordering states with societal (civil and ethnic) MEPV.

MID: is a binary dummy variable that is 1 if the country is in a conflict in that year and 0 otherwise. The variables represent *dyadic* conflict in our analysis.

Anticipated conflict/persistent conflict (AC): As conflict in South Asia has been persistent and longstanding, the threat of a possible conflict/violent episode will enter into the profit calculations of individual agents at all times irrespective of its actual occurrence or translation into reality. As anticipation of conflict adds to the risk of an enterprise engaged in international commerce, it may be appropriate to include a variable that operationalizes expectations of conflict. All else equal, pairs of states with poor political relations are likely to have a higher level of threat than states with good bilateral relations. Morrow, Siverson and Tebares (1998, 1999) have argued that in cases of hostile or poor interstate relations the expected return on trade is negative and subject to a large element of risk leading to the traders' lack of participation in the market. Therefore, strategic rivalry, which is understood to be borne out of long-standing conflict or poor inter-state relations, is considered to be an appropriate proxy for anticipated inter-state conflict in our estimation process.

Thompson (2001) explains that strategic rivals states may be classified as such based upon selection criteria for rivals, as the actors regarding each other as competitors, enemies and a source of actual or latent militaristic threats to their own state and during a rivalry, 'both sides expect hostile behaviour from the other side'. Further, it is stated that strategic rivals are most likely to generate conflict. In the post-1945 era strategic rivals opposed one another in 91.3 per cent of the conflicts that meet the criteria of an inter-state war, according to the COW project.[13] Additionally, typically characteristic of the South Asian situation, Thompson (2001) describes rival states' conflict as not independent of time and part of a historical process in which a pair of states creates and sustains a relationship of atypical hostility for some period of time. Their relationship in the present is conditioned by what they have done to each other in the past. The interpretation of these intentions leads to expectations about the likelihood of conflicts and their escalation into physical attacks. In our estimable specification we therefore provide for anticipated conflict by specifying the variable indicating strategic rivals in a trading pair using Thompson's[14] dataset. Anticipated conflict is thus represented by a dummy variable that is coded as 1 if the states are involved in a strategic rivalry according to Thompson (2001) and 0 otherwise. The coefficient of the strategic rivalry/persistent conflict/expectations of conflict variable is expected to be negative.

While both civil (domestic) and inter-state conflict is considered to be equally likely to impact bilateral trade, expectations for private firms/trading agencies are considered possible to be formulated for inter-state conflicts rather than civil conflict. For the former, which are likely to be a fall-out/spill-over or a function of the prevailing/long-standing political relations between a pair of countries, private trading agents are more likely to have sufficient information to formulate expectations with reasonable accuracy, while for the latter the information may be with the partner state, confidential and may not be in public domain. The expectation of conflict is therefore understood with respect to dyadic inter-state conflict only.

A related and relevant proposition in the South Asian context, as discussed by Morrow, Siverson and Tebares (1999), is that if conflict is anticipated it may prevent trade from growing, rather than the realization of conflict leading to its disruption. In other words, owing to anticipated risk of conflict and consequent expected losses, the existing trade may be so small that an actual conflict event may not evidently impact trade, at least not in measurable terms. It may also be possible that conflict may impact trade in the years following the actual conflict. Li and Sacko (2002) have accordingly drawn a distinction for onset, duration and severity of conflict that may differentially influence firm behaviour and response towards partner-country firms, and new information thus revealed.

We make an attempt to understand these implications of unexpected/unanticipated conflict by using the estimated coefficients of our augmented gravity model to examine if the strategic rivals, that is, the countries with persistent conflict, are the countries with maximum gap between the actual and potential trade. If this holds true it would imply that expected conflict nullifies trade possibilities. We also undertake a cross-section gravity model estimate for the year 2000 for the South Asia sub-sample, that is, for the year immediately following the 1999 Kargil conflict, which was close to being a full-fledged war between India and Pakistan, but that was also unanticipated given the multi-faceted CBMs that immediately preceded the conflict event. Minimum trade disruption as evident from the gap between actual and potential would again be revealing in terms of persistent conflict, which is an underlying risk incorporated in the South Asian trader's profit function.

The basic gravity model as augmented to include non-policy variables, policy variables and conflict variable/s is thus represented as follows.

Conflict augmented gravity model

Log (T_{ij}) = α + $\beta 1$ log (Y_iY_j) + $\beta 2$log(D_{ij}) + $\beta 3$(Borderij/ Adjacency/ contiguity) + $\beta 4$(Langij) + + $\gamma 1$ (Comcol) + $\gamma 2$ (Col) + $\gamma 3$ (landlocked) + $\gamma 4$ (Island) + $\gamma 5$(**RTA**) + $\gamma 6$ **(political regime)** ++$\gamma 7$ **(durability of political regime)** $\gamma 8$ **(Conflict)** + $\gamma 9$ **(AC)** + U_{ij}

Where i and j denotes countries and Tij denotes the value of bilateral trade between i and j.

U_{ij} is a log-normally distributed error term and represents the myriad other influences on bilateral trade. E (lnU_{ij}) = 0.

The functional form of the gravity model is semi-logarithmic. The dependent variable and all the gravity model variables are log transformed, except the political, conflict and dummy variables. Log transformation of the variables is consistent with the functional form of the economic model that allows the estimates to be interpreted as elasticities.

Country sample/sub-samples

The gravity model has been estimated using a global sample with maximum possible coverage of global trade. In addition a smaller sample for South Asia has been constructed to get a more nuanced understanding of the region and its long-standing instability impacting economic exchange in the region. Further, a sub-period analysis has been undertaken for the full sample and South Asia subset to take note of the shift in *economic regimes* post-1991 when South Asia as a region as well as the developing world really opened up to the outside world with an accelerated pace of global trade integration. Further, given the significance of the India–Pakistan dyad in South Asia, an attempt is also made to undertake the estimation with the country sample defined for this one dyad only. Even though the sample is immensely constrained, we hope to derive some interesting observations from this estimation.

Reference time period

The reference time period for our estimation is 1965 to 2000. The starting and endpoints of the reference period coincide with two major conflicts between the most hostile dyad in South Asia – India and Pakistan. As indicated in our analysis of visual impressions in Chapter 5, regional conflict intensity replicates to a large extent the intensity of conflict between India and Pakistan. The reference period is appropriately representative of all the tension-ridden phases in South Asia – be it an outcome of the India–Pakistan conflict or among other bilateral pairs in South Asia. While it is desirable to extend the data backwards to 1947–48 when the first war between India and Pakistan took place, it is precluded by non-availability of data for most countries in the dataset. The end date of 2000 is closest to the end of one of the most tense periods in India–Pakistan relations. The estimation is undertaken with panel data at five-yearly intervals over the reference period, and by 2005, the next possible end point, India–Pakistan relations were well into a positive phase. Our reference time period allows for inclusion of the other major war/war-like conflicts between India and Pakistan, which are the India–Pakistan war in 1971 that was critical in terms of having led to the creation of a new country, Bangladesh being carved out of Pakistan, and the more recent conflict over Kashmir, in Kargil in 1999. Other major conflicts in the region are also well covered by this reference period. In the period after 2000 South Asia has not been witness to any major episode of inter-state political violence/conflict. When the MEPV database is analyzed it is observed that none of the South Asian countries are involved in any inter-state violence or war within or outside the region after 2000–01. According to the SIPRI (Stockholm International Peace Research Institute) database on armed conflict, 2001 onwards all conflicts are intra-state. In fact SIPRI database Yearbook consistently maintains India–Pakistan to be the only inter-state conflict and characterizes it as ongoing, a feature that is explicitly incorporated in our analysis through the strategic rivalry/anticipated conflict variable. The exception is Afghanistan, which is not part of South Asia as per our definition till 2007 when it became a member of SAARC. Further, the Afghan conflict, according to SIPRI Yearbook, is one that escapes a neat classification as 'inter'- or 'intra'-state. Additionally it may also be noteworthy that post-2001 the world focus has been on international security being re-defined by the new threat of global terrorism. The data on terrorism is more recent and in the nature of location-specific events/terrorist attacks. It is quite possible that the target locations in such attacks may not necessarily be the location of origin of conflict. We therefore restrict our analysis to upto 2000 only.[15] Additionally, economic regime change that began in 1990, while continuing its onward movement in the twenty-first century, is considered to show signs of 'reform fatigue' across the world by 2000.[16]

Estimation methodology

The estimation has been undertaken using a panel dataset over the reference period ranging from 1965 to 2000, with observations at five-year intervals and all country pair combinations as defined by available data on bilateral trade. The MID conflict variable is defined for dyads, and, as some conflicting dyads may not be trading with each other or trade may go unreported between such countries, the dataset is restricted by the conflict dataset. Specific bilateral events and/or decades of intense conflict are analyzed for their impact on trade through separate cross-section estimation, as, for example, for the year 2000. As discussed in detail in the last chapter and given the contextual realities of South Asia as well as the economics tradition, the estimation is undertaken for log trade as a dependent variable.

The direction of causality is not subjected to econometric confirmation. This is considered appropriate and in accordance with the regional context. While a separate analysis dedicated to determining the direction of causality may be worthy in cases where the research objective so requires, this is not the case in our analysis. The objective of our book, the economic perspective and the contextual reality of South Asia make it imperative for us to define the estimation framework with causality running from conflict to trade. Furthermore, with an annual dataset, as for our analysis, the granger causality test may not provide informative results given the short horizon profit calculations of traders. This has already been pointed out by Reuveny and Kang (1996). More importantly, considering that the results of such an analysis have been largely inconclusive, and even for the relatively more conclusive tests by Reuveny and Kang, cautionary notes are inserted to make these specific to dyad selection, conflict and trade level and the included time lag. We consider it best, therefore, to make this choice specific to context and objective.

The estimation is undertaken using panel data with OLS methodology. Several variants of the model are estimated so as to perform robustness and sensitivity checks for our analysis. The gravity model estimates with panel data have also been undertaken using country pair fixed effects (CPFE-within) only, as well as CPFE with time dummies.[17] Results are qualitatively similar across model variations.

Impact of conflict on intra-regional trade 127

Estimations using instrumental variables such as population for economic size have also been undertaken to correct for possibilities, if any, of income-trade endogeneity. No major variations in the results are noted, so the considered endogeneity does not cause any significant distortion of the originally postulated relationship in the gravity model.

The results of our estimation process are presented in Table 7.1.

Conflict augmented gravity model: estimation results[18]

The econometric results obtained from the above-specified augmented gravity model incorporating the economic, political and conflict variables are analyzed below.

The model fits the data well, explaining over 66 per cent of the variation in bilateral trade flows across our sample of countries. The baseline variables (GNP and distance) are very highly significant and of reasonable magnitude. The added control variables are economically and statistically significant with meaningful interpretations. All signs and coefficients of the basic gravity model are in accordance with our expectations. The higher the economic size of the two economies as measured by the GNP the greater the bilateral trade. The coefficient for GNP is positive, statistically highly significant but less than 1 (0.89) implying that bilateral trade increases with GNP but less than proportionately. Bilateral trade is negatively related to distance, so that the larger the distance between any two economies the lower their trade with each other. The coefficient for log distance is slightly more than 1, so that a unit increase in distance leads to more than proportionate decline in bilateral trade. Common language leads to a 58 per cent increase in bilateral trade. The coefficient for landlocked is negative as the geographical feature implying lack of ocean ports is such as to inhibit individual economies' abilities to trade. For our sample, landlockedness reduces trade by 50 per cent. The coefficient for island is positive but not statistically significant. Historical and colonial relationships lead to disproportionately high trade as coefficients for representative dummy variables are positive and highly significant.

Border/contiguity

Countries that are land or water contiguous are revealed to engage in more bilateral trade. Border and contiguity variables, alternatively used in the estimable equation, are observed to positively and very significantly impact bilateral trade. When border is replaced by contiguity that denotes a broader concept inclusive of land or water masses/bodies connecting two countries, the results remain the same with negligible differences in coefficient value and level of statistical significance.

Common border and conflict

To estimate the impact of conflict at the border we introduce an interactive term for border and conflict in the regression. The results show the coefficient for the interactive term to be negative (−0.90) and statistically highly significant, indicating that countries with a common land border that are also involved in conflict[19] suffer a 59 per cent loss in their bilateral trade.[20]

Conflict in neighbouring countries

We also consider the impact of societal conflict (civil and ethnic) in neighbouring states (totciv/nciv) on bilateral trade. Neighbouring states as defined by the MEPV database are states in immediate proximity and also those in general proximity (that is, in the 'politically relevant' regional system).[21] The coefficient of the variable for neighbourhood societal conflict is negative and significant, implying that civil or ethnic conflict in either of the partner countries or in both countries' neighbourhood may have a negative impact on bilateral trade for the dyad under reference. This is further reinforced when we control for the number of bordering/ neighbouring states in our model. Again the coefficient appears with a negative sign and is also statistically significant. The possible interpretation could be in terms of neighbourhood conflict leading to a general regional instability or spill-over effects such that trading abilities would be impinged upon with negative consequences. The observation would certainly support the low intra-regional trade in South Asia, where almost all the regional economies are involved in some civilian conflict or other, which have cross-border implications. Interestingly though, and again in character with South Asia, our results show the variable representing the number of bordering states (nborder) with a positive sign. The higher the number of states, therefore, with which any country shares borders, the greater, naturally, the ability to trade. However, if borders are under conflict or if neighbours are in conflict the positive effect of common borders may very well be negated!

Truly reflecting this result is the case of South Asia, in which case the positive impact of common borders with the most dynamic economy is more than offset by conflicts involving the border. The trade facilitating borders are converted into trade-restricting barriers owing to disputed boundaries in the region!

Political regimes

Our regression results support the proposition that democratic regimes trade more. Joint democracy leads to almost 25 per cent additional trade between countries. To test if more trade is true for all same-regime pairs, irrespective of the regime type, we test the obverse by including the dyads where both members are autocracies/predominantly with autocracy characteristics. Our results reveal that when both reporter and partner countries are specified such that they have autocracy characteristics, bilateral trade is adversely impacted. The coefficient for political regimes in this case is negative and significant, with the impact on trade amounting to a loss of 26 per cent. It is interesting to note that joint democracies and autocracies exert an equal but opposite force on bilateral trade. It may only be natural for the impact of similar political systems to be positive for democracies than other forms of political regimes, as democracies are characterized by more open and transparent polities and fair judicial systems,[22] which would in turn contribute to lower risk of trading. Open polities are also likely to make protectionist policies more visible and subject to opposition by affected commercial lobbies, thereby restricting the scope for the protectionist element in trade policy. Interestingly, incorporating political regimes thus also presents an alternative means to test for trade barriers that may be an outcome of institutional characteristics of prevailing political regimes in a country.

Further, the more durable a political regime, the higher the trade for the country pair. Durability[23] of a political regime has positive implications for trade. The longer a regime lasts, the greater the element of stability and therefore credibility in the political institutions as well as policies and economic framework governing trade and economic exchange, thereby reducing the element of risk in trade transactions.

Conflict

MONADIC CONFLICT (INTTOT)

The coefficient of the variable indicative of third-party effects, that is, the total of inter-state warfare and violence with a third party that either state or both states are involved in outside of the dyad, is positive and significant. This implies that the greater the country's conflict with the rest of the world, the greater the tendency to trade within the dyad – that is, the greater the bilateral trade among the dyadic pair. The impact of conflict with the outside world is in terms of 5–10 per cent additional bilateral trade. Quite naturally, involvement in international wars/violence is likely to limit the trade possibilities with the outside world to fewer countries. The corollary of this result, in a way, substantiates the notion that multi-lateralization or multiple trade partners reduce the incentive for making peace bilaterally. Alternative trading partners lower the emphasis on bilateral trade, thereby allowing the predominant play of bilateral political relations.

DYADIC CONFLICT

The MID variable, which is indicative of the dyadic conflict, is negative and significant and implies a cost in terms of 68 per cent loss in bilateral trade.

Anticipated conflict/persistent conflict

The coefficient for strategic rivalry-based anticipated conflict variable that is incorporated in the estimable regression is as per a priori expectations, negative and significant, with a value of the coefficient indicating a cost of 65 per cent in terms of bilateral trade. However, strategic rivals are not necessarily revealed to have the maximum gap between potential and actual trade levels. Interestingly, among strategic rivals the maximum gap between actual and potential levels of trade is for the India–Pakistan dyad over the reference years of 1995 and 2000.

The potential trade is close to 14 and 11 times the actual trade for the India–Pakistan dyad in 1995 and 2000 respectively.[24]

Regional trading arrangements

The RTA effect varies across different regions. The net effect of reporter-partner membership is positive and significant for both AFTA and MERCOSUR, negative and significant for SAPTA, and negative but not significant for NAFTA. The South Asian RTA is not trade-creating. An extension of the RTA specification for South Asia to beyond SAPTA years yields the same result, indicating the negligible trade-creating effects of a trade agreement for the region. The variable that accounts for conflict and RTA membership may shed better light on this aspect.

Strategic rivals and RTA membership

Estimation for two interaction terms, one between the RTAs and conflict, and two between RTAs and anticipated conflict (strategic rivals), are also undertaken only for South Asia. The coefficient of the interaction terms is negative and highly significant in both cases. An implication of the estimation that is thus clear is that the South Asian RTA has not been trade-creating, and when reporter and partner are both RTA members and are involved in conflict and/or long-standing rivalries, the impact on trade is negative and significant. Conflict and its anticipation further amplifies the negative impact of a regional trading arrangement in South Asia. The highest cost to the trading arrangement occurs when the members are strategic rivals – that is, are in persistent conflict. In other words, when conflict is a constant or countries make an attempt to establish trading arrangements in a conflictual atmosphere with an underlying expectation of conflict, the outcome of a FTA is close to null.

Sub-period analysis: economic regimes

As discussed, a sub-period estimation is undertaken to analyze the implications of a shift of economic regime, as evident through greater economic openness and trade liberalization undertaken around 1991, particularly by developing countries and transition economies. South Asia specifically started its economic liberalization programme in 1991. Our estimation results reveal that in the two economic regimes the traditional gravity model variables do not undergo a change in sign or significance. The magnitudes of the variables are in close proximity to each other in both the sub-periods. The conflict variables, however, show clear and significant distinctions. The coefficient of the anticipated conflict variable that we represent by strategic rivalry, although negatively signed, is not significant in the more recent period relative to its high significance levels in the earlier regimes. One obvious explanation for this result could be the decline in the number of strategic rivalries in this period. Out of a total of 174 strategic rivalries in the entire period, less than a third, only 40, are sustained post-1990 (Thompson, 2001). Interestingly, India–Pakistan is one of the strategic rivalries that have persisted even after 1990. The dyadic conflict variable MID is negative and highly significant in the first period and remains so in the liberalized economic regime period as well, but with its significance reduced again, apparently because of reduced episodes of bilateral war and armed conflict in this period. The monadic conflict variable, which is the dyad member's involvement in international warfare and violence with third parties, continues to positively impact bilateral trade with little change in magnitude and significance, and the neighbourhood civil conflict continues to negatively impact on bilateral trade in the first sub-period. In the second sub-period – that is, after economic liberalization – the signs on these variables are reversed, with monadic conflict being insignificant and civil conflict becoming significant and positive in its impact on bilateral trade. This may probably be on account of an increase in the magnitude of civilian conflict relative to international warfare in the latter period around the world and in the nature of its greater spill-over effects to international participation, as is true of Afghanistan. In that context civilian conflict, which replaces international warfare/violence participation, may reduce trade partners, making bilateral trade more significant. The negative impact of countries that share a border and are in conflict, which is significant in the pre-liberalized economic regime, becomes insignificant in the period after economic liberalization is undertaken.[25]

Our results and analysis show a declining impact and significance of international monadic conflict, dyadic and border conflict on bilateral trade in the period after 1990. This is also a period when international conflicts and enduring rivalries are observed to have registered a decline at the global level, supporting our initial choice of direction of causality and hypothesis of prior peace that ensures successful trade expansion. This is reflected and reaffirmed by our results on the strategic rivals variable, implying that expectations of conflict becoming redundant precedes/ coincides with more liberalized global trade regimes. However, one enduring rivalry among the few that remain in the world is between India and Pakistan. To test the significance of this continuing conflict we estimate a separate model for South Asia and the India–Pakistan dyad.

South Asian model[26]

The results of the South Asian model are interestingly different from the full sample. The basic gravity model variables remain loyal to the a priori expectations and the model provides a good fit with almost 70 per cent explanatory power. The model provides the most interesting revelation in terms of border, which has a negatively signed and statistically significant coefficient. A common border acts more as a barrier than facilitator for trade in South Asia. The many conflicts that revolve around the border in the region are presumably at the base of such behaviour of the border variable in the gravity model. Our estimates show that a common border in South Asia implies costs to the extent of a 52 per cent loss in bilateral trade. The negative impact of conflict is further confirmed when estimation is undertaken by addition of explicit conflict variables in the regression. Thus on netting out the impact of conflict, the border variable acquires a positive coefficient of negligible significance. Quite obviously, South Asia needs to seriously take up conflict resolution and trade facilitation at its borders. Among the conflict variables, anticipated conflict implies maximum costs to total trade, to the extent of a 90 per cent loss of trade, and actual militarized disputes have meant a 75 per cent loss in bilateral trade. It is imperative that while announcing positive trade measures the one enduring strategic rivalry in the region works on a more holistic approach to redefining their relationship from antagonism to friendship. It may also be noted that for South Asia the joint democracy variable was replaced by the variable indicating 'mixed regimes', as that better characterizes the polity of South Asia. The coefficient of the variable is negatively signed and modestly significant. A combination of political regimes, which have been the predominant political structures in South Asian countries, has not been a positive factor in promoting trade for the regional economies. An attempt is also made to undertake estimation for the sub-samples to observe the differential impact of economic regimes and the year 2000 to take note of the unanticipated conflict event, as indicated in the methodology section. While the broad scenario remains close to the full sample results, the MID is only marginally significant in the year 2000 and anticipated conflict consistently remains as the most significant negative influence on trade. Clearly the element of anticipated conflict is overpowering in South Asia, and in the tradition of Barbieri and Levy (1999) actual MID/conflict event makes an insignificant dent on economic activity of trade in the region. The RTA membership is consistently negative in the full and sub-sample estimates.

India–Pakistan

A sub sample analysis of the India–Pakistan dyad is undertaken to analyze the impact of the most enduring conflicts on trade for these two economies. Reconfirming our earlier impressions from the visual analysis in Chapter 5, the regional South Asian scenario on trade and conflict appears to echo the India–Pakistan dyadic behaviour. In this case too, the simple gravity model formulation, without the conflict representation, reveals a common border as significantly negatively related to trade. The cost of a common border is to the extent of a 58 per cent loss of trade, presumably on account of the border conflicts that have defined the India–Pakistan relationship. In the model formulation with these conflict representative variables incorporated – that is, on netting out the effects of both anticipated conflict and bilateral MIDs – a common border has a positive effect, but statistically the coefficient is insignificant. Further, anticipated conflict continues to have the most overpowering effect on trade, followed by actual MIDs. While anticipation of conflict leads to a 93 per cent loss of trade, actual MIDs imply a cost of a 76 per cent loss of trade. Political regimes, joint democracy or mixed regime representations remains an insignificant variable and the regional trade agreement appears with a negative and significant coefficient. Monadic conflict in terms of involvement in international warfare with third parties is also an insignificant variable. In this case the conclusion holds relevance as the MEPV database for more recent years reveals only Afghanistan among South Asian countries to be among any instances of any country's involvement in international warfare.[27] Prior to 2000, through 1965 into the 1990s, the database shows India and/or Pakistan to be involved in international violence/warfare among the small set of countries in the world so involved. For India and Pakistan involvement in international violence is apparently with each other and may therefore be the reason for the insignificant impact of the variable on bilateral trade.

Table 7.1 Conflict augmented gravity model: estimation results

Variables/Model	I	II	III	IV	V	VI	VII	VIII
GDP	0.89				0.89, 1.05	1.03	0.86	0.83
Distance	−1.29				−1.19, −1.27	−1.44	−1.52	−1.6
language	0.46				−0.14, 0.33	0.38	0.30	0.18
Island	0.108				0.14, 0.20	0.19	0.35	
Landlocked	−0.703				−0.45, −0.41	−0.28	−0.93	−0.48
Comcol	0.86				0.73, 0.87	0.87	0.89	1.13
Colonizer	0.98				2.01, 1.04	1.3	1.33	1.5
Comctry	1.355				2.11	2.15		
Contiguity	1.18				0.70, 0.47	1.09		
Border	(1.04)						0.47 (−0.53)	0.46, (−0.64)
RTA	−2.91	−0.40			−0.33	−3.83	−0.40	−0.68
RTAconf				−2.18				
AC	−1.04	−0.11		−0.52	−0.50, −0.41	−1.6	−2.22	−2.56
MID	−1.12				−1.25, −0.31	−0.91	−1.33	−1.44
ACRTA				−3.66				
Inttot1, Intott2	0.05, 0.09				0.006, 0.03; −0.02, 0.01			
Nborder	0.08							
Borderconf			−0.90		−1.5, −0.29			
Nciv1, Nciv2	−0.10, −0.11							
Totciv1, Totciv2	−0.03, −0.005				−0.06, −0.06; 0.04, 0.006			
Polity	0.22(JD); −0.30(JA)				0.63, 0.21	0.13 (JD)	−0.09 (MR)	
Durable1	0.004				0.006, 0.001	0.004	0.001	0.003*
Durable2	0.004				0.007, 0.0004	0.002	0.004	0.354*
Adj. R²	0.66				0.62, 0.73	0.69	0.69	0.71

Notes: Border coefficient within parentheses before netting out for conflict; MR: mixed political regimes; all coefficients except * are statistically insignificant; JD: joint democracy; JA: Joint autocracy; RTA coefficients are reported only for South Asia RTA; Civilian conflict variables-have been alternatively estimated; Relevant coefficients are presented for specific models.

Key:
II: Inclusion of interaction term for border and conflict
III: Strategic rivalry and membership of RTA, reported for SAPTA only
IV: Conflict and membership of RTA, reported for SAPTA only
V: With distinction in economic regimes, 1990 followed by post-1991 period coefficients
VI: Country pair fixed effects (within) and time dummies (coefficients not reported)
VII: South Asia sub-sample
VIII: India–Pakistan sub-sample

Irrespective of the country sample that we consider for estimation and analysis the implication of conflict in negating the positive benefits of geographical proximity attributable to shared boundaries and common borders is unmistakable. A conclusion that we can therefore draw from our analysis is that states that are involved in long-drawn border/boundary disputes are most likely to be adversely impacted in terms of their bilateral trade relationships, which is reflected not just in terms of higher transaction costs and lower-than-potential levels of trade, but also and quite significantly in terms of their inability to formulate or effectively implement preferential trading arrangements between themselves. Given that India and Pakistan in South Asia have and continue to be bogged down by this phenomenon, it is not surprising to have seen low and stagnant levels of intra-regional trade and the regional agreements performing below par in South Asia.

8 Summary findings and an assessment of the way forward

This concluding chapter proceeds in two sections. The first section deals with a summary presentation of the key findings of our analysis with regard to the trade-conflict relationship. The explicit consideration of conflict as a variable that influences or, more appropriately, chokes the process of economic integration in South Asia brings forth many significant revelations on how persistent hostilities can make ineffective the most positive attribute of a region with regard to its potential and abilities for economic exchange. We elaborate on each of the outcomes of our analysis in the first section. The second part discusses specific initiatives that, in the light of our findings, are considered imperative to take the idea of economic integration forward in South Asia. Lessons as available from comparative contexts of economic integration initiatives in other regions are also included so as to facilitate policy shaping in these critical areas.

Summary findings

That South Asia is unique in its experience of regional economic integration is a notion, a priori, with whichthis book was initiated. The analysis of the regional profile, trends in trade and investment and nature and implementation of preferential trading agreements provide evidence towards the fact that South Asia, a perfect fit for regionalism as theoretically defined, has been unable to translate this inherent advantage to achieving economic integration in the region.

South Asia's growth patterns have been among the most dynamic in the world, both pre- and post-global financial crisis. India, with an 8 per cent rate of economic growth in 2010, has been among the first few economies in the world to have regained their positive, pre-crisis levels of growth. In fact South Asia as a region was among the least impacted by the global financial crisis, as in 2009 it registered growth at 8 per cent, which was higher than its pre-crisis levels and well above the rate for 2008, the year of the crisis. The rate of growth for South Asia in 2009 was the highest among all regions in the world as the other regions recorded negative or very low rates of growth. Even prior to the crisis, in 2008, the average rate of growth in South Asia was comparable with the maximum registered by other regions. Commendable as this trend is, it has had only limited, if any, significance for the progress of economic integration in South Asia, which was and continues to be the least-integrated region in the world. Given that all the South Asian economies, starting in the 1990s, made a successful transition from inward-looking to outward-oriented economies with respect to their growth strategies, there has been very little evidence of the growth dynamism and open economy orientation having combined to take forward the idea or process of economic integration in South Asia.

Among other reasons that are made prominent by our analysis, one point of concern that is apparent from the manner in which trade liberalization has been undertaken in these economies is the co-existence of opposing forces of increasing openness and continued restrictiveness. This contradiction is even more apparent in the context of the region when trends for trade are analyzed. The openness index that measures the trade-to-GDP ratio has doubled since the initiation of economic reforms in 1991, reflecting a pace of trade integration that is the highest among all regions in the world. Yet, the value of the index is lower than its value for other regions. The rapid pace of global trade integration is, however, also accompanied by a restrictiveness that is observed in the trade policy of the region's economies. In the most obvious form it can be seen in the region's MFN trade tariff structure, which is more restrictive than the average in comparator low- and lower-middle-income country groups. The South Asian region maintains a high potential for protectionism and policy manoeuvrability through the gap between bound and applied tariff rates, overall and in specific commodity groups like the agricultural products. While this may account for the region's growing, though as yet small, contribution to global trade, the constancy of intra-regional trade appears to have its rationale embedded elsewhere.

The regional trade trends show an expansion of South Asia's trade with the developing 'South' as also developing Asia. However, the latter does not encompass developing South Asia in its fold. The increasing movement away of the South Asian economies from their traditional markets in the west to developing countries has been in terms of expanding trade with South East Asian and East Asian economies that in turn is predominantly a reflection of India's increasing trade with China. Trade among South Asian economies has been disappointingly stagnant at around 5 per cent of their total trade for successive decades. Within the South Asian region our analysis has shown that India is the largest exporter though not the largest importer for other regional economies. India figures among the top ten trade partners for the other South Asian economies, though none of the other economies appear in a similar position among India's trade partners. India has trade agreements with three South Asian economies – Sri Lanka, Bhutan and Nepal – and is negotiating a free trade agreement with Bangladesh. The only other bilateral agreement in South Asia is between Pakistan and Sri Lanka, with far less success to its credit in terms of expansion in bilateral trade and diversification in composition relative to that between India and Sri Lanka. India's geographical omnipresence in South Asia, through a common border with all other South Asian economies, thus spills over to the economic sphere as well. Also, the geographical asymmetry is replicated in the economic asymmetry of the region. The balance of its bilateral trade with all the South Asian economies is in favour of India, with the exception of Bhutan.

Summary findings and way forward 137

The implications of this economic asymmetry and omnipresence have not been positive for South Asian economic integration. The smaller economies in the region have constantly been in fear of being flooded by Indian goods that would feed into larger bilateral deficits with India, if concessional access was to be provided through the tariff liberalization programmes of regional FTAs. Notwithstanding the success of the non-reciprocal India–Sri Lanka bilateral FTA, therefore, the extent of coverage of traded goods in regional FTAs, SAPTA or SAFTA, have been small, resulting thereby in large-sized negative lists (or a small positive list!) that has rendered the FTAs meaningless. Even though the year 2010 has seen positive growth in exports from and imports by India from the SAARC region, apparently as South Asia and India are substituting for the traditional western markets that have yet to completely recover from the global financial crisis, it has come after successive declines since 2005 and negative growth rates for 2008 and 2009. The previous two years' trends are surprising as during this time India has announced giving special and favourable treatment on a non-reciprocal basis to least-developed countries of SAARC – that is, Bhutan, Bangladesh, Maldives, Afghanistan and Nepal – removed import tariffs on over 4,800 products from the four neighbouring countries on January 1, 2008, and in April 2008 announced an offer of preferential market access to all least-developed countries of the region. Trust in the larger economy obviously doesn't come easily to the smaller economies of the region.

Importantly, this period has also seen the implementation of the SAFTA agreement that was initiated with the objective of establishing a FTA in South Asia in 2006. Six years into the FTA, the region has almost no developments to list as achievements in this direction. On the contrary it is still struggling to set right the many design and implementation flaws in the FTA. The biggest challenge that SAFTA has faced in this time period until recently has been the consistent defiance of Pakistan of the SAFTA provisions of specifying a negative list. Pakistan has followed a positive-list approach to the implementation of the Agreement vis-à-vis India, even though it has been with the other six participants (seven with Afghanistan's entry into SAARC in 2007) a signatory to the Agreement as initially formulated. Pakistan's violation of the Agreement has deeper roots in the history of the region. Persistent conflict between this pair appears to be at the core of the unexpectedly anaemic performance of South Asia with respect to its regional FTAs. Even the earlier SAPTA agreement had to be suspended on account of high-intensity hostilities between India and Pakistan. Given that two regional FTA initiatives have thus been held hostage by the hostilities between India and Pakistan, with the other South Asian economies also being politically motivated to keep preferences to a minimum, provides justification to formulate the framework of our formal econometric estimation in terms of the impact of conflict on trade.

Our analysis of the conflict-trade relationship has been undertaken in three stages. Starting with a narrative of the history of conflict and confidence-building measures (CBMs) in South Asia, we draw a few initial observations to ascertain the structure of our estimable equation and country sub-samples, supported as they are by theoretical and contextual realities of the region. It is well known that South Asia has been plagued by conflict since independence. The nature of conflict and its intensity has varied over time. India has been central to the conflict history of South Asia. However, we observe that the bilateral conflict history as it relates to the bilateral economic relationship varies across country pairs in the region. Conflict is persistent and overriding in the relationship between India and Pakistan. There are periods where the number and nature of CBMs by the two economies can only be marvelled at, stretching as they do from no-war pacts to non-interference in bilateral affairs to regular communication through establishment of military and heads of state hotlines. There have been many economic CBMs between the two nations too, with the promise of granting most favoured nation (MFN) status to India coming twice from Pakistan without ultimately seeing the light of day on either occasions. Most often during the periods of CBM bonhomie or immediately after, the pair has also experienced some of their most intense conflicts. This has been evident in the successive decades of the 1980s and 1990s, most notably in the Kargil conflict in 1999. The CBMs have invariably amounted to little in terms of changing the core of the relationship that continues to be defined by hostile attitudes. Our graphical analysis confirms the political predominance over economics in this relationship. A graphical plot of trade and conflict intensity over time leaves us in no doubt that for India and Pakistan, trade indeed follows the flag! Business or trade has not been the lead actor in this relationship and instead every time there is a peak in the intensity of conflict, whether or not this is marked by a violent episode, there has been a dip in bilateral trade, which is otherwise very low given the economic performance of the two countries. This has not necessarily been true of the other bilateral relationships in South Asia, also identified as they are with reference to India given the conflict framework as evident in the region. With Nepal, Bangladesh or Sri Lanka trade has followed its own course quite independent of the political relationship with India. The peaks and troughs observed for bilateral trade are consonant in these cases with friendly or not-so-friendly terms and changes therein of the bilateral trade treaties. This is true of Nepal and Sri Lanka. In the case of Sri Lanka, in fact, the signing of the bilateral FTA eased off the tensions caused by India's alleged involvement in the smaller economy's domestic civil strife. Bangladesh has been a variant with the ruling party defining both the political and economic relations. However, as our analysis reveals, it is the India–Pakistan relationship that defines the South Asian region. The intensity of conflict for the region at any point in time replicates the intensity of conflict between India and Pakistan. The other relationships have little reflection on regional stability. The character of the India–Pakistan relationship, marked as it is by persistent conflict, defines our analytical and estimable framework. We elaborate on this below.

We estimate the trade-conflict relationship in South Asia using a conflict augmented gravity model. The objective is that in a region where trade has been stagnant for long and it is hard to find a theoretically sound economic argument to justify this trend, political variables need to be recognized as probably the crucial actors. The precept becomes important in the context of the region actually defying the economic argument wherein it is predicted that preferential trade agreements with geographically proximate countries are potentially more trade-creating and

Summary findings and way forward 139

less trade-diverting. Unfortunately South Asia, which abounds in not just geographical proximity but also historical and cultural proximity, has revealed no such inclinations. The political contours of the region therefore need to be factored in the estimation process to get an understanding of low intra-regional trade. The outcome, it is hoped, will in turn help formulate policy to correct the anti-home bias that is evident in trade patterns of the South Asian region. For this purpose we extend the gravity model as normally formulated in economic analysis with bilateral trade as a function of distance, cultural and historical proximity, membership of a regional trading agreement by including representative variables for political influences, and conflict with its multiple dimensions.

From our analysis of South Asia and the nature of conflict, which has prevailed in the region, our additional variables take into account the political framework within which the predominant bilateral relationship has allowed its economics to operate. The gravity model that we use for estimation includes representative variables to study the impact of conflict as it has played itself out, multi-dimensionally in the region, on trade. This is achieved by including monadic and dyadic conflict in the estimation process. That is, we not only make provision for conflict between the trading pair, but also for violence or warfare that individual countries in a trading pair maybe involved in with third countries, as has been the case in Afghanistan. Further, for comparative and inclusive analysis we consider civil conflict in the model as there is always a possibility of it acquiring international dimensions through interstate spillover effects. This has been amply reflected in South Asia where, between India and Pakistan, India and Sri Lanka or India and Bangladesh, secessionist movements have crossed over to find support across borders, leading to the extension and sometimes transformation of intra-state conflicts to inter-state conflicts. Finally, apart from conflict events, violence, warfare and militarized interstate disputes, we also include the expectation of conflict as a distinct and separate variable in our analysis. The expected conflict or anticipated conflict is defining for the South Asian region. Given that India–Pakistan conflict dominates the South Asian conflict landscape it is important to incorporate anticipated conflict in our model. Theoretically it is proposed and well accepted that while actual conflict definitely endangers trade transactions, expectation of conflict also increases the element of risk in the transaction undertaken with a conflict-prone region or country, as it may lead to higher transaction costs through increased possibilities of currency instability, breach of contract, low institutional credibility, increased government restrictions (e.g., through tariffs and non-tariff barriers), and thus reduce the scope for profitable trade. Where firms anticipate conflict owing to a state's violent relations with its neighbours there will be ex ante reduction in trade because economic actors factor in the risks of a political conflict, existing and future, and make their profit calculations accordingly. In such situations traders are likely to undertake transactions much lower in number than they would if peace was the norm between two countries. We try and estimate this effect using strategic rivalry as indicative of long-standing and therefore expected conflict to assess both the cost of anticipated conflict over and above that due to the actual conflict episode and to examine if the gap between actual and potential trade is at maximum for economies that have for long been in such conflictual relationships. In a further effort to draw upon the South Asian context we also include a variable for number of bordering states and their conflict involvement in our estimable framework.

In addition, we also estimate the impact, if any, of political regimes on trade, again to examine if the democratic peace theory holds true for South Asia. The results are relevant as South Asia, other than India and Sri Lanka, has yet to see its member economies experience durable democratic regimes. Finally, the novelty of our estimation process extends to the inclusion of economic as well as political regimes as a determining factor in the bilateral trade analysis. Given that the developing world and South Asia in particular has opened up to global trade and market largely in the 1990s, we consider it relevant to analyze the differential behaviour of the variables in the more open period. Apart from economic regimes, we have also undertaken separate sub-sample analysis of the South Asian region and individually for the India–Pakistan dyad. Overall the trade-conflict estimation in the gravity model framework has been undertaken for the global sample and for the period 1965–2000, which is inclusive of the major conflicts in South Asia and precedes the global change in security perceptions as an outcome of the 9/11 terrorist attacks in the US. The post-2001 period is also marked by a relative decline in the enthusiasm and pace of economic reforms as well as the number of inter-state conflict episodes around the world. South Asia itself has shown reluctance to implement 'the second generation' of economic reforms in the twenty-first century, even while the earlier reforms continue. Also post-2003, interruptions notwithstanding, the region has seen India and Pakistan enter into a relatively peaceful period with some new economic initiatives. The period of reference therefore holds relevance for our analysis. Our estimation, we hope, will be the basis of the policymakers' collective effort at preventing a reversion to high-intensity conflict in the region.

The estimation has been undertaken using a panel dataset. The direction of causality from conflict to trade is considered appropriate with reference to the South Asian contextual reality. Econometric robustness has been ensured by using alternative methodologies and variables. Our results are most enlightening.

Overall the gravity model performs satisfactorily with a reasonably good power of fit. In the global and in all sub-samples the traditional gravity model variables are in accordance with a priori expectations. Trade is positively related to GDP and negatively related to distance. The impact of a unit increase in the former implies a less-than-proportional increase in trade and more-than-proportional decline in trade for the latter. Further, in the global sample, the impact of adjacency represented by border or the broader concept of contiguity is more than proportionately positive for bilateral trade. However, countries that share a border and are also involved in bilateral conflict suffer a loss of 59 per cent of trade. Neighbourhood conflict in general leads to regional instability such that civil or ethnic conflict in either of the partner countries or in both countries' neighbourhood may have a negative impact on bilateral trade. Our results for the global sample also show that joint democracies and autocracies exert an equal but opposite force on bilateral trade. While the democratic peace theory provides one explanation for this result, the more economic argument is presented in terms of the open democratic polity, implying lower risk and thereby transaction costs owing to greater transparency of policy and institutions that would also restrict the scope for trade barriers and increase the probability of opposition from affected parties in such a case.

Regarding the variable of core interest to us, quite naturally the involvement in international wars/violence is likely to limit the trade possibilities with the outside world to fewer countries and hence increase bilateral trade. Alternatively, multi-lateralization, which allows for multiple trading partners, lowers the emphasis on bilateral trade thereby allowing the predominant play of bilateral political relations thereby reducing the incentive for making peace bilaterally. However, if relations outside the dyad are conflictual the dependence on dyadic trade would be that much greater. Our model estimates for the global sample show this effect to be of the magnitude of 10 per cent additional trade. Understandably, dyadic conflict has a negative and significant impact on trade such that it has a cost in terms of 68 per cent loss in bilateral trade. In addition, if conflict has been persistent and a pair of countries is in a relationship of strategic rivalry, the costs are higher. Anticipated conflict in these cases implies a cost of 65 per cent in terms of loss of bilateral trade. In the global sample strategic rivals are not necessarily revealed to have the maximum gap between potential and actual trade levels. Interestingly, though, and of relevance to the South Asian context is the noteworthy result that among strategic rivals the maximum gap between actual and potential levels of trade is for the India–Pakistan dyad over the reference years of 1995 and 2000, a period of heightened tensions that culminated in a war-like conflict in 1999 over the longest-standing territorial dispute over Kashmir between the two countries. Our result also reveals that the positive effect of a common border on bilateral trade is magnified as the number of states with which the border is shared increases, but the same effect is negated if the countries sharing a border are also in conflict. The result appears to reflect the South Asian scenario. Conflict and its anticipation also amplify the negative impact of a regional trading arrangement in South Asia. The highest cost to the trading arrangement occurs when the members are strategic rivals. In other words, when conflict is a constant or countries make an attempt to establish trading arrangements in a conflictual atmosphere with an underlying expectation of conflict, the outcome of a FTA is close to null.

The shift in economic regimes impacts the conflict variables such that anticipated conflict becomes less significant a variable in trade transactions relative to its value in the pre-liberalization phase. To some extent this is accounted for by a prior dilution of rivalries that is evident from the reduced number of strategic rivalries to a third of its number in the pre-1990 period. Interestingly India–Pakistan is among the most enduring pairs of strategic rivalries in the world. Dyadic conflict, though, continues to be significant in both the periods; it is less so in the liberalized economic regime, again apparently because of reduced episodes of bilateral war and armed conflict in this period. It has been well documented[1] that the number of episodes of armed and violent conflicts have been on a decline in recent decades and civil conflict is on the increase. Probably on that account the neighbourhood civil conflict positively impacts upon bilateral trade in the post-liberalization phase and in a significant manner relative to its impact in the pre-1990 period and to the impact of involvement of states in international violence and warfare.

The model when estimated for the South Asia, while confirming our results on the interaction between border and conflict in the overall sample, makes some additional fascinating revelations with regard to the adjacency factor in the region. It is observed that in South Asia, as against theoretical expectations and in a reversal of our full sample results, a common border acts more as a barrier than facilitator for trade. Our estimates show that a common border in South Asia implies costs to the extent of a 52 per cent loss in bilateral trade. The negative impact of conflict is further confirmed when estimation is undertaken by addition of explicit conflict variables in the regression. On thus netting out the impact of conflict the border variable acquires a positive coefficient but with negligible statistical significance. The conflict variables behave as expected in our model for South Asia. Anticipated conflict implies maximum costs to total trade, as would be expected in South Asia, which has had its member nations in dispute ever since independence. The loss of trade on account of persistent hostilities and consequent anticipation of conflict is to the extent of 90 per cent. Actual militarized disputes have meant a 75 per cent loss in bilateral trade. As a combination of political regimes has characterized the South Asian political structure, our representative variable in the model is 'mixed regimes' rather than joint democracies/autocracies. Political regimes have not been a positive factor in promoting trade for the regional economies in South Asia. Sub-sample results do not show any major difference across time periods and economic regimes from the results. Anticipated conflict consistently remains as the most significant negative influence on trade in South Asia. Clearly the element of anticipated conflict is overpowering in South Asia. For this reason an actual MID/conflict event such as the 1999 conflict in South Asia makes an insignificant dent on the economic activity of trade in the region. The impact of RTA membership is consistently negative in the full and sub-sample. Finally, the model estimates for the India–Pakistan dyad confirm that the regional picture is a fall-out of the bilateral relationship for the most enduring strategic rivalry in South Asia.

Our estimation results provide a clear understanding of the critical input to trade enhancement in the South Asian region. As the many conflicts that revolve around the border in the region are presumably at the base of the negative implications that common borders have for the region in terms of low intra-regional trade, the solution to this thus far intractable problem lies in decongestion and de-regulation of the borders in South Asia. There is a need for South Asia to take cognizance of the impact that hardened borders have on limiting economic exchange and potential of the region and formulate corrective policies to ease movement of goods across borders. A combination of economic and political policy measures will have to be implemented to achieve this objective. Singular focus on either may result in only short-term and possibly reversible gains.

In the following section we consider three issues that have been brought forth by our analysis and that may have a direct and immediate bearing on the path towards economic integration in South Asia.

Way forward

Common borders

The implication of our results for common borders in South Asia, which are only insignificantly positive even after netting out the effect of conflict, is close to what has been shown earlier with case studies from Latin America: that just disputing a border will eliminate its possible positive effects. Settled borders act as a signalling instrument that says that military conflict is less likely, economic development has higher priority than territorial acquisition so that hostile harassment at the border will not be the norm (Simmons, 2006). A disputed territory or unresolved boundary disputes are invariably likely to be reflected in the form of subtle negative policy instruments like imposition of non-tariff barriers, customs regulations (barriers at the border) or creation of other obstacles for goods to cross the border, and sometimes even in terms of overt policy to reduce economic exchange so that economic interdependence is of the minimum order. The operation of both the overt and covert policy measures are amply evident in South Asian trade policy and patterns. Pakistan did not give MFN status to India until 2012 even though India granted the same to Pakistan in 1995. Pakistan chose to operate the SAFTA using a positive list even though a negative-list approach had been stipulated in the agreement. Non-tariff barriers imposed in the form of excessive and time-consuming checks and documentation at the border are all examples in this respect. The average logistics performance of South Asia is lower than for the lower-middle-income group of countries and only marginally higher than that of the countries in the low-income group. Individual performance for South Asian economies reveals customs procedures and transport and IT infrastructure as areas most in need of improvement to further ease the behind-the-border constraints for trade enhancement in the region. This requires individual country efforts at improving these areas so as to reduce trade costs, which could and should be complemented by a coordinated approach among the South Asian countries so that a coherent and similar regional performance across a range of business and trade-facilitation areas could significantly increase trade competitiveness.

Our analysis leads us to recognize the fact that acceptance of an international boundary implies an element of normalized relations between two erstwhile competing claimants to territory. In terms of economic logic, an institutionalized border will contribute to reducing the element of risk and transaction costs at the border. The policy instruments for trade facilitation will be more effective in that context. Other than trade facilitation in South Asia, therefore, there is a need to decoagulate the borders. A consequence of the disputed boundaries and borders in South Asia has been observed over time in terms of hardening and thickening of the borders, which is reflected in the form of 'separation barriers' like barbed-wire fencing, bunkers and trenches, troops stationed at the border, and closure of the possible/high-potential border routes for trade, all in the name of security against neighbours.

It is observed that during relatively peaceful periods border trade is opened and the free flow of people and goods is allowed, with positive spillover implications for border towns that may until then be among the least-developed and most-neglected regions owing to the repercussions of boundary and territorial disputes. The opening of the border trade along the Srinagar-Muzaffarabad road in 2008, for the first time in 61 years, has in this context been one such initiative in the nature of building greater confidence through opening the border for commercial exchange. The road had been re-opened earlier to passenger traffic in 2005 and was further extended to an additional route in 2006. Since trade re-opened a reasonably high turnover of trade has been observed at the point. Simultaneously, the opening of the trade route has added impetus to the growth of the town and has increased its potential for economic development. Already the impact of trade on development of the involved border towns is evident in that town planning[2] now includes the setting up of a trade centre to give Baramullah the impetus as a growth centre for its hinterland. Baramullah was an important historical trade centre as a consequence of the Srinagar-Rawalpindi trade route, which gradually lost its significance as a trade route to only strategic significance. Business and transit centres are now planned along border towns to facilitate trans-boundary trade as a result of the Srinagar-Muzaffarabad trade route. Agriculture, horticulture and tourism sectors are being encouraged and promoted as a consequence. However, only 21 goods, largely agricultural commodities, are allowed for trade across this route as per the agreement between India and Pakistan. The other border trade route at Attari-Wagah has been opened up and India's first Integrated Checkpost (ICP) became operational for trade in April, 2012. Only 137 of the 1,209-item negative list specified by Pakistan are yet being allowed through this trade point, with the promise that the rest of the list will be phased out by end of 2012 under its MFN programme for India.

Possible other sites that have been identified in the Indian states of Punjab and Rajasthan along the border include a trading point at Munabao-Khokhrapar in Rajasthan, which opens up into Sindh province in Pakistan, and the Hussainiwala and Fazilka border points in Punjab in India. There are also plans to have 13 ICPs constructed on the border of Pakistan along with those for trade with Bangladesh and Nepal for fewer procedural delays and hassles. Apart from the fact that more crossings are being announced along the 2,900km-long India–Pakistan border, facilitating institutional changes are also planned. As regards the ICP, state-of-the-art facilities for security, customs and immigrations, and passenger amenities like waiting areas, restaurants and refreshment areas, duty-free shops, parking, warehousing, truck-parking, container yards, offices of transport and logistics companies, banks and financial services, dormitories and all related facilities like service stations and fuel stations are on the anvil. Already, though, defence and security issues are being raised by the armed forces at the border citing increased vulnerability of these commercial points.

Success of the commercial initiatives, therefore, has to have a prior in peace, whatever the mode. The India–Pakistan dyad has all its frictions rooted in unresolved territory/boundary and border issues. It is time for the region to find and settle for long-lasting peace by creating mutually acceptable solutions. This process will have to precede or accompany the trade process. Until then the small steps of MFN with a limited number of tradable commodities, the limited opening of border trade routes, and the slow and only partial establishment of infrastructure may be the only way to do trade, but that will also be easy and susceptible to reversal or closure if and when there is a resurgence of conflict or change in political regimes. More concrete structures for trade will be set up and invested in by either country only when they establish greater trust in each other.

Additionally, when expansion of trade through the border routes is discussed, an important lacuna that is often highlighted in the South Asian context is the lack of infrastructure along these trade routes, particularly in the form of road and rail links, which are so essential to developing land trade routes. The issue has been briefly touched upon in the context of transit arrangements in South Asia in Chapter 3. In this section we discuss connectivity in a broader context to take forward the idea of economic integration in South Asia.

Connectivity

In South Asia, connectivity has to be seen in terms of the physical, which is established through multiple modes of transportation, but also the equally important but less-stressed aspect of financial connectivity, and, in a visionary manner, of extending to beyond the South Asian region to other sub-regions of Asia, also encompassing in its fold the scope for achieving regional energy security in Asia. Further, connectivity in South Asia, apart from contributing to enhancing intra-regional trade, has to be viewed in the larger context of making the region globally competitive. The underlying function of integrated transport and communication systems is to improve access to sub-regional markets, in response to which individual countries would be required to make structural changes in their production capacities, which can then help expand and diversify the basket of goods available for exports. Well-connected regional markets are also more attractive as destinations for foreign direct investment than individual countries. The larger connected markets provide scope for exploiting economies of agglomeration and integrated production networks that contribute to more efficient and competitive production possibilities. The positive spillover effects of physical infrastructure across borders are particularly beneficial for smaller economies that may otherwise be constrained by their size, limited resources and markets. For South Asia regional connectivity holds relevance, as cross-border connectivity can be an essential contributory factor to the region's developmental prospects by connecting economies at varying levels of development and thereby helping to leverage complementary strengths and synergies in the region. In South Asia in particular, connectivity ought to be promoted to take advantage of the economic dynamism that India and the rest of the region has experienced over the last decade. A rate of growth of over 5 per cent experienced by almost all the economies, combined with an average annual rate of growth of over 8 per cent of the Indian economy, prior to the global financial crisis augurs especially well for a cooperative and collaborative economic agenda, and regional connectivity would give it the necessary push. India has also been among the first few economies in the world to regain its pre-crisis growth of 8 per cent in 2010. The emphasis on regional connectivity gains added significance in the wake of the global financial crisis when looking inwards for growth impulses, which has become imperative for all regions. South Asian countries that have predominantly looked westwards for export markets now need to re-orient themselves towards South Asian markets as the former may yet take a long time to regain their pre-crisis growth levels. Physical connectivity is therefore imperative for regional prosperity, and this may also be able to provide a stepping stone towards realizing the vision of a South Asian economic community in the long run.

To a certain extent the relevance of connectivity in the region has already been recognized. The 14th SAARC summit in 2007 was held in New Delhi with the central theme of connectivity. As an outcome of the summit heads of governments of member countries agreed to improve intra-regional physical, economic and people-to-people connectivity. Since the summit, there have been four ministerial meetings organized to focus on areas of physical, financial, and security connectivity. At the 16th SAARC Summit at Thimpu in Bhutan, the 2010–20 decade was jointly declared as the decade of intra-regional connectivity in SAARC. The centrality of connectivity to further deepen and consolidate regional integration was reiterated in the joint declaration, as was the importance of developing transport infrastructure and transit facilities in the region and especially for landlocked countries.

In order to take the agenda of connecting South Asia within and with other sub-regions forward some important transport corridors have been proposed. These include the Lahore–Delhi–Kolkata–Petrapole–Benapole–Dhaka–Akhaura–Agartala (2,453 km), Kathmandu–Nepalganj–Delhi–Lahore–Karachi (2,643 km), Kathmandu–Birgunj–Kolkata–Haldia (1,323 km) and the Thimpu–Phuentsholing–Jaigon–Kolkata–Haldia (1,039 km) routes. Simultaneously two priority routes have also been identified in the Asian Highway network touching upon South Asia. One of these routes connects Iran, Afghanistan, Pakistan, India, Bangladesh, Myanmar, Thailand, and Vietnam, while the other route links Iran, Pakistan, India, Nepal, Bangladesh, and Myanmar. Some other proposed and possible links that can be established and would go a long way to establish regional connectivity include bringing the railways of India and Bangladesh under the Trans-Asian Railways, which consists of the railway systems of Pakistan, India, and Bangladesh; integrating Ganga, Brahmaputra, and Meghna waterways with the sea ports in India and Bangladesh; initiating ferry service between Colombo and Kochin, and Colombo and Tuticorin; and establish air links so that tourism can receive a great boost. Airports in Nepal and Bhutan should be upgraded to promote tourism.

It may be insightful in the context of regional connectivity to draw a comparison between South Asia and ASEAN. ASEAN has been observed to face similar challenges to South Asia with regard to physical connectivity, such as poor quality of roads and incomplete road networks; missing railway links; inadequate maritime and port infrastructure, including dry port, inland waterways and aviation facilities; widening of the digital divide; and growing demand for power. To resolve these connectivity constraints the regional organization has drawn up seven strategies, including a multimodal transport system, an enhanced information and communications technology (ICT) infrastructure and a regional energy security framework. To establish institutional connectivity ASEAN has adopted ten strategies that include harmonization of standards and conformity assessment procedures among regional economies; operationalizing key transport facilitation agreements, including the ASEAN Framework Agreement on the facilitation of goods in transit; inter-state transport; and multimodal transport. ASEAN also requires that its member states fully implement their respective national single windows towards realizing the ASEAN Single Window by 2015 to bring about seamless flow of goods at, between and behind national borders. Simultaneously, an ASEAN single aviation market and an ASEAN single shipping market is to be pursued in order to contribute towards the realization of a single market and production base, which is the ASEAN goal of an economic community. As regards people-to-people connectivity, two strategies have been formulated. These include promotion of deeper intra-ASEAN social and cultural interaction and understanding through community-building efforts. Greater intra-ASEAN people mobility is also facilitated through progressive relaxation of visa requirements and development of mutual recognition arrangements (MRAs) to provide the needed impetus for concerted efforts in promoting awareness, collaboration, exchange, outreach and advocacy programmes to facilitate the ongoing efforts to increase greater interactions between the peoples of ASEAN. In all aspects ASEAN has a master plan and identified prioritized projects. Therefore, there is in ASEAN's case a clear and firm desire to overcome the constraints in regional connectivity. Towards the objective of regional connectivity formal strategies and plans with programmes of implementation have been taken up by respective authorities at the national and regional level. In addition and alongside the master plan, critical inputs like mobilization of required financial resources and technical assistance to implement the key actions and prioritized projects stipulated under the adopted strategies have been taken care of through innovative approaches like the establishment of an ASEAN fund for infrastructure development, public-private sector partnerships (PPP), and development of local and regional financial and capital markets, particularly to finance the key deliverables identified to be achieved by 2015. ASEAN has also set up an institutional mechanism for coordination and monitoring the progress of its various programmes for connectivity. An essential component in this process is a performance score card that is reviewed on a regular basis. South Asia, in comparison while recognizing the importance of connectivity, is more ad hoc in its approach. The region continues to lack an integrated plan for such an important aspect of economic integration. Several programmes and projects, as listed above, have been announced, but none of these have any significant progress on the grounds to their credit. A more proactive and cooperative approach to achieving regional connectivity is imperative if South Asia is serious about pursuing its goal for economic integration.

A mention need also be made of Afghanistan, for which the issue of transit is strategic given its geographic location. Afghanistan has the potential to serve as an energy transit corridor in Asia. Thus far Afghanistan has had difficulties in trade and transit owing to internal disturbances/civil wars that have affected its transit trade through Pakistan. Domestic political instability has also prevented it from fully exploiting its rich resources of oil, gas, coal, iron, chrome and copper for trade purposes. Besides security issues, poor quality of roads and logistical hurdles also hamper Afghanistan's accessibility in the region. Also, continued unofficial trade, including opium trade and re-export trade, is an increasing source of tension with Pakistan. Under the 2010 trade and transit agreement between Afghanistan and Pakistan, Afghanistan has been allowed to export consignments to the Indian border via the Wagah border. In return Pakistan gets access to the central Asian republics (CARs) through Afghanistan. The agreement, however, does not allow Delhi a trade corridor to Afghanistan via Pakistan.

Energy transit from Afghanistan has been given a boost through the encouraging progress in the proposed Turkmenistan–Afghanistan–Pakistan–India (TAPI) gas pipeline. The 1,680 km TAPI proposal has seen substantial movement forward and appears set to take off as India has agreed to pay US$13 per unit for buying natural gas through the pipeline and also agreed to take indirect responsibility for safe transit of the fuel through high-security-risk regions of Afghanistan and Pakistan. The agreement, signed by India in May, 2012, has it buying natural gas from Turkmenistan at a rate equivalent to 55 per cent of the crude oil price with an additional payment as a transit fee and transportation charges. This inter-sub-regional gas pipeline thus initiates connectivity beyond South Asia.

The issue of conflict and security has been at the heart of earlier proposals that have been discussed, debated and suspended in that order so far. In 2008 India pulled out of the Iran-Pakistan-India gas pipeline owing to dragged out negotiations regarding pricing and issues of security of transit. The other proposed project that was to link Myanmar and India through Bangladesh did not materialize either on account of reservations, political in nature, from the Bangladesh side.

Another aspect of connectivity that has received relatively less focus but is of equal importance for trade enhancement and, in the long-run, competitive production abilities of the region is financial connectivity. As initiatives in the former context have already begun with the opening up of border trade, the necessity to simultaneously augment South Asia's financial connectivity becomes immediate and paramount. As an example the trade across the line of control in Kashmir to be operational has to be supported by adequate communication and banking facilities. Currently trade is largely on a barter basis. The model for the banking mechanism has only just been proposed in April 2012, four years after the opening of the border for trade in 2008. But it may be emphasized in this context that financial connectivity in South Asia as yet needs to be understood as distinct from financial integration. Given the level of financial development in the region, particularly with respect to financial markets, it may be early days for thinking about financial integration. For building trade capacity at the borders, however, necessary financial support measures need to be established. This is very important to border trade where banking channels are currently limited. One way could be for South Asian countries to enter into regional and bilateral financial arrangements to facilitate trade. There could be local currency-swap agreements with assistance from the central banks for settling payments in local currencies of cross-border charges and fees for cross-border movements of goods. For India and Pakistan and the newly opened border trade routes, negotiations are being held and the central banks of the two countries are in touch regarding reopening of banking channels on both sides of the border. The possibility of India's EXIM bank extending operation could also be considered, particularly in areas like developing context-suitable trade finance instruments like export credit insurance, which would go a long way in diversification of exports beyond the traditional agricultural commodities (of course, this would be subject to extension of the currently limited number of tradable items!) Another area of operation could be risk assessment for small producers and exporters with potential for export development. Access to affordable domestic financial services is important, particularly for border trade to expand beyond the immediate term. It may also be appropriate to consider establishing a regional or bilateral fund for border trade and joint information access and exchange for better risk assessment between the participating countries.

A third relevant aspect and that is also a direct outcome of our analysis is related to the role of production networks in South Asian economic integration.

Production networks

There has been a lot of emphasis of late on developing regional production networks. It is easy to identify the source of this thought process as a possible means for furthering economic integration in South Asia. Quite naturally, having seen the experience of network production in the neighbouring East Asian economies as a precursor to both high intra-regional trade and the subsequent formalization and institutionalization through the ASEAN, South Asia has had reason to explore this possibility. While a lot of focus is now being placed on identifying sectors and industries for this mode of integration, there ought to be some scope for introspective analysis on why production networks have not evolved in South Asia on their own as they did in South East Asia. Often the argument that is put forward in this context is the lack of complementarities in the comparative advantage structures of the South Asian economies. There is undoubtedly some truth in this given the almost similar resource endowment of these economies and the inward-looking growth strategies that these economies followed until around the 1990s. However, while sequentially advancing production complementarities may not be identifiable to the extent and on the scale of South East Asian economies, there is still scope for production networks, and these could in fact be in sectors where all the major economies of South Asia have developed expertise internationally. In our analysis in Chapter 5 we have identified such possibilities in the textile and clothing sector, one of the dominant sectors in the export profile of South Asian economies. So what are the questions that the region needs to deal with to make this networked production a success and to in general replicate the South East Asian production networks?

First and foremost, South Asian production networks may not be able to evolve in the manner of the South East Asia assembly-line manufacturing production that has China as its hub and for which different production stages would need to be located in different countries. For example, our identified complementarities in the textiles and clothing sector would broadly imply that cotton moves from India to Pakistan, from where yarn, fibre and fabric could move to Bangladesh,which could then export garments to the rest of the world. The overlaps of India and Pakistan's specialization in terms of yarn may have complementarities at a more detailed commodity classification or else would call for some industrial restructuring in the two economies, a process which in any case is inevitable when network production evolves in a region. This is also the most difficult part of establishing production networks in South Asia. Is the region coordinated enough in terms of policy and labour markets for this structural reorganization, even in a single industry? Do wage differentials across the region favour this kind of industrial restructuring as they did in South East Asia? Most of these aspects, if not far-fetched to think of in the South Asian context, require an immense amount of commitment and willingness on the part of the member economies of the region to share regional resources for regional development. In East Asia, MNCs have played a crucial role in establishing regional production linkages. In South Asia, few MNCs exist, and those that do have their origins in India. India, though, is not as yet in any significant manner a participant in the global production networks. So what kind of time span does South Asia visualize for developing the right structures within the region for production networks to evolve and become lead actors in promoting intra-regional trade?

While, of course, the South Asian economies would need to overcome their insecurities vis-à-vis India for such processes to take form in the region, India's capabilities of leading such production networks in South Asia may in itself be doubtful given its limited participation in international production networks. India has only a 17 per cent share in networked products in manufacturing exports and 40 per cent in imports versus China's 58 and 63 per cent respectively (Athukorala, 2010).[3] In addition, production linkages are facilitated by transport and infrastructural connectivity, which South Asia at least at present is severely lacking in, a weakness that over the years has been aggravated on account of thickened borders and persistent conflict, aspects that we have highlighted in our preceding discussion.

Ultimately production coordination calls for positive administration of the differences between partners, removing obstacles like border difficulties, differences in scale of production, market access and funding. One possible approach in this context for South Asia could be as adopted by MERCOSUR,where production integration has been seen as a necessary tool in overcoming the regional asymmetries. This could be tactical in removing the trust deficit while also enhancing intra-regional trade and development prospects.With the help of private-sector-industry chambers it may be possible to select the most dynamic sectors across the region and devise ways to institutionalize regional production in these areas. Private-sector involvement will provide long-term perspective to such initiatives, as then they are likely to be based on profit calculations. A support fund for production integration and the restructuring involved would be necessary, and this could be undertaken through funds pooled regionally, with large contributions from India and/or aided by multilateral lending agencies like the ADB.

In this concluding section we have thus taken up three areas for focused discussion to identify the lacunae and possible directions and alternative paths to take the idea of economic integration in South Asia towards realization. The clear and distinct outcome of this process is that there is a lot of prior work that South Asia still needs to accomplish to enhance intra-regional trade beyond the low-level equilibrium that it has been caught in now for several decades. Positive intentions are evident, but strategic thinking needs to evolve. There is a growing sentiment of allowing economic initiatives to take shape in the region. These initiatives need to be accompanied or preceded by a commitment to resolving long-standing disputes through some or the other mutually respected and accepted solutions. While closure of disputes may not be immediately possible, pushing dispute resolution to an indeterminate future date is also not the solution for the region that has far too often witnessed reversal of confidence-building measures.

Appendix

List of members of RTAs included for estimation: SAPTA: Bangladesh, Bhutan, India, Maldives, Nepal, Pakistan, Sri Lanka; NAFTA: USA, Canada, Mexico; AFTA: Brunei, Indonesia, Malaysia, Philippines, Singapore, Thailand, Vietnam, Cambodia, Laos, Myanmar; MERCOSUR: Argentina, Brazil, Paraguay, Uruguay.

Neighbouring countries for South Asia: MEPV, Polity IV classification: Afghanistan, Bhutan, Bangladesh, China, India, Iran, Kyrgyzstan, Kazakhstan, Burma, Nepal, Pakistan, Sri Lanka, Tajikistan, Turkmenistan, Uzbekistan.

Table A.1 SAFTA sensitive list: revisions underway

Countries	No. of Products in Sensitive List	No. of products agreed to be reduced during second meeting in 2011	Proposed no. of products in the sensitive list w.e.f. 1.11.2011
Afghanistan	1072	214	858
Bangladesh	**1233**	**246**	**987**
	1241	248	993
Bhutan	150	0	150
India	**480**	**96**	**384**
	868	173	695
Maldives	681	136	545
Nepal	**1257**	**251**	**1006**
	1295	259	1036
Pakistan	1169	233	936
Sri Lanka	1042	208	834

Note: In bold: sensitive list for LDCs

Table A.2 Phase-out period for the SAFTA sensitive list

	Years	Tariff Reduction
NLDC to NLDC	3	0–5%
Sri Lanka	6	
LDC to all contracting states	8	
NLDC to LDC	3	

Table A.3 Textile and clothing sector: exercise details on production networks

Bangladesh Exports-and Sri Lanka imports

Commodity Code	SA Trade Partner	Major Trade Partner
560721		China, RoK
570249	India	China, Singapore
570250	India	India
570490	Bangladesh	UAE, China
630691	Pakistan, India	Pakistan

Pakistan Exports-Sri Lanka imports

Commodity Code	SA Trade Partner	Major Trade Partner
510111		RoK
520534	Pakistan	Pakistan
520544	India, Pakistan	India
520614	India	India
520623		RoK
520624		China
520812	India, Pakistan	Italy, India
520813	India, Pakistan	Hong Kong, China
520823	Pakistan	Pakistan, Thailand
520833		Hong Kong, China
520851	India	Italy, China
520912	Pakistan, India	Pakistan, India
521011	India, Pakistan	USA
521021		China, Hong Kong
521112	India	Hong Kong, India
521120	India	Hong Kong, India
521131		Hong Kong, China
521143		USA, Hong Kong
521221	India, Pakistan	Hong Kong, India
540773	India	India
540781		USA,, China, Hong Kong
550190		Japan, China
551030		Thailand
551423	Pakistan	Malaysia
551634		Hong Kong
551641	India	Singapore, Thailand, India
570249		Portugal
580211	Pakistan, India	India, Pakistan
600521		Indonesia
630240	India	India, Thailand
630691	Pakistan	Pakistan

No common commodities between Sri Lanka exports and Pakistan imports

Table A.3 Continued

Pakistan's exports–Bangladesh imports

Commodity Code	SA Trade Partner	Major Trade Partner
520515	Pakistan, India	
520526	India	
520528	Pakistan, India	
520534		China
520613	Pakistan	
520625	Pakistan. India	
520632	Pakistan	
520843	Pakistan, India	China
521021	Sri Lanka, India	China, Sri Lanka
521112		China
521143	Pakistan	China, Pakistan
521152	India	Thailand, Korea
521212	India, Pakistan	
551030		China
551221		RoK, Hong Kong
551291	Pakistan	China
551423	India	China
551614	India	India
551641		China, Hong Kong
600524		Canada
600623	India	Hong Kong, China
600644		China, Hong Kong

Pakistan imports–Bangladesh exports

Commodity Code	SA Trade Partner	Major Trade Partner
510510	India	India. Australia
520291		Bahrain, USA
531090	Bangladesh	Bangladesh, China
570490		China, Egypt, UAE
610331		China, Hong Kong
611530		China, USA, Italy
620191		China, RoK

India imports-Sri Lanka exports: No common commodities

India exports–Sri Lanka imports

Commodity Code	SA Trade Partner	Major Trade Partner
520528	Pakistan, India	China, Pakistan, India
520531	India, Pakistan	Hong Kong, Indonesia, India,
520533		Hong Kong
520535		Malaysia
520541	India	Hong Kong, India, China
520611	Pakistan, India	RoK, China, Pakistan,

Table A.3 Continued

Commodity Code	SA Trade Partner	Major Trade Partner
520621	Pakistan, India	Pakistan, India
530720	Bangladesh, India	Bangladesh, India
540771	India	RoK
551644	India	Italy, Turkey

India imports–Pakistan exports

Commodity Code	SA Trade Partner	Major Trade Partner
510111		Australia,
551634		Turkey, Italy

India exports–Pakistan imports

Commodity Code	SA Trade Partner	Major Trade Partner
530720	Bangladesh, Sri Lanka	Bangladesh

India imports–Bangladesh exports

Commodity Code	SA Trade Partner	Major Trade Partner
611231		China, Italy

India exports–Bangladesh imports

Commodity Code	SA Trade Partner	Major Trade Partner
520528	Pakistan, India, Bangladesh	China, Pakistan, India, Bangladesh
520533	Pakistan, India	Pakistan
520535	India, Pakistan	India, Pakistan, Vietnam
520611	India, Pakistan, Bangladesh	India, Pakistan, Hong Kong
520613	Pakistan	Thailand, Pakistan
520614		China
520621	India	India, Thailand
520641	Pakistan, India	Pakistan, China, India
521222		China
540771	India	India
551644		China, RoK
580230	Pakistan	China, Pakistan

Source: UNCOMTRADE and author's calculations
Note: SA: South Asia; RoK: Republic of Korea

Notes

1 Introduction

1 Given that regional economic cooperation is the subject of this book, the analysis has been undertaken for the region defined as per membership of the South Asian Association for Regional Cooperation (SAARC). Seven countries are founding members of the organization and Afghanistan joined as the eighth member in 2007.
2 According to the Wonnacott and Lutz (1989) version of the hypothesis, preferential trade agreements with geographically proximate countries are potentially more trade creating and less trade diverting. Higher trade creation is attributed to lower transport costs.
3 Ahmed *et al.* (2010).
4 Even though Sri Lanka initiated its economic liberalization in 1978, the process gained momentum only in the 1990s. Prior to the 1990s South Asian economies were inward looking with trade as a relatively low-importance economic activity in their growth process that was based largely upon a policy of import substitution and aimed at self-reliance.
5 This approach is referred to as the positive list approach and is more tedious to negotiate than the negative list that specifies the number of items to be excluded from concessional treatment.
6 An agreement for liberalization of services in South Asia was signed in 2010 at the 16th SAARC summit held in Thimpu, Bhutan. Agreement towards investment liberalization among the member countries is yet to be finalized.
7 It may be noted that Pakistan has made announcements towards a change in both granting MFN status to India and negative list delineation in September 2011. However, soon after the announcement a clarification was issued stating that the Pakistan cabinet had decided to normalize trade relations with Pakistan, and granting the MFN status was a part of that process that is expected to be completed by end of 2012. Work towards this objective was initiated in March 2012. Announcements towards granting India the MFN status have been made by Pakistan earlier in 1975 and 2004, but not fulfilled in terms of implementation. It is considered that continuing with and implementing the announcements vis-à-vis India will be a function of the interest and inclination of the political regime, as well as the politically influential classes at any point in time in Pakistan. This has been the experience vis-à-vis India and Pakistan in the past.
8 Nepal being the sole exception to this trend.
9 Ahmed *et al.* (2010).
10 It is relevant to note that many studies have shown that US trade has increased more quickly with its NAFTA partners than with non-NAFTA partners. Since the announcement of NAFTA in 1993, real US exports to Mexico have increased by 95 per cent and Canada by 35 per cent in contrast with the 20 per cent increase observed for non-NAFTA partners. Real US imports from Mexico have increased by 190 per cent

Notes 157

in comparison with 69 per cent for Canada and 59 per cent for non-NAFTA partners: Agama and McDaniel (2002).
11 Trade between India and Pakistan may provide the most obvious and significant evidence of this trend. Batra (2004) has shown econometrically the large gap between potential and actual trade for India and Pakistan. Also, while the trends on formal trade that is officially recorded trade show dismal progress over the years, it is also an acceptable fact that a large amount of trade in South Asia is undertaken through the informal or illegal routes. Some estimates on this aspect have also been made and indicate a fairly high magnitude of trade in the region. However, considering that these are estimates of trade undertaken on an informal basis the estimates may not be entirely accurate. In case of Pakistan, in addition trade takes the circular route as large amounts of goods are routed to India via Singapore or Dubai.
12 Mukherjee (2010).
13 India and Pakistan have in particular differed in their approach and stance at the UN vis-à-vis proposing a solution on Kashmir.
14 This concept derives from the Kantian philosophy of democratic peace.
15 Issues like the Malaysia-Philippines dispute regarding their territorial claims over Sabah and the Malaysia-Indonesia suspicions following the 1963 confrontations did prevent significant progress in the initial years. This, however, changed with the holding of the first summit meeting of the organization in 1976 (Sridharan, 2007).
16 At the second ASEAN summit in 1977 President Marcos of Philippines renounced his country's claim on Sabah (Sridharan, 2007).
17 Athukorala and Kohpaiboon (2009).
18 Sridharan (2007).
19 The relative importance of the India–Pakistan dyad to the task of economic integration in the region becomes more evident as we proceed in our analysis in subsequent chapters of this book.
20 Source: http://dgft.gov.in/.
21 The gravity model in its basic form derives from the Newtonian notion of gravity and predicts bilateral trade to be a positive function of the product of GDP (mass) and a negative function of the distance between the two economies. The model has been used to predict the gap between actual and potential trade for a pair of countries within the global and regional context (Batra, 2004). Econometric evidence from this model reveals some of the highest potential for trade among the South Asian economies.

2 South Asia: the region

1 In some classifications where the reference is to Southern Asia rather than South Asia the region is extended to cover countries like Myanmar on the east and Iran on the west. Historical and contemporary explanations have been provided for such extensions. Myanmar was a part of British India and shares a long land boundary with two SAARC members, India and Bangladesh. Geographically it is like a bridge that connects South Asia to South East Asia. Iran is included in the UN-classified Southern Asia.
2 This is an important aspect as granting transit rights to these economies by India is important for them as well as to enhancing regional trade.
3 All data in this section is culled from the World Development Indicators (2011), World Data Bank, World Bank, and is for the year 2010 unless otherwise specified. Where appropriate, pre-global-financial-crisis trends and changes during and after the crisis are discussed separately.
4 Classification as per the World Bank: country and lending groups database.
5 Data on the East Asia and Pacific region is presented to provide a perspective for South Asian trends as the two regions are in immediate neighbourhood and similar in terms of member countries in varying stages of development.
6 Source: http://hdr.undp.org/en/statistics.

158 *Notes*

7 Published for the first time in the 2010 report, this measure complements the money-based measures by considering multiple deprivations and their overlap.
8 Percentage of population below the poverty line.
9 The latest year for which headcount poverty estimates are available.
10 Ahmed *et al.* (2010).

3 Trade and FDI patterns of South Asian countries

1 The classification of economic regimes is not undertaken econometrically as economic growth strategy in the 1990s is dramatically different from the earlier period and almost at the same time for all South Asian economies. Prior to economic reform external transactions in terms of trade and investment are negligible in the region.
2 Sri Lanka started its economic liberalization process in 1978 but the process was intensified only in the 1990s.
3 The new economic policy regime included de-licensing of the industrial sector and fiscal consolidation, followed later by financial sector liberalization. Given the objective of the analysis in this book, the focus of this section is limited to policy changes in trade and FDI regimes only.
4 Prebisch (1950, 1984).
5 To ease the transition to a market-determined exchange rate system a limited exchange rate management system (LERMS) that used a dual exchange rate was introduced as a transitional system in 1992.The dual rates were merged and the market-determined exchange rate was introduced in 1993.
6 Jain and Singh (2009).
7 Most of the mining sector is on the 100 per cent automatic route.
8 Khan, Ashfaque A. (1998).
9 Some policy reversals in this domain were undertaken during 1994–95 and March 1997 for fiscal considerations: Khan, Ashfaque A. (1998).
10 Ijaz Nabi (1997).
11 Khan and Kim (1999).
12 Investment Policy Review, UNCTAD (2003).
13 Country note UNESCAP (2007).
14 Openness index is defined as the ratio of export plus imports of goods and services to GDP.
15 1991 is taken as the benchmark year, as in this year the process of economic liberalization took off in India followed by other economies in the ensuing years. Sri Lanka began its economic reform programme in 1978 that was further intensified in the 1990s.
16 Jain and Singh (2009).
17 India's Foreign Trade Policy (2009–14). Source: http://dgft.gov.in.
18 As reported in World Bank. 2010. *World Trade Indicators 2009/10: Country Trade Briefs*. Washington, DC: World Bank. Available at http://www.worldbank.org/wti.
19 The index summarizes the trade restrictiveness of the MFN tariff schedule of a country. It is equivalent to the uniform tariff that would maintain the country's aggregate import volume at its current level (given heterogeneous tariffs). It is expressed in percent as if it were a tariff rate: Islam, Roumeen and Gianni Zannini, 2008, World Bank.
20 Over 95 per cent of Bhutan's exports are sent to India, which is also the source of nearly 75 per cent of its imports. Under various free trade agreements in place since the 1970s, imports from India have not been subject to tariffs. However, the Royal Government of Bhutan (RGoB) does employ a sales tax that applies only to imported goods, which it uses to protect its domestic industries.
21 Although Sri Lanka has continued to liberalize its tariff regime since the late 1990s, there has been some backpedalling. Recent taxes on imports introduced primarily for revenue purposes often have a protectionist impact on trade.
22 South Asia Economic Update (2010) World Bank.
23 Akanda (2012).

Notes 159

24 5.21 per cent in 2007. In the subsequent years 2008–10 the share has fallen to a little over 4 per cent, possibly on account of the adverse impact of the global financial crisis. Source: http://aric.adb.org/indicators.
25 Aggarwaland Mukherjee (2008).
26 India posts a positive trade balance for preferential trade under SAPTA also. In analyzing India's preferential trade with Bangladesh, Maldives, Pakistan, and Sri Lanka for the period 1996–97 to2002–03, Mukherjee (2004) finds that India generally had a positive preferential trade balance with all SAPTA countries except Bangladesh during 1997–98 to 2000–01. The preferential trade balance, however, is not as much in India's favour as India's overall trade with these countries. It is, however, too early to make this assessment as regards the implementation of SAFTA.
27 Agama and McDaniel (2002).
28 Qamar (2005).
29 Source: www.tradingeconomic.com/pakistan/balance of trade.
30 See SDPI (2005). Indian products routed their Pakistan bound products by ship through Dubai in a 28-days journey that is 40 times more expensive than trucking it over their shared land border.
31 While estimation of informal/illegal trade has been attempted in some studies, these are very rough approximations and can at best be considered with huge margins of error. In many studies, for example, the estimation is based on a highly selective sample of 'important' smuggling centres that are surveyed to estimate the extent of trade. The figures thus attained are then extrapolated to arrive at national figures. The procedure thus adopted is more in the nature of a 'guess' than a serious estimation and is therefore highly prone to large error elements. We therefore desist from quoting a figure for informal trade in the SAARC region.
32 ADB and UNCTAD (2008).
33 Iqbal (2012).
34 Baldwin (2005)
35 The limited transit rights are invariably politically motivated, but sometimes security conditions may also prevail as rationale for imposition of such restrictions and barriers.
36 Faye *et al.* (2004).
37 Statement by SAARC Secretary General at the Inaugural Session of the 15th SAARC Summit held in Colombo in August, 2008. Source: www.saarc-sec.org.
38 In September 2011in a meeting of the commerce secretaries of both nations, Pakistan expressed its intention to extend the MFN status to India. The process of extending MFN status was initiated in March 2012 and is expected to be completed by the end of 2012.
39 This has been discussed on p. 43.
40 The MFN,which is understood to translate as mera pyara desh,'my friend nation' in urdu, will, it is feared, hurt the Pakistani nationalistic sentiment.
41 This is evident from the fact that, even when the commerce secretary talks in April 2011 led to Pakistan showing a likelihood of granting MFN to India, the announcement was followed the day after by a clarification that granting MFN was part of an overall trade normalization process with India and that it will happen in due course.
42 At the border procedures may be understood mainly at customs clearance procedures and related trade documents and regulations, as well as procedures at the port, cargo handling etc.
43 Duval and Utoktham (2009).
44 In 2009, though capital flows were up from the previous year by 26 per cent this was largely on account of a turnaround in portfolio equity inflows: Global Development Finance (2011).
45 Kumar(2010) and UNCTAD, FDI Database (2010).
46 *Doing Business*, World Bank (2010).
47 Mauritius and the Netherlands appear as major sources of FDI. However, this reflects the relocation of traditional FDI via these countries given the special tax treatment accorded to transitional capital in these countries.

48 Madhukar, Rana and Pradhan (2005).
49 Kelegama and Mukherjee (2007).
50 Alamand Zubayer (2010).
51 UNCTAD online database (2010).
52 World Investment Report (WIR) (2010).
53 Giroud (2009). Source: www.unctad.org.
54 The latest trade data available for Bangladesh is for 2008.
55 This is a preliminary exercise that is indicative of the scope for production networks and future research towards economic integration in South Asia. Details are available on request from the author.
56 See Table A.3 in the Appendix.
57 Tewari (2008).
58 Tewari (2008) states synthetic yarn and other new varieties as one of the reasons for South Asian countries to import from South East Asia. But in our analysis South Asian potential for networks has been identified for South Asian imports that can be substituted by existing comparative advantage /specializations structure of the South Asian economies.
59 Trade Policies in South Asia: An Overview. Report No. 29949, September 2004.

4 Preferential trading agreements in South Asia

1 The discussion in this chapter is focused upon PTAs by the South Asian economies within the region.
2 ADB, http://aric.adb.org, January, 2011.
3 As per ADB definition, FTAs at the proposed stage are those where the concerned parties are in the process of forming joint study groups to conduct feasibility studies. The FTAs that are under negotiation are doing so on the basis of the contents of a framework agreement, or proceeding without one. Signed agreements have concluded negotiations and, where applicable, are awaiting legislative or executive ratification. FTAs are under implementation when their provisions, such as those relating to tariff reductions, are effective.
4 Feridhanusstyawan (2005).
5 For a definition of the 'natural trading partner' hypothesis see Note 2.
6 Mansfield, Milner and Rosendorff (2000) prove that two democracies are more likely to enter into reciprocal trade agreements. Democratically elected politicians are motivated by a desire to be re-elected, the chances of which are higher with increasing consumer welfare and campaign contributions from organized industry lobbies. Reciprocal trade agreements ensure local export industry support for trade policy.
7 Batra (2010).
8 IMF DOTS Database.
9 Enabling Clause of the text of the 1979 GATT decision allows preferential trade in goods among developing countries. It is more flexible in comparison with GATT article XXIV that specifies that substantial trade (understood as 85–90 per cent) should be liberalized in an FTA.
10 Mukherjee (2004).
11 Detailed list provided in the Appendix.
12 The ADB initiated a South Asia Sub-Regional Economic Cooperation (SASEC) initiative under its umbrella programme of Regional Cooperation and Integration (RCI). Six priority areas of cooperation, including transport, tourism, trade investment and private-sector cooperation, energy and power, environment and ICT, have been indentified under the SASEC. ADB provided the first Technical Assistance for the SAARC multi-modal transport study. Other initiatives have been in the energy sector.
13 That is after the setting up of a democratic government in Nepal in 1990.
14 UNCOMTRADE.

15 For example, vanaspati vegetable oil.
16 Mukherjee (2010).
17 Provided an exemption from export duties for goods from Bhutan to third countries.
18 2009, source:http://www.indianembassythimphu.bt/relation.
19 The beneficial outcome for both Bhutan and India of cooperation on the Chukha hydroelectricity project has been an eye-opener for the region (Batra,2005).
20 India follows more stringent RoOs with its other partners like Thailand (40 per cent), Singapore (40 per cent), Mercusor (60 per cent–proposed).
21 Weerakoonand Thennakoon.
22 Shahzad et al.(2011)state that thePSLFTA resulted in a rise in Pakistan's exports to Sri Lanka by 41 per centand Sri Lanka's exports increased by 28 per cent.
23 Deshal de Mel, IPS, Colombo.
24 As simple average of all items, Source: http://www.unescap.org/tid/apta/factsheet08.pdf.
25 Source: http:// www.unescap.org/tid/apta.asp.
26 Batra (2010).
27 Batra (2010).

5 Conflict in South Asia

1 According to the partition plan for India the princely states were given the option to join either India or Pakistan.
2 Wirsing and Jasparro (2007).
3 Sahai (2007).
4 Incorporating provisions for flood control, power generation and irrigation.
5 Bhattarai, D. (2009).
6 Khatri.and Kueck (2003).
7 Inter-state conflict that has been interpreted by one party as internal disturbance with uncalled-for interference by the other – e.g., the 1948 and 1965 India–Pakistan war described as Pakistan's interference with India's internal developments in Kashmir and vice versa for the 1971 war are excluded from this section.
8 Ghani and Iyer (2010).
9 Also Ref.: Khan, Shaheen Rafi (2009).
10 CBMs can be defined as mutually agreed actions that set processes in motion such that parties move from a condition of mutual hostilities to reduced hostilities or increased accommodation. These actions may be military-strategic, non-military, political, social and/or cultural actions undertaken by state, non-government organizations. CBMs are invariably temporary in nature and do not necessarily ensure long-term change or establishment of trust between hostile parties.
11 Post-1988 data is sourced from South Asia Confidence Building Measures Timeline: Stimson-Research pages. Source: http://www.stimson.org/research-pages/confidence-building-measures-in-south-asia-/.
12 Yasmeen and Dixit (1995).
13 Wetter (1971).
14 Source: http://www.stimson.org/research-pages/confidence-building-measures-in-south-asia-/.
15 Chandran (2001).
16 Talks were resumed in 2004, suspended in 2008 after the Mumbai attacks and then resumed again in 2011.
17 India withdraws later on account of differences over pricing and transit fee with Iran and Pakistan respectively.
18 This was extended to four days a week since July 2011.
19 Preparation for implementation of the same is expected to be completed by the end of 2012.

162 *Notes*

20 About 11 miles below Farraka, India, the Ganges forms the common boundary between India and Bangladesh and continues about 63 miles before entering Bangladesh at Rajshahi. The Ganges dispute was recognized in 1951. While negotiations between India and Pakistan (before 1971) had taken place, there was no convergence towards an acceptable sharing arrangement. The issue became more complex and many other issues were related to sharing arrangements. In November 1977 the two countries proposed a five-year agreement on water sharing.
21 The new arrangement is as follows: if the Ganges flow at Farraka is 70,000 cubic feet per second (cusecs) or less, both countries are to receive 50 per cent; with a flow of between 70,000 and 75,000 cusecs Bangladesh receives 35,000 cusecs and India receives the rest; with a flow of more than 75,000 cusecs or more India receives 40,000 cusecs and Bangladesh receives the balance. Further provision is made for the situation where the flow falls below 50,000 cusecs. The sharing arrangements are to be reviewed every five years and if no agreement can be reached on adjustments, India is to release at least 90 per cent of Bangladesh's share (Devabhaktuni, 1997).
22 India's centrality in major conflicts in the South Asian region is evident from the analysis undertaken in the preceding sections.

6 Theoretical foundations of the economic integration and conflict relationship in South Asia

1 Schiff andWinters (2003).
2 See Batra (2004).
3 Keshk, Pollins and Reuveny (2004).
4 McMillan (1997).
5 South Asia has experienced one of the fastest growth rates in trade in the world, averaging 10.8 per cent in 2007, following growth of almost 12 per cent during 2005–06, which was the highest among all regions: Ahmed and Ghani (2008).
6 The term is used in a broad sense, inclusive of all forms of conflict and specific conflict events.
7 But it also may be kept in mind that for these measures to be effective beyond goodwill gestures other facilitating institutional changes need to be installed. These have, however, been slow to come.
8 These trends have been discussed in detail in Ch. 3.
9 Refer to Ch.3, p. 43.
10 Long's (2009) analysis is based on the economic agents having perfect information and forming accurate expectations about conflict in the future.
11 Refer to Ch. 5 section 'Conflict intensity and trade: visual impressions'.
12 For a survey of literature, see Reuveny (2000). Others include Barbieri and Schneider (1999) and Mansfield and Pollins (2003), Barbieri (1996), Mansfield (1994), Mansfield and Pevehouse (1999), Pollins (1989), Chang, Polachek and Robst (2004) and Oneal and Russet (1999).
13 Barbieri (1996).
14 Reuveny and Kang (1996).
15 The discussion in Ch. 5 amply reveals the role of history, India's centrality and economic and geographical asymmetry in conflict initiation and perpetuation in South Asia.
16 Barbieri (1996).
17 Conference Report (2008)'Weak States and South Asia's Insecurity Predicament, McGill University, October,.
18 Hegre, Oneal and Russet (2009).
19 Studies like Gartzke (1998), Oneal and Ray (1997), Oneal and Russet (1997), Oneal *et al.* (1996) and Polachek (1994).
20 As discussed in Ch. 5, p. 95.
21 Schiff and Winters (2003).

Notes   163

22   Reuveny and Kang (1996) present a review of the literature in this context.
23   Aitken (1973) and Brada and Mendez (1985), Rose (2000a, b).

7   Impact of conflict on intra-regional trade in South Asia: A gravity model analysis

1   This section draws from Batra (2004).
2   The results remain unchanged with population indicating economic size. The magnitude of the coefficient remains large, though is smaller than when GNP is used.
3   Coefficient sign remains unchanged with PPP-based GNP figures.
4   In accordance with Baldwin and Taglioni (2006) all variants are attempted with real values for GDP, time dummies, country pair fixed effects (CPFE-within), the last by defining the panel by unique identity for each country pair and year. The results show minor variations in the size and significance of the coefficients but broadly our conclusion with reference to the objective of our analysis remain unchanged. Results for alternative formulations are reported in Table 7.1.
5   Four different levels of water contiguity are recorded, based on the distance between the two states' territories: up to 12 miles (reflecting the widely recognized 12-mile limit for territorial waters), 24 miles (reflecting the maximum distance at which two states' 12-mile territorial limits can intersect), 150 miles (from the original 1816–1965 version of the data set, reflecting what was considered the average distance that a sailing ship could travel in one day), and 400 miles (the maximum distance at which two 200-mile exclusive economic zones can intersect), as from: Correlates of War Project. Direct Contiguity Data, 1816–2006, Version 3.1.and Stinnett et al. (2002).
6   Higher values are indicative of higher levels of joint democracy.
7   Wacziarg and Welch (2003), in their analysis of trade liberalization, experience accounts for 49 countries over the period 1990 and 2002, and in his paper, Francisco Rodriguez (2006) argues that Wacziarg and Welch (2003) actually underestimate the extent of globalization during this period.
8   Refer to analysis in Ch. 3.
9   Rose (2000).
10   The list of member countries for the RTAs is provided in the Appendix.
11   Alternative regressions with civil conflict are undertaken as some of these conflicts may have inter-state spillover effects.
12   Maoz (2005), source: http://psfaculty.ucdavis.edu/zmaoz/dyadmid/html.
13   Long (2009).
14   William R. Thompson (2001). Strategic rivalry data is available for upto 1999. For our estimation we extrapolate the 1999 data to 2000 taking these rivalries as persisting over the following year.
15   A separate analysis using the database on terrorist attacks may be more appropriate and a subject for future research.
16   Rodriguez (2006).
17   Refer to Baldwin and Taglioni (2001).
18   Coefficient estimates presented in this section are an outcome of the model specification in each context. Addition/deletion/substitution of alternative variables does not lead to any major qualitative changes in variable coefficients and hence reported elasticity values.
19   In this case, MID is used as the representative of conflict as MEPV variables for regional and bordering states in conflict would be overlapping and imply collinear terms. For this reason, therefore, neither MID nor MEPV neighbourhood conflict variable is included as a separate variable in the same regression.
20   $(e^n) - 1$.
21   Source: http://www.systemicpeace.org. List of countries in the neighbourhood for South Asia as in the MEPV database are given in the Appendix.

22 Fair judicial systems ensure that in case of legal disputes contracts would be recognized with a fair interpretation.
23 The variable is of particular interest to us as some countries in South Asia – Pakistan, Bangladesh and even Nepal – have had frequently changing political regimes.
24 Results are available from the author on request.
25 It is often said that globalization and increased economic integration at the global level has rendered borders insignificant. This is, however, a much-debated proposition. Refer to Kahler and Walter (2006).
26 Alternative estimation with a subset of the panel that is restricted to only South Asia reporter and partner countries, although extremely restricted, is undertaken to get a picture, even if constrained by the sample size and design of the region vis-à-vis conflict.
27 The country is, however, not part of our analytical sample as also of South Asia until 2007, when it becomes a member of SAARC.

8 Summary findings and an assessment of the way forward

1 Suba Chandran, source: http://www.ifa.org.np.
2 As part of the Government of India, the Jawaharlal Nehru Urban Renewal Mission started in 2006 for the development of towns and cities in explicit recognition of the role of urban areas as engines of growth.Ref. Draft Master Plan Greater Baramullah-2027, March 2011.
3 Athukorala (2010).

Bibliography

Agama, Laurrie Ann and McDaniel,Christine A. (2002) "The NAFTA Preferences and U.S. – Mexico Trade", Office of Economics Working Paper, Washington DC: US International Trade Commission.
Aggarwal, Vinod K., and Mukherjee, Rahul (2008) "India's Shifting Trade Policy: South Asia and Beyond", in Vinod K. Aggarwal and Min Gyo Koo (eds), *Asia's New Institutional Architecture*, Berkeley, CA: Springer.
Ahmed, Sadiq and Ghani, Ejaz (2008) "Making Regional Cooperation Work for South Asia's Poor", *World Bank Policy Research Working Paper* No. 4736, Washington, DC: World Bank.
Ahmed, Sadiq, Kelegama, Saman and Ghani, Ejaz (2010) *Promoting Economic Cooperation in South Asia: Beyond SAFTA*, New Delhi: Sage Publications.
Aitken, Norman D. (1973) "The Effect of EEC and EFTA on European Trade: A Temporal Cross Section Analysis", *American Economic Review*, 63.
Akanda, Aminul Islam (2012) Global Market Dynamism: Export Potentials for Bangladesh, Financial Express, March 24, 2012, www.mof.gov.bd/en/budget/rw/external_sector
Alam, M. Sayeed and Zubayer, Mahmud (2010) Intra-regional FDI Prospect in SAARC Region, *International Journal of Economics and Finance*, 2 (3).
Anderton, Charles H., and Carter, John R. (2001) "The Impact of War on Trade: An Interrupted Time Series Study", *Journal of Peace Research*, 38 (4).
Arad, Ruth and Hirsch, Seev (1981) "Peacemaking and Vested Interests" *International Studies Quarterly*, 25.
Arad, Ruth and Hirsch, Seev (1983) *The Economics of Peacemaking: Focus on the Egyptian-Israeli Situation*, New York: St. Martin's Press.
Athukorala, Prema-Chandra and Kohpaiboon, Archanun (2009) "Intra Regional Trade in East Asia: The Decoupling Fallacy, Crisis and Policy Challenges", *ADBI Working Paper Series*, No. 177, December.
Athukorala, Prema-Chandra (2010) "Production Networks and Trade Patterns in East Asia, Regionalization or Globalization", August, *ADB Working Paper Series on Regional Integration*, No. 56.
Baldwin, Richard E. (2005) Sequencing and Depth of Regional Economic Integration: Lessons for the Americas from Europe, www.nd.edu
Baldwin, R. and Taglioni, Daria (2006) "Gravity for Dummies and Dummies for Gravity Equations", Working Paper 12516, National Bureau of Economic Research (NBER), Cambridge MA.
Barbieri, Katherine (1996) "Economic Interdependence: A Path to Peace or a Source of Interstate Conflict?", *Journal of Peace Research*, 33 (1).

Bibliography

Barbieri, Katherine (2002) *The Liberal Illusion: Does Trade Promote Peace?* Ann Arbor: University of Michigan Press.

Barbieri, Katherine and Levy, Jack S. (1999) "Sleeping with the Enemy: The Impact of War on Trade", *Journal of Peace Research*, 36 (4). Special Issue on Trade and Conflict.

Barbieri, Katherine and Schneider, Gerald (1999) "Globalization and Peace: Assessing New Directions in the Study of Trade and Conflict", *Journal of Peace Research*, 36 (4).

Batra, Amita (2010) "Indo ASEAN Agreement Boosts India's Image", Policy Commentary, Sigur Centre for Asian Studies, George Washington University, February, 2010.

Batra, Amita (2005) "India-Country Study", in *South Asia Free Trade Area, Opportunities and Challenges*, Washington, DC: USAID.

Batra, Amita (2004) "India's Global Trade Potential: The Gravity Model Approach", *Working Paper No. 151, Indian Council for Research on International Economic Relations (ICRIER)*, New Delhi.

Bergstrand, Jeffrey H. (1985) "The Gravity Equation in International Trade: Some Microeconomic Foundations and Empirical Evidence, *Review of Economics and Statistics*, 67.

Bhattarai, D. (2009) "Multi-purpose Projects", in Dwarika Nath Dunghel and Santa B. Pun (eds), *The Nepal-India Water Relationship: Challenges*, New York: Springer.

Bliss, H. and Russett, B. (1998) "Democratic Trading Partners: The Liberal Connection, 1962–1989", *Journal of Politics*, 60 (4).

Blomberg, S. Brock and Hess, Gregory D. (2006) "How Much Does Violence Tax Trade?", *The Review of Economics and Statistics*, 88 (4).

Blomberg, S. Brock, Hess, Gregory D. and Orphanides, Athansios (2004) "The Macroeconomic Consequences of Terrorism", *Journal of Monetary Economics*, 51.

Brada, Joesph and Mendez, Jose A. (1985) "Economic Integration Among Developing and Centrally Planned Economies: A Comparative Analysis", *The Review of Economics and Statistics*, 67.

Chandran, Suba (2001) "Indo-Pak Summits – A Profile", Monograph, Institute of Peace and Conflict Studies, New Delhi.

Chandran, Suba (n.d.) "Intra State Armed Conflict in South Asia, Impact on Regional Security", http://www.ifa.org.np

Chang, Yuan-Ching, Polachek, Solomon W., and Robst, John (2004) "Conflict and Trade: The Relationship between Geographic Distance and International Interactions", *Journal of Socio-Economics*, 33 (4).

Conference Report (2008) 'Weak States and South Asia's Insecurity Predicament", McGill University, October.

Deardorff, Alan (1995) "Determinants of Bilateral Trade: Does Gravity Work in a Classical World?" Paper presented at conference on The Regionalization of the World Economy, NBER, Woodstock, Vermont.

Deshal de Mel (n.d.) "India–Sri Lanka, Pakistan Sri Lanka Free Trade Agreements", Institute of Policy Studies, mimeo Colombo.

Devabhaktuni, Sony (1997) "Regional Cooperation in South Asia, Prospects and Problems", Occasional Paper 32, The Henry L.Stimson Centre, Washington, DC.

Duval, Yann and Utoktham, Chorthip (2009) "Behind the Border Trade Facilitation in Asia-Pacific: Cost of Trade, Credit Information, Credit Information, Contract Enforcement and Regulatory Coherence", Asia Pacific Research and Training Network on Trade, Working Paper Series No. 67, May 2009.

Faye, Michael, McAurthur, John W., Sachs, Jeffrey D. and Snow, Thomas (2003) 'The Challenges Facing Landlocked Developing Countries", *Journal of Human Development*, 5 (4).

Feridhanusetyawan, Tubagus (2005) "Preferential Trade Agreements in the Asia Pacific Region", *IMF Working Paper* WP/05/149, International Monetary Fund (IMF), Washington DC.
Frankel, Jeffrey A., Stein, Ernesto and Wei, Shang-Jin (1997) *Regional Trading Blocs in the World Economic System*, Washington, DC: Institute for International Economics.
Frankel, Jeffrey A. and Rose, Andrew (2000) "Estimating the Effect of Currency Unions on Trade and Output", *NBER Working Paper* No. 7857, NBER, Cambridge, MA.
Gartzke, Eric (1998) "Kant We All Get Along? Opportunity, Willingness and the Origins of the Democratic Peace", *American Journal of Political Science*, 42 (1).
Gartzke, E., Li, Quanand Boehmer, C. (2001) "Investing in the Peace: Economic Interdependence and International Conflict", *International Organization*, 55 (2).
Gasiorowski, Mark J. (1986) "Economic Interdependence and International Conflict: Some Cross National Evidence," *International Studies Quarterly*, 30.
Gasiorowski, Mark J. and Polachek, Simon W. (1982) "Conflict and Interdependence" *Journal of Conflict Resolution*, 26.
Ghani, Ejaz and Iyer, Lakshmi (2010) "Conflict and Development – Lessons from South Asia", Economic Premise, No. 31, Poverty Reduction and Economic Management (PREM), World Bank, September.
Giroud, A. (2009) "Regional Integration and South-South FDI: A Global Perspective", Presentation to the Expert Meeting on International Cooperation, www.unctad.org
Glick, Reuvan and Taylor, Alan M. (2005) "Collateral Damage: Trade Disruption and the Economic Impact of War", *NBER Working Paper* No. 11565.
Gowa, Joanne and Mansfield, Edward D. (1993) "Power Politics and International Trade", *American Political Science Review*, 87.
Hegre, Havard, Oneal, J.R. and Russet, B. (2009) "Trade Does Promote Peace: New Simultaneous Estimates of the Reciprocal Effects of Trade and Conflict", Mimeo.
Helpman, Elhanan and Krugman, Paul R. (1985) *Market Structure and Foreign Trade: Increasing Returns, Imperfect Competition, and the International Economy*, Cambridge, MA: MIT Press.
Ijaz, Nabi (1997) "Outward Orientation of the Economy: A Review of Pakistan's Trade and Exchange Rate Policy", *Journal of Asian Economics*, 8 (1), Spring.
Islam, Roumeen and Zannini,Gianni (2008) *World Trade Indicators: Benchmarking Policy and Performance*, Washington, DC: World Bank.
Iqbal, Ashiq (2012) "Non Tariff Barriers in South Asia, Addressing the Challenges", Presentation at a ARTNeT/WTO Research Workshop on Emerging Trade Issues in Asia and the Pacific, meeting contemporary challenges, organized by ARTNeT in Thailand, April.
Jain, Rajiv and Singh, J.B. (2009) "Trade Pattern in SAARC Countries, Emerging Trends and Issues, *RBI Occasional Papers*, 30 (3), Winter, Reserve Bank of India, New Delhi.
Jones, D.M., Bremer, S.A. and Singer, J.D. (1996) "Militarized Interstate Disputes, 1816–1992: Rationale, Coding Rules and Empirical Patterns", *Conflict Management and Science*, 15 (2).
Kahler, Miles and Walter, Barabara F. (eds) (2006) *Territoriality and Conflict in an Era of Globalization*, New York: Cambridge University Press.
Kaplan, Robert D. (2010) "South Asia's Geography of Conflict", Centre for a New American Security, Washington DC.
Kelegama, Saman and Mukherjee, I.N (2007) "India–Sri Lanka Bilateral Free Trade Agreement: Six Years performance and Beyond", *RIS Discussion Paper No. 119*, New Delhi.

Keshk, Omar M. G., Pollins, Brianand Reuveny, Rafael (2004) "Trade Still Follows the Flag: The Primacy of Politics in a Simultaneous Model of Interdependence and Armed Conflict", *Journal of Politics*, 66 (4).

Khan, Ashfaque A. (1998) "The Experience of Trade Liberalization in Pakistan", *Pakistan Development Review*, 37 (4), Part II, Winter.

Khan, Ashfaque H. and Kim, Yun Hwan (1999) "Foreign Direct Investment in Pakistan: Policy Issues and Operational Implications", *Economic and Development Resource Centre (EDRC) Report Series* No. 66, July 1999, Asian Development Bank, Manila, Philippines.

Khan, Shaheen Rafi (2009) *Regional Trade Integration and Conflict Resolution*, London: Routledge.

Khatri, Sridhar K. and Kueck, Gert W. (2003) *Terrorism in South Asia: Impact on Development and Democratic Process*, Colombo: RCSS/New Delhi: Konrad Adeneur Foundation/Delhi: Shipra Publications.

Kim, Hyung Min and Rousseau, David L. (2005) "The Classical Liberals Were Half Right (Or Half Wrong): New Tests of the 'Liberal Peace', 1960–88", *Journal of Peace Research*, 42 (5).

Kumar, Nagesh (2010) "Capital Flows and Development: Lessons from South Asian Experience", MPDD Discussion Papers WP/10/11, UNESCAP, November.

Levy, G. and Razin, R. (2004) "It Takes Two: An Explanation for the Democratic Peace", *Journal of the European Economics Association*, 2 (1).

Linnemann, Hans (1966) *An Econometric Study of International Trade Flows*, Amsterdam: North Holland.

Li, Quan and Sacko, David (2002) "The (Ir) Relevance of Militarized Interstate Disputes for International trade", *International Studies Quarterly*, 46.

Long, Andrew G. (2009) "Bilateral Trade in the Shadow of Armed Conflict", *International Studies Quarterly*, 52 (1).

McMillan, Susan (1997) "Interdependence and Conflict", *Mershon International Studies Review*, 41.

Madhukar, S.B.J. Rana and Man Pradhan, Stalin (2005) "Implementation Evaluation of FDI Policy in Nepal", *Economic Policy Network, Policy Paper* 1, August.

Mansfield, Edward D. (1994) *Power, Trade and War*, Princeton, NJ: Princeton University Press.

Mansfield, Edward D., Pevehouse, Jon C. and Bearce, David H. (1999) "Preferential Trading Arrangements and Military Disputes", *Security Studies*, 9 (1).

Mansfield, Edward D. and Milner, Helen V. (1999) "The New Wave of Regionalism", *Industrial Organization*, 53 (3).

Mansfield, Edward D. and Pevehouse, Jon C. (2000) "Trade Blocs, Trade Flows and International Conflict", *International Organization*, 54 (4).

Mansfield, Edward D., Milner, Helen V. and Rosendorff, B. Peter (2000) "Free to Trade: Democracies, Autocracies and International Trade", *American Political Science Review*, 94 (2).

Mansfield, Edward D. and Pollins, Brian M. (eds) (2003) *Economic Interdependence and International Conflict: New Perspectives on an Enduring Debate*. Ann Arbor, MI: Michigan University Press.

Martin, Philippe, Mayer, Thierry and Thoening, Mathias (2007) "Make Trade Not War", *Review of Economic Studies*, 75 (3).

Milner, Helen V. and Kubota, Keiko (2005) "Why the Move to Free Trade? Democracy and Trade Policy in Developing Countries", *International Organization*, 59 (1).

Morrow, James. D. (1999) "How Could Trade Affect Conflict? *Journal of Peace Research*, 36 (4).
Morrow, J.D., Siverson, R.M and Tabares, T.E. (1998) "The Political Determinants of International Trade: The Major Powers, 1907–90", *American Political Science Review*, 92 (3).
Morrow, J.D., Siverson, R.M and Tabares, T.E. (1999) "Correction to The Political Determinants of International Trade", *American Political Science Review*, 93 (4).
Mukherjee, I.N. (2004) "Towards a Free Trade Area in South Asia: Charting a Feasible Course for Trade Liberalization with reference to India's Role", *RIS Discussion Paper* No. 86, Research and Information Systems, New Delhi.
Mukherjee, I.N. (2010) "Revision of India–Nepal Treaty of Trade and its Implications for Strengthening Bilateral Trade and investment", *RIS Discussion Paper* No. 161.
Oneal, John R., Oneal, Frances H., Maoz, Zeev and Russet, Bruce (1996) "The Liberal Peace: Interdependence, Democracy and International Conflict, 1950–85", *Journal of Peace Research*, 33.
Oneal, John R. and Ray, James Lee (1997) "New Tests of the Democratic Peace: Controlling for Economic Interdependence, 1950–85", *Political Research Quarterly*, 50 (4).
Oneal, John R. and Russet, Bruce (1997) "The Liberal Peace with Alternative Specifications: Trade Still Reduces Conflict", *Journal of Peace Research*, 36 (4), Special Issue on Trade and Conflict.
Oneal, John R. and Russet, Bruce (1999a) "Assessing the Liberal Peace with Alternative Specifications: Trade Still Reduces Conflict", *Journal of Peace Research*, 36 (3).
Oneal, John R. and Russet, Bruce (1999b) "Is the Liberal Peace Just an Artifact of the Cold War?" *International Interactions*, 25 (3).
Polachek, Solomon W. (1994) "Cooperation and Conflict Among Democracies: Why do Democracies Cooperate More and Fight Less?" Paper presented at the Peace Science Society (International) Meeting, Urbana-Champaign, IL.
Polachek, Solomon W. (1980) "Conflict and Trade", *Journal of Conflict Resolution*, 24 (1).
Pollins, Brian M. (1989a) "Conflict, Cooperation and Commerce: The Effects of International Political Interactions on Bilateral Trade Flows", *American Journal of Political Science*, 33 (3).
Pollins, Brian M. (1989b) "Does Trade Still Follow the Flag?" *American Political Science Review*, 83.
Poyhonen, Pentti (1963) "A Tentative Mode for the Volume of Trade Between Countries", *Weltwirtschaftliches Archiv*, 90.
Prebisch, R. (1950) "Commercial Policy in Undeveloped Countries", *American Economic Review*, Papers and Proceedings, May.
Prebisch, R. (1984) "Five Stages in My Thinking on Development", in G.M Meir and D. Seers (eds), *Pioneers in Development*, New York: Oxford University Press.
Qamar, Abid (2005) "Trade between India and Pakistan: Potential Items and the MFN Status", State Bank of Pakistan, Research Bulletin, 1 (1).
Quantification of Benefits from Economic Cooperation in South Asia (2008) Asian Development Bank and UNCTAD, New Delhi: Macmillan India.
Reuveny, Rafael (2000) "The Trade and Conflict Debate: A Survey of Theory, Evidence and Future Research", *Peace Economics, Peace Science and Public Policy*, 6.
Reuveny, R and Kang, H. (1996) "International Trade, Political Conflict/Cooperation, and Granger Causality", *American Journal of Political Science*, 40 (3).
Rodriguez, Francisco Rafael (2006) "Openness and Growth: What Have We Learned?" Working Paper No., United Nations Department of Economic and Social Affairs.

170 Bibliography

Rose, Andrew K. (2000a) *EMU's Potential Effect on British Trade: A Quantitative Assessment*, Berkeley, CA: University of California.

Rose, Andrew K. (2000b) *One Money, One Market: Estimating the Effect of Common Currencies on Trade*, Berkeley: University of California.

Sahai, I.M. (2007) "Baglihar Decision – An End to the Dispute?"*International Water Power and Dam Construction*, 59 (4).

Schiff, M. and Winters, L.A. (2003) *Regional Integration and Development*, Washington, DC: The World Bank.

Shahzad, Shafiq A., Sarfraz, M. Irfan, Quddus, Maliha, Aslam, M. Rizwan (2011) "Evaluation of Trade Agreements: A Case Study of Pakistan–Sri Lanka FTA", PITD Working Paper 02/2011.

Simmons, Beth (2006) "Trade and Territorial Conflict in Latin America: International Borders as Institutions", in Miles Kahler and Barabara Walters (eds), *Territoriality and Conflict in an Era of Globalization*, Cambridge: Cambridge University Press.

Sridharan, Kripa (2007) *Regional Cooperation in South Asia and Southeast Asia*, Institute of Southeast Asian Studies, Singapore.

Stinnett, Douglas M., Tir, Jaroslav, Schafer, Philip, Diehl, Paul F., and Gochman, Charles (2002) "The Correlates of War Project Direct Contiguity Data, Version 3." *Conflict Management and Peace Science* 19 (2): 58–66.

Sustainable Development Policy Institute (SDPI) (2005) Qualifying Informal Trade between Pakistan and India. SDPI, Pakistan.

Tewari, M. (2008) "Deepening Intra-Regional Trade and Investment in South Asia, the Case of the Textiles and Clothing Industry", *ICRIER Working Paper* No. 213, New Delhi.

Thompson, William R. (2001) "Identifying Rivals and Rivalries in World Politics", *International Studies Quarterly*, 45.

Tinbergen, Jan (1962) "An Analysis of World Trade Flows", in Jan Tinbergen (ed.), *Shaping the World Economy*, New York: The Twentieth Century Fund.

Wacziarg, R. and Welch, K.H. (2003) "Trade Liberalization and Growth: New Evidence". NBER Working Paper No. 10152, NBER, Cambridge MA.

Weerakoon, Dushni and Thenakoon, Jayanth (n.d.) "India Sri Lanka FTA: Lessons for SAFTA", www.commonwealth.org.

Wetter, J. Gillis (1971) "The Rann of Kutch Arbitration", *The American Journal of International Law*, 65 (2), April: 346–357.

Wirsing, Robert G. and Jasparro, Christopher (2007)"River Rivalry: Water Disputes, Resource Insecurity and Diplomatic Deadlock in South Asia", *Water Policy*, 9.

Wonnacott, P. and Lutz, M. (1989), "Is There a Case for Free Trade Areas" in J. Scott (ed.), *Free Trade Areas and U.S. Trade Policy*, Washington, DC: Institute for International Economics.

Yasmeen, Samina and Dixit, Aabha (1995) "Confidence Building Measures in South Asia", Occasional Paper No. 24, Henry L. Stimson Centre, Washington, DC.

Reports

Government of India, *Foreign Trade Policy: August 2009–March 2014*, Ministry of Commerce and Industry, Department of Commerce. http://dgft.gov.in

Group of 15, A Survey of Foreign Direct Investment in G15 Countries, *Working Paper Series*, Volume 7, February 2010, mimeo, Summit Level Group of Developing Countries.

India–Bhutan Bilateral Relations, Embassy of India, Thimpu, Bhutan, http://www.indianembassythimphu.bt/relation

South Asian Association for Regional Cooperation (SAARC), Statement by SAARC Secretary General at the Inaugural Session of the Fifteenth SAARC Summit held in Colombo in August, 2008, SAARC Secretariat, Kathmandu, Nepal.www.saarc-sec.org

United Nations Conference for Trade and Development (UNCTAD), *World Investment Report*, various issues, Geneva, Switzerland.

United Nations Conference for Trade and Development (UNCTAD), *Investment Policy Review*, various issues, Geneva, Switzerland.

United Nations Economic and Social Commission for Asia and the Pacific (UNESCAP), Asia Pacific Trade Agreement, Trade and Investment Division, Bangkok, Thailand. http://www.unescap.org/tid/apta.asp and http:// www.unescap.org/tid/apta/factsheet08.pdf

United Nations Economic and Social Commission for Asia and the Pacific (UNESCAP), *Country Note: Economic and Social Survey of Asia and Pacific*, various issues.

World Bank, *Doing Business*, various issues, Washington, DC.

World Bank, *South Asia Economic Update: Moving Up, Looking East, 2010*, Washington, DC.

World Bank, 2004, *Trade Policies in South Asia: An Overview*, Report No. 29949, September, Washington, DC.

World Economic Forum, *Global Competitiveness Report*, various issues, Geneva, Switzerland.

Databases

Asian Development Bank, Asia Regional Integration Centre, Databases: http://aric.adb.org

Asian Development Bank (ADB), Water Knowledge Centre, Statistics, Country Profiles – India. www2.adb.org/Water/Indicators/cwsi-country-profile.asp

Centre for Systemic Peace, Polity IV Project: Political Regimes and Transitions, 1800–2010. www.systemicpeace.org/polity/polity4.htm

CIA, *The World Fact Book*, several issues.

International Monetary Fund, (IMF) Directions of Trade Statistics (DOTS), various issues, Washington DC.

International Monetary Fund, (IMF) World Economic Outlook, 2012, April, Washington DC.

Pakistan Balance of Trade: www.tradingeconomic.com/pakistan/balance-of-trade

South Asia Confidence Building Measures Timeline, Stimson Centre, Washington, DC. http://www.stimson.org/research-pages/confidence-building-measures-in-south-asia-/

United Nations Conference for Trade and Development (UNCTAD): Statistical databases online: http://archive.unctad.org

United Nations Commodity Trade Statistics Database: UNcomtrade: hhtp://comtrade.un.org

United Nations Economic and Social Commission for Asia and the Pacific (UNESCAP), Asia Pacific Research and Training Network (ArtNET) databases, http://www.unescap.org/tid/artnet/database

World Bank, 2011, World Data Bank, *World Development Indicators*. Available at http://databank.worldbank.org/data

World Bank, 2010, *World Trade Indicators 2009/10: Country Trade Briefs*. Washington, DC: World Bank. Available at http://www.worldbank.org/wti

Zeev Maoz, 2005, Dyadic Militarized Interstate Dispute Dataset (version 2.0), http://ps faculty.ucdavis.edu/zmaoz/dyadmid/html

Index

ADB 68, 72, 78, 151
adjacency 117–19, 124, 140, 142
adult literacy 25
Afghanistan 1, 5, 11, 17, 40, 43; bilateral FTA with India 71; boundary dispute with Pakistan 76–7; conflict 82; connectivity 146, 148; FDI 52; gas pipeline 86; international warfare 131–2, 139; refugees 81; role of transit agreement 46–8; South Asia neighbourhood 152
Agreements of Double Taxation Avoidance 54
aid 11, 82, 86
Anderton, Charles H. and Carter, John R. 128
anticipated conflict 104–5, 123–4, 126; coefficient of 129; costs to trade 132, 139, 142; and RTA membership 130
anti-dumping measures 44–5
APEC 110
APTA 26, 72
Arad and Hirsch 106
Argentina 7, 110, 152
ASEAN 5–8, 10, 14, 64, 72–3; FTA with India 109–10; production networks 149; regional connectivity 146–7; regionalism 99
ASEAN Economic Community 6
ASEAN Framework Agreement on Services liberalization (AFAS) 6
ASEAN Free Trade Area agreement (AFTA) 6, 121, 130, 152
ASEAN Investment Area (AIA) 6
ASEAN plus-three 8
asymmetry 5, 8, 107; economic 70, 111, 113, 136, 137; geographic 136
Athukorala, Prema-Chandra 150
Attari-Wagah/Wagah-Attari 86, 144

augmented gravity model 124
autarkic policies 3
autocracies 6, 64, 108–9, 128, 140; joint 142
Awami League 109

Baglihar dam 79
balance of payment crisis 29
Bangladesh 5, 7–8, 11, 17, 18; bilateral trade relationship with India 138; LDCs 137; production networks 57–9; RTA members 152
Bangladesh Nationalist Party (BNP) 95, 109
Barbieri, Katherine 106, 107
Barbeiri, Katherine and Levy, Jack S. 112, 122, 132
bargaining power 47–8
barriers 36, 46, 66, 99, 113, 128; behind the border 15, 28, 50; non-tariff 3, 30–1, 34, 44–5, 65, 102, 139, 143–4; trade 2, 14, 33, 108, 129, 141
Batra, Amita 115
Bergstrand, Jeffrey H. 116
Bharatiya Janata Party (BJP) 109
Bhutan 1, 5–6, 8, 17, 45, 66, 68, 72, 82, 136; India-Bhutan 4, 69–70; 146; LDCs 137; RTA membership 152
bilateral conflicts 4, 7, 75, 81; globalization and 103–4; relates to bilateral economic relationship 138; RTAs and 111; trade as a consequence of 113; trade loss 140
Bilateral Investment Protection and Promotion Agreements 54
bilateral trade agreements 4, 48, 61, 68
BIMSTEC 26, 72, 73
Bliss, H. and Russett, B. 108
Bloomberg, S. Brock and Hess, Gregory D. 101

Board of Investment (BOI) 31, 33
border 11, 17, 25, 26, 43–4, 47–9, 80; charges 32; common 5, 17, 110; and conflict 127–8, 131–2, 134, 136; cross-border 46, 75, 81–2, 102, 128; disputes 5, 75–7; fencing 88; hardening of the 102; independent variable 117–19, 124, 133; shared 118, 119; thickened 150; trade 45, 102, 108, 119, 143, 144, 148, 149; trade loss 140–2, 143
border trade routes 119, 145, 149
Brasstacks 83
Brazil 7, 110, 152
Bureau of Indian Standards 45

CACM 110
capital inflows 20, 21, 26, 30, 51
ceasefire line 76
Central Asia 11, 19, 35, 62
Central Asian Republics 148
CES preferences 116
change in tariff heading (CTH) 68, 71
Chiang Mai Initiative (CMI) 6
China 12, 13, 20, 23, 24, 38, 39; assembly line manufacturing production 150; Bangkok Agreement 72; FDI 51, 56; India's trade with 136; neighbouring countries for South Asia 152; Pakistan and 43; source of imports 57–9
circular trade 43
civil conflict 4, 75, 93–7, 117, 139
Cobb-Douglas preferences 116
Colombo 7, 11, 33, 146
comparative advantage 6, 10, 42, 56–7, 106, 149
comprehensive dialogue: India–Pakistan 85
comprehensive economic partnership agreement 4, 8
confidence building measures/CBMs 15, 75, 82–7; conflict and 90–1; democratic regimes 98; history of 137–8; India's trade with Pakistan 93; multi-faceted 124; regional 89
conflict intensity 93, 94–7, 112, 138
conflict prevention 7
connectivity 25, 48, 68, 119, 145–50
contiguity 82, 117–19, 124, 127, 133; impact on trade 140
Correlates of War (COW) 121
cost of conflict 75, 91, 100–4; economic 109; quantitative estimates of 115
countervailing measures 44
cross-section estimation 126
customs procedures 44, 50, 66, 143

Deardorff, Alan 116
deeper economic integration 6, 14
democracy 5, 6, 32, 64, 75, 93–4, 96–8, 108–9; joint 120, 128, 132–3
democratic peace 98, 119, 140–1
dependent variable 112, 117, 124, 126
dispute settlement 3, 66, 67
distance 62, 83, 115–19, 127, 133; bilateral trade related to 139–40
Doha Development Agenda (DDA) 63–4
doing business 23, 32, 51
Dubai 43, 49
dummy variables 113, 118–24, 127
Durand line 76–7
dyadic conflict 101, 121, 123, 129–30; in the estimation process 139; impact on trade 141

early harvest programme (EHP) 65
East Asia 6, 9, 10, 12–13, 18–20, 22, 35; bilateral FTAs 62; BIMSTEC 73; integrating South Asia with 64; investor regions 56; production networks 150
East Asia Summit (EAS) 8, 10
econometric modelling 26
economic conflicts 82
economic cooperation 2, 7, 26, 42, 87, 106; intra SAARC 65–6, 68
economic dynamism 1, 10, 18, 24, 109, 145
economic interdependence 5, 14, 105, 106, 143
economic profile 20
economic reforms 1, 9, 14, 18, 29, 32–4; initiation of 136; pace of 140
economic regime 28–9, 57, 63, 109, 117; shift in 125–6, 130–3, 140–2; South Asian 120
economies of scale 42
ECSC 110
EEC 110
embargoes 102
enabling clause 66
endogeneity 127
energy security 102, 145, 147
ethnic conflict 89, 128, 140
EU/European Union 5–7, 11, 14, 35, 110; case of 46, 99; FTA with 62; traditional markets like 38
Europe 19, 35, 53, 110
expectation of conflict 104–5, 123, 130–1, 139

174 Index

exchange rate 18, 28–31, 33–4, 117
export-import policy 29
export-led growth 13
export processing zones 33

Farakka 80–1, 88
FDI 10, 15–16, 20, 28, 30, 31–4; collaborations 63; South Asia's share 51; trade agreements and 69–71
financial integration 20, 148, 149
five-year plans 28
fixed effects: country pair (CPFE) 126, 133
Foreign Investment Promotion Board 30
Foreign Investment and Technology Act 33
foreign portfolio investment 30
Foreign Private Investment Promotion and Protection Act 31
foreign trade policy 30
Franco-German 7
Frankel, Jeffrey A. 116

Gandak agreement 80
Ganges water agreement 88
Gasiorowski, Mark J. 112
Gasiorowski, Mark J. and Polachek, Simon W. 106, 112
GATT 30, 66
GDP 1, 3, 4, 10, 13, 19–23, 26, 33; gravity model 115, 120, 133, 136, 140
genetically modified (GM) 45
geo-political 63
Glick, Reuvan and Taylor, Alan M. 101–2
global competitiveness report 23
global financial crisis 6, 9, 10, 12, 34, 38, 63; impact of 21, 55; intra regional trade 40; post 14, 18, 135; prior to the 20; recover from 137
global imbalance 12
globalization 32, 101, 103
Gowa, Joanne and Mansfield, Edward D. 122
granger causality test 112, 126
gravity model 15, 100, 101, 105, 113; analysis 115–17, 119; conflict augmented gravity model 16, 124, 127, 133, 138; estimated 125–7, 130–2, 139–40; specification 122
Greater Colombo Economic Commission 33
gross national income, per capita (GNI PC) 18–19

harmonized system 30, 34, 65
Hecksher-Ohlin 109, 116–17
Hegre, Harvard, Oneal, J.R. and Russet, B. 112
Helpman, Elhanan and Krugman, Paul R. 116
Hirschman index 39
Hong Kong 43, 53, 58, 154–5
Human Development Index/HDI 24, 25
Hussainiwala and Fazilka 144

import duty: peak rate 30
import-substitution 17, 19, 28, 34, 109
independent variables 115, 117, 119
index of openness 34–5
India-ASEAN FTA 64, 109; Treaty of Trade and Commerce 68
India-Bangladesh 44, 77, 88, 91, 92, 95
India Bhutan Trade and Commerce Agreement 4, 69
India's centrality 1, 26, 41, 119
India and China 8, 9–11
India and Nepal 4, 68–9, 77, 87–8; economic frictions 90–2, 96; transit 48; water relations 80–1
India and Pakistan conflict 8, 61, 63–4, 81, 111, 113, 125, 129–34, 139; deficit 49; Trade 43–4
India–Sri Lanka Bilateral Free trade Agreement (ISLFTA) 4, 55, 97, 137
India and Sri Lanka Peace Accord 89
India–Thailand FTA 64
Indo–Bangladesh Border Agreement 88, 95
Indonesia 110, 152–4
Indo–Pak Joint Commission 84
Indo–Sri Lanka Joint Commission 89
Indus water treaty 78, 79, 84
Industrial Policy and Industrial Enterprise Act 32
infant-industry argument 29
informal trade 28, 43, 44
instrumental variables 127
Integrated Checkpost (ICP) 144
interactive/interaction term 128, 130
inter-state conflict 15–16, 75, 82, 101, 105; anticipated 123–4, 126, 140; between a trade partner and third party 117; of the dyad members 121; in South Asia 110; transformation of intra-state to 139
intra-regional trade 6, 15, 27, 40, 65–7; diversification of 48; facilitating 46, 49; impact of conflict on 16, 82; India and 26, 41–2; production network 57, 60,

149–50; RTA contribution to 111; stagnant/low level of 2–4, 28, 63, 101, 103, 128, 134, 136, 139, 142
intra-state conflict 75, 82, 139
inter-sub-regional: agreements 71–3; groupings 26
investment promotion board 33
inward-looking 10, 19, 28–9, 34; economies 9, 109, 120, 136
IPKF 89
Iran-Pakistan-India gas pipeline 102
island 4, 17, 33, 77, 88–9, 119; coefficient of 127; gravity model 124, 133

Japan 8, 11, 53, 64–5, 153
Jones, D.M., Bremer, S.A. and Singer J.D. 122

Karachi Agreement 76
Kargil 76, 83, 91, 124–5, 138
Kashmir 75–6, 78–9, 81–5, 125, 141; trade across Line of Control (LoC) in 86, 148
Kathmandu 2, 146
Keshk, Omar G, Pollins Brian and Reuveny, Rafael 112
Kim, Hyung Min and Rousseau, David L. 112
Kishenganga dam 79
Korea/South Korea/RoK/Republic of Korea 8, 11, 53, 55, 58, 64, 72, 153–5
Kosi Agreement 80, 87

Lahore declaration 85, 90
landlocked 17, 21, 25, 46–50, 146; dummy variables 119; gravity model 124, 127, 133
latent conflict 90
least-developed countries/LDCs 40, 46, 65, 137
letter of credit authorization 45
Levy, G. and Razin, R. 119
Li, Quan and Sacko, David 120, 124
Liaquat Nehru Pact 83
life expectancy 24–5
Line of Control/LoC 76, 85
Linnemann, Hans 116
lobbies 63–5, 129
Logistics Performance Index/LPI 50
Long, Andrew G. 102, 104–5, 108–9
look east policy 8, 73
look west policy 73
low-income countries 36, 38
lower-middle-income countries 36–8
LTTE 89–90

Index 175

Mahakali river 77, 88; agreement 80
Major Episodes of Political Violence/ MEPV 121–3
Malaysia 110, 152–4
Maldives 1, 17, 62, 66–7, 89, 137, 152
Maoists 82
Maoz, Zeev 121
Martin, Phillipe, Mayer, Thierry and Thoening, Mathias 103
Mauritius 11, 55
Mcmillan, Susan 106
MEPV database 94–7, 121–2, 125, 128, 132, 152
MERCOSUR 7, 110, 121, 130, 150, 152
migration 75
militarized armed conflict 76
militarized inter-state dispute (MID) 121–3, 126, 129, 131–3, 142
military regimes 5, 6, 64
Milner, Helen V. and Kubota, Keiko 109
mixed regimes 120, 132, 142
MNCs 53–6, 150
monadic conflict 117, 122, 129, 131–2
monarchy 5, 75, 98
Morrow, James D., Siverson, R.M and Tebares T.E. 104, 122–4
most favoured nation (MFN) 34, 54, 65, 69, 136; applied tariff 32, 37; India, Pakistan and 43–4, 49, 64, 82, 84–6, 91, 94, 111, 138, 143–5; Tariff Trade Restrictiveness Index (TTRI) 36, 37; trade tariff structure 136
Muhurichar river island 77
multilateral trade openness 103
Munabao-Khokhrapar 86, 144
mutual recognition agreements 46
Myanmar 11, 17, 72, 146, 148, 152

NAFTA 42, 99, 121, 130, 152
Nathu-la pass 11
National Democratic Alliance 109
national income 115
national treatment 31, 33, 54
natural resource based conflicts 78
natural trading partner 1, 63
negative list 3, 8, 30, 67, 70–1, 137, 144
negative-list approach 90, 143
negotiations 4, 26, 62, 84, 102–3, 110, 119, 148–9; Bangkok Agreement 72; BIMSTEC 73; India–ASEAN FTA 64, 109; product-by-product approach of 66; SAFTA 67; SAPTA 2, 65–6
neighbourhood civil conflict 131, 142
neighbourhood conflict 128, 140

176 Index

Nepal's trade policy 35
New Moore island 77
non-discriminatory 49, 54
non LDCs (NLDCs) 67
non-policy variables 117–18, 124
non-reciprocal 8, 40, 137
North America 110
Northeast and eastern states/regions, India 11, 45, 48, 81–2
NTBs database 68

OLS methodology 126
open regionalism 12
overlap 73, 150

Pakistan 1, 3, 43, 66–7, 77
Pakistan-Sri Lanka FTA 71
panel dataset 126
Paraguay 7, 152
partition 1, 5, 65, 75, 83
persistent conflict 1, 9, 15, 65, 90, 117; connectivity and 150; gravity model 123–4, 129, 130; impact of 122; India-Pakistan 137–8
Petrapole-Benapole border crossing 45
pharmaceuticals 39, 54
Polachek, Solomon W. 106, 111, 113
policy-related costs 117
policy variables 115, 124
political economy 63–4
political regimes 5, 6, 64, 75, 90, 94, 142, 145; authoritative 96; determinant of trade policy 108–9; gravity model 117, 119–20, 128–9, 132–3; impact of 140; Nepal-Sri-Lanka 98; in Pakistan 102
polity IV 94–5, 120–1, 152
Pollins, Brian M. 100, 112–13
Pollins, Brian M. and Reuveny, rafael 112
positive list 143
positive-list approach 64, 67, 90, 137
poverty 24–5
Poyhonen, Pentti 115
preferential tariffs 2, 65
preferential trading agreements 61–73, 135
pre-shipment inspection (PSI) 44–5
production networks 6–7, 10, 15, 28, 56–7, 145, 149
protectionist 38, 63, 106, 129
proximity 2, 4, 17, 62–3, 128, 130, 134, 139
purchasing power parity (PPP) 18, 118

quantitative restrictions 29–30, 32, 120

Rann of Kutch 84
rational expectations 105
readymade garments 8, 39, 59
reform fatigue 126
refugees 76, 81
region, definition 17
regional conflict 93–5, 118, 125
regional conflict intensity 93–7, 125
regional instability 91, 93–4, 128, 140
regionalism 8, 12, 17, 61, 64, 99, 135
regression 108, 127, 129, 131, 142
resource disputes 5
Reuveny, R. and Kang, H. 112, 126
Rose, Andrew K. 121
rules of origin/RoO 3, 44, 55, 65–8, 70

SAARC 3, 5, 8, 72, 99, 114, 126; expansion 12; institutional mechanism 2; intra regional trade 40; observers 9; Region/economies/member nations/ states 18, 26, 32, 42–6, 56, 65–6, 71, 137; regional CBM 89; regional transit 49; Summit 7, 11, 61, 67, 84–6, 90, 111, 146
SAFTA 2–4, 18, 40, 49, 61, 64, 66–8, 73, 90; and BIMSTEC 143; Pakistan's positive list approach 111, 137; progress of 99; sensitive list 152
Salal dam agreement 84
sanitary and phyto sanitary (SPS) 44–6, 69
SAPTA 2, 18, 61, 65–6, 90; progress of 99, 137; RTAs included for estimation 121, 130, 133, 152
SASEC 72
secessionist movement 82, 139
sector-wise 22, 53
security externalities 110
sensitive list 66, 152
shallow trade agreement 67
Siachen 76, 83, 90
Simla Agreement 76, 84
Simmons, Beth 143
Singapore 10, 43, 49, 53, 58, 152–3
SIPRI (Stockholm International Peace Research Institute) 125–6
Sir Creek 76
smuggling 43–4, 48, 59
social indicators 24
South Asia Growth Quadrangle (SAGQ) 26, 72
South East Asia 8, 10, 18, 28, 56, 62, 64, 72, 149; South East Asian 6, 7, 59, 71, 136, 150

south-south 38, 56, 60, 64
sovereignty 5, 14, 77, 80, 84, 107, 119
special and differential treatment 34, 65
special industrial zones (SIZ) 31
spillover effects 5, 82, 139, 145
Srinagar–Muzaffarabad road 102, 144
Stolper Samuelson theorem 109
strategic rivalry 123, 126, 129, 133, 139, 141; coefficient of 130; enduring 132, 142
structural adjustment programme 29
sub regional agreements 71
Sub-Saharan Africa 18–19, 24, 35
Sugauli Treaty 77
supra-national 14, 46
synchronization costs 116

tariff liberalization 3, 71, 137
tariff rate quotas 70–1
Tashkent agreement 84, 90
technical barriers to trade (TBT) 44–6
Teesta river water management 81
territorial conflict 110
territorial disputes 5, 75, 110, 118, 144
terrorism 75, 85, 101; cross border 81; global 126,
textile and clothing sector 15, 28, 56, 59, 150, 153
Thailand 10, 55, 58, 65, 72–3, 146, 153–5
theoretical modelling 100, 111
Thompson, William R. 123
time dummies 126
Tinbergen, Jan 115–16
trade balance 41, 70, 91, 104,
trade barriers 2, 14, 33, 99, 108, 129
trade blocs 7, 42
Trade Competitiveness Institute of Pakistan 31
trade-conflict 15–16, 99–101, 106, 115; bi-directional causality 16, 99, 111–12; estimation 138, 140; liberal proposition 105; neo-marxist 105–6
trade creation 62
trade deflection 68, 91
Trade Development Authority of Pakistan 31
'trade as an engine' for growth 109
trade facilitation 49–51, 66–9, 72, 132, 143
trade-to-GDP ratio 19, 35, 136
trade integration 2, 3, 34, 48, 111; global 125, 136; multilateral 103
trade intensity 41

trade loss 100, 103–4, 113
trade policy space 38
trade potential 1, 9, 100
Trade and Transit Agreement (APTTA) 47, 148
transaction costs 42, 49, 102, 119, 134; risk and 139, 141, 143; transport and/or 104, 116
transit agreement: regional 48–9
transit rights 26, 48, 82, 102
transport costs 48
Treaty of Rome 46
treaty of transit 46
Turkmenistan-Afghanistan-Pakistan-India gas pipeline (TAPI) 148

UAE 38, 53, 153–4
UNCTAD 51
under-declaration 59
UNESCAP, Trade and Investment Division 72
unilateral trade liberalization 3
United Progressive Alliance (UPA) 109
University of Maryland's Centre for Systemic Peace 121
University of Michigan 121
Uruguay 7, 152

value addition (VA) 68, 70–1
Vietnam 59, 146, 152, 155
violent conflict 90, 91, 141

war 1, 7, 14, 16, 101, 103, 139; between India and Pakistan 75–6, 83–4, 90, 124–5; bilateral 131; civil 52, 89, 121; costs of 102; gulf 29; hegemonic wars 106; impact on trade 112; India–China 11; international 132–3, 141–2; inter-state 123, 129; overt 105; shadow of 104; threat of 110, 122
welfare benefits 62
World Association of Investment Promotion Agencies (WAIPA) 32
World Bank 23, 26, 51, 78–9, 120
World Economic Outlook (WEO) 26
World Intellectual Property Organization (WIPO) 32
World Investment Prospects Survey 51
WTO 30, 36, 63–4, 68–9, 111; accession 32, 34; agreements 34; defined FTA 4, 65; norms 49; notified to the 61, 62; rules 38
Wular barrage 79

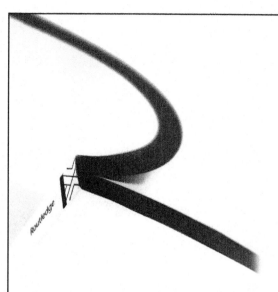

Routledge Paperbacks Direct

Bringing you the cream of our hardback publishing at paperback prices

This exciting new initiative makes the best of our hardback publishing available in paperback format for authors and individual customers.

Routledge Paperbacks Direct is an ever-evolving programme with new titles being added regularly.

To take a look at the titles available, visit our website.

www.routledgepaperbacksdirect.com

ROUTLEDGE
Revivals

Are there some elusive titles you've been searching for but thought you'd never be able to find?

Well this may be the end of your quest. We now offer a fantastic opportunity to discover past brilliance and purchase previously out of print and unavailable titles by some of the greatest academic scholars of the last 120 years.

Routledge Revivals is an exciting new programme whereby key titles from the distinguished and extensive backlists of the many acclaimed imprints associated with Routledge are re-issued.

The programme draws upon the backlists of Kegan Paul, Trench & Trubner, Routledge & Kegan Paul, Methuen, Allen & Unwin and Routledge itself.

Routledge Revivals spans the whole of the Humanities and Social Sciences, and includes works by scholars such as Emile Durkheim, Max Weber, Simone Weil and Martin Buber.

FOR MORE INFORMATION

Please email us at **reference@routledge.com** or visit:
www.routledge.com/books/series/Routledge_Revivals

www.routledge.com

CPSIA information can be obtained
at www.ICGtesting.com
Printed in the USA
BVOW09*2306070218
507575BV00006B/52/P

9 780415 602099